BARBARY GENERAL

Books by
Samuel Edwards

BARBARY GENERAL
DAUGHTER OF GASCONY
FIFTY-FIVE DAYS AT PEKING
MASTER OF CASTILE
THE WHITE PLUME
THE QUEEN'S HUSBAND
THE NAKED MAJA
THAT RANDALL GIRL
DEVIL'S PRIZE
THE KING'S MESSENGER
THE SCIMITAR

BARBARY
GENERAL

The Life of William H. Eaton

SAMUEL EDWARDS

PRENTICE-HALL, INC. * *Englewood Cliffs, N.J.*

iii

Barbary General   The Life of William H. Eaton
by Samuel Edwards

© 1968 by Samuel Edwards

Library of Congress Catalog Card Number: 68–11551

Printed in the United States of America

T

Prentice-Hall International, Inc., London
Prentice-Hall of Australia, Pty. Ltd., Sydney
Prentice-Hall of Canada, Ltd., Toronto
Prentice-Hall of India Private Ltd., New Delhi
Prentice-Hall of Japan, Inc., Tokyo

For

EDWIN J. HARRAGAN

CONTENTS

If the President, the Congress and the Navy—above all, the Navy—will take my advice, the United States will win the greatest victory in her history, and the pirate states of North Africa will be totally defeated, never to rise up against us or other civilized nations again.

William H. Eaton, to
Secretary of State James
Madison, October 1804.

CHAPTER ONE

THE SHORES OF TRIPOLI

First Lieutenant P. N. O'Bannon and his small detachment of United States marines, consisting of one junior officer and six enlisted men, marched endlessly across the desolate wastes of the North African desert. Their destination was Derna, the powerful fortress-city on the shores of Tripoli, and the marines, along with more than five hundred other members of the strangest "army" ever assembled, were making their way across uncharted wastelands, where the temperature soared to 100°F. by day and dropped nearly to freezing at night.

The marines slept on their rifles to prevent their comrades-in-arms from stealing them, and one member of the detachment stood guard duty every night to protect their meager supplies of food, their horses and equipment. Nearby were hundreds of Arabs, most of them members of the expedition because of promised loot. There were about fifty Greeks, too, all combat veterans, and a sprinkling of other Europeans. The officer corps was made up almost completely of international adventurers. One was a renegade English gentleman, another a Serbian with a dubious background; the deputy commander was of unknown nationality, used an Austrian name and was known to have been a deserter from the armies of the French Emperor, Napo-

1

leon. There were several Italians, a ferocious Bulgarian and an able cavalryman who claimed to be a noble Bourbon refugee from France, but in actuality was the bastard son of the late Marie Antoinette's personal chambermaid.

It was small wonder that the marines did not think of themselves as immortals whose exploits would be forever remembered in the official Hymn of their Corps, in words set to a light opera tune composed by Jacques Offenbach. All they knew was that they were participating in one of the weirdest military campaigns ever conceived and executed by allegedly sane men.

In the beginning, back in January, 1805, when they had been assigned to the expedition by their immediate superior, Lieutenant Isaac Hull, captain of the sloop-of-war, U.S.S. *Argus*, the marines had entertained doubts about the enterprise. So had Lieutenant Hull. Commodore Samuel Barron, commander in chief of the United States squadron in the Mediterranean, had been even more dubious, as had Colonel Tobias Lear, principal Consul General of the United States to the Barbary nations of North Africa.

When traveling to Cairo, then to Alexandria, in search of the claimant to the throne of Tripoli, Hamet Karamanli, the marines had found it difficult to believe that such a person existed. Twice they had been threatened by mobs of Egyptians, and once, for 24 hours, they had been under close arrest, guarded by a whole regiment of Turkish infantrymen.

But Hamet was real, sometimes all too real, and when not complaining, interfering and conniving against the men who were trying to restore him to the throne held by his brother, the Bey Yusef, he slept in a pavilion of silk, guarded by four Tripolitanian Arabs who hated each other so passionately that no one of them dared to approach the sleeping person of Hamet for fear the others would plunge knives into his back. Hamet, who trusted no one, had chosen them deliberately as his escort.

Only one man enjoyed the respect of every other member of the expedition. Even the marines, who had laughed at him behind his back in January, had become his most enthusiastic supporters in less than two months. "Wherever General Eaton leads, we will follow," wrote Lieutenant O'Bannon. "If he wants to march us to hell, we'll gladly go there. Last week we thought we were in hell; we spent almost five days without water. Two days ago, when we were drenched by a cold rain in a gully and thought we would drown, we were certain it was the River Styx. But no matter. General Eaton overcomes every obstacle. He is the great military genius of our era!"

• William H. Eaton of Connecticut was indeed a military genius, but he had no right to call himself General. The highest military rank he had ever held had been that of a captain in the United States Army, and his present title was that of Consul to the Barbary nations, attached to the Navy as a special advisor. His authority for leading a march on Derna was questionable. It was true that President Thomas Jefferson had approved of his plan to depose Yusef Bey, who had declared war against the United States, and replace him with Hamet, but by no stretch of the imagination had Jefferson dreamed that Eaton himself would recruit and direct such a force.

The State Department was opposed to such a venture. In the War Department there were a few enthusiastic supporters of Eaton's scheme, but not even they had thought he intended to command the assault force in person. The Navy was opposed to his plan, although Commodore Barron had been persuaded to give him several cannon, place three warships at his disposal and order Hull to assign him several marines. Barron and the outraged Tobias Lear claimed that Eaton had fooled them, and were promising each other they would send him home in chains when they got their hands on him.

At the moment he was beyond their reach, having started his long march from Burj el Arab, the Arab's Tower, forty miles west of Alexandria. Derna was five hundred and twenty miles away, and Eaton, traveling without maps or reliable guides, was destined to march closer to seven hundred miles in one of the most remarkable feats of this or any other period. The

3

obstacles he faced were overwhelming, and a lesser man would not have attempted what he was trying.

Acting solely on his own authority, he had rented hundreds of camels and purchased supplies worth the better part of $100,000. He had also contracted for the services of his "army," and every officer, every desert Arab, expected to be paid—by the United States of America. Eaton was blithely incurring obligations left and right, even though Secretary of the Treasury Albert Gallatin had warned him, specifically and in so many words, that the United States would not honor any of the debts he contracted.

His cash reserves were gone, having been stolen by an English adventurer whom he had made a staff officer. Eaton was making his long journey with only $53 in cash in his wallet, and he owed the better part of that sum to the physician accompanying the expedition. Dr. Mendrici, as the man called himself, declared he had paid for medicines and unguents out of his own pocket, but at no time had he been seen treating a patient. The marines, who were open-minded, insisted that Mendrici was an Egyptian, not an Italian, as he claimed, and swore he was a baker's assistant, not a physician. Such trivial details were unimportant to William H. Eaton.

● The march was the culmination of four years of observation, experience and romantic daydreaming. Eaton had badgered President Jefferson, made life miserable for a number of high-ranking Navy officers, who disliked him intensely, won the enmity of his colleagues in the consular service, and had, by intense lobbying, gained the support of influential members of both Houses of Congress.

Until now, few people had ever heard of him. Within a few weeks he would become one of the most renowned, highly honored heroes in Christendom, although there would be those who would claim he was, in Commodore Barron's words, "a lucky bastard."

On the surface, few men were less likely candidates for the role of international hero. Eaton was 41 years of age, and for

4

years had led a sedentary life that, combined with his love of good food, had made him soft and overweight. But no one seeing him in the saddle would have believed him at home anywhere else. No one would have believed he made his permanent residence in Brimfield, Massachusetts, that only a few years earlier he had earned his living as a schoolmaster there, and that he was married to a shrew almost old enough to be his mother.

There was one member of the expedition who was, indeed, familiar with the General's background, but he kept his mouth shut. Eli Danielson, Eaton's stepson, was his personal aide-de-camp, and thought him the greatest man who had ever lived.

Wearing flowing Arab robes and a scimitar in his belt, the heavily tanned Eaton looked at first glance like a leader of the Bedouin, the ferocious Arab nomads who were respected throughout all of North Africa as fighting men. He rode a huge, spirited stallion with easy grace, and at the end of a long day's march, when other, far younger men were bone-weary, he was as fresh as he had been at daybreak. When others complained of hunger, he nibbled a little cheese made of goat's milk, drank a gourd or two of stagnant rainwater and was refreshed.

His mastery of his subordinates' languages was astonishing. He spoke at least four Arab dialects without an accent, and was so fluent that each might have been his native tongue. He was equally at home in the patois, part Italian, part Turkish and part Egyptian-Arabic, that was the lingua franca of the North African pirate states. He had first heard all of these languages less than five years earlier.

But he had always had a gift for foreign tongues, having studied French, Latin, and Greek at Dartmouth College. As his stepson knew, he spoke four different North American Indian dialects with the ease of a forest warrior.

His Arabs admired him because he was their superior in all they did. No Bedouin was his equal as a horseman, no Algerian or Tunisian marksman could match him as a rifle shot. He was a demon cannoneer, as his gun crews learned, and he was so completely the Arab in his personal mannerisms that wandering tribesmen whose path crossed that of his column automatically assumed that this tall man with the air of command was Hamet Karamanli, future Bey of Tripoli and rightful heir to the throne that his cunning grandfather had stolen from the Turks in a night of bloody treachery. Anyone looking at Eaton carefully would have known he was a Westerner, however; no Arab had pale blue eyes.

He awed the international adventurers whom he had hired as his officers, and was more ruthless, crafty and resilient than the hardest of them. He could hit a target with a knife at eighty feet, demonstrated calm presence of mind when attempts were made on his life on two occasions, and was incredibly resourceful in finding food when there seemed to be no supplies anywhere.

What endeared him most to his men was instinct for command. "The General," wrote Lieutenant O'Bannon, "always knows what to say and do, in any situation. One day the Arabs in our army mutinied, all four hundred and fifty of them, and the General's courage was almost beyond belief. He handed me his rifle, pistols and scimitar, and went into their midst unarmed.

"They swarmed around him, all but obscuring him from sight, although he is much taller than any of them. My men and I were troubled, and I would have given the order to plunge into the throng with bayonets fixed had I not feared that they would kill him before we could reach his side. As well can be imagined, I blamed myself for negligence, and would not have forgiven myself had he been harmed.

"Suddenly, however, a single voice began to dominate that mob of shouting, swearing, gesticulating Arabs. The voice was that of General Eaton. I am familiar with no more than a few words of the Arabic tongue, and know not precisely what he said to them. Later he told me that he had derided them, calling them women who were afraid of battle, and who wanted to run away rather than taste the glory that would belong to those who captured Derna from the Bey Yusef.

"Bey Hamet Karamanli was himself one of those who was taking part in the mutiny, but so great was the force of the General's speech that Hamet covered his face with his hands and sobbed like a child. Other Arabs also wept, and some threw themselves onto the ground and covered their faces, so ashamed were they of being less than manly.

"The General continued to revile them until I thought he would lose his voice. Then, all at once, his manner changed, and now he sounded joyous. He was encouraging the Arabs, and in a few moments they began to cheer him. To our amazement they lifted him onto their shoulders and paraded around the oasis with him in a victory march, trampling the tender grass beneath their boots. The next Bedouin who bring their sheep to that water-hole to graze will not thank our troops, I can promise you.

"When the General decided there had been enough of the parade, he commanded them to put him down and go about their business. They obeyed him with alacrity, and the mutiny came to a swift and inglorious end. But the General was not yet finished with the insurrectionists. He had singled out two fellows who were the ringleaders of the uprising, and after he had recovered his weapons from me, sent for them.

"When they came to him, the General told them they had broken the basic military law, that of loyalty and obedience, and that he would require them to pay the penalty for their transgression. So saying, he drew his scimitar and decapitated each of them with a single stroke, performing this grisly act with a tranquility of spirit astonishing in one who so frequently displayed a tenderness to all of his fellow human beings.

"Thereafter he had the dripping heads of the culprits mounted on pikes and placed in the rock wasteland beyond the oasis. There, when the march was resumed, the other Arabs saw what had happened to their comrades, and learned a salutary lesson.

7

"To my mind the aspect of this entire incident that best illustrates the inner nature of the General lies in a postscript. After supper that evening I remonstrated with him for the carelessness he had displayed in walking unarmed amongst the Arabs, whom he knew to be among the most treacherous of beings to walk the face of the Earth, more treacherous by far than the savages who inhabit the nether wilderness of our own Continent. Such action, I told him, was not courage but foolhardiness of the blindest and most stubborn sort.

"By way of reply, the General laughed and raised the sleeves of his loose-fitting Arabian robe. There I could see, lightly strapped to his wrists and lower arms, two superbly fine-balanced knives with bone handles, which he can throw great distances, and with remarkable accuracy. A slight tug at the handle of either knife would have brought the weapon instantly into his hand. So it was that General Eaton made a show of disarming himself before treating with the mutineers, when all the while he was prepared to take any violent measures required for his self-protection, had it been necessary for him to strike up a defense.

"Other men are tacticians who think only in terms of the one or two steps they intend to take beyond their own immediate, present actions. But the General is ever a strategist, one whose thinking is attuned to the making of plans well in advance, for any eventuality. Such a man as this cannot help but capture any goal he has determined to conquer. Those who command the enemy at Derna would be wise to lay down their arms when they first see the approach of General Eaton toward their gates! They may know it not, but they are doomed!"

Early in the campaign Eaton had an opportunity to demonstrate the peculiar qualities of leadership that his followers required. The motley company left Burj el Arab on March 8, and four days later the first crisis arose.

From the outset Eaton made it his custom to ride ahead of his vanguard, a lone figure who made a perfect target for possible snipers. But he refused to accept the protection of an escort or to conceal himself in the center of his column, stating repeatedly that it was the duty of a commander to lead his men. The route, on March 12th, carried the little army past a series of rock-strewn ridges and cliffs that looked down on sand-swept valleys in which not even a single blade of resilient Bedouin grass could grow. Enemy sharpshooters, or anyone who carried a grudge against Eaton, could find perfect cover for himself in such country, as the officers of the General's staff emphatically pointed out to him.

He rejected their advice, however, and rode alone. Twice during the morning someone shot at him, but missed. It was the private belief of O'Bannon and several of the international adventurers that the culprit was one of Eaton's own Arabs. Perhaps the man was an agent in the employ of Bey Yusef Karamanli. Perhaps he had some private reason of his own to hate the General. Or perhaps he wanted to throw the army into chaos so he would be given the opportunity to steal a horse or a rifle.

Whoever the marksman may have been, his identity remained undiscovered, and Eaton was unmoved by the experience. His officers, understandably, were jittery when, shortly before sundown, a halt was called for the day near the ruins of an ancient Roman castle at Alem-el-Halfa, where water was relatively plentiful. There the troops made their bivouac, dividing into three sections or groups. The Arabs remained together in one part of the camp, the Greeks and other Christians withdrew to the opposite side, and in the middle was Eaton, with his officers erecting their tents near his.

Eaton sat down with the members of his staff to eat, and at his insistence they sat cross-legged, each man dipping his left hand, Arab style, into a pot of lamb stew. Only Eaton appeared at ease, although some of his subordinates had spent many years living in the Arab world.

Before they finished their meal, several of the Greek mercenaries, whose portion of the camp lay toward the west, came to the General with a courier from Derna, a man whom Eaton

9

recognized from the period he had lived in Tripoli. The courier had been a junior officer in the pay of Bey Yusef, but it was evident he wanted no more to do with his former master.

There had been an uprising of the garrison at Derna, he said, and the Governor, who was loyal to Yusef, had been thrown into the dungeons beneath his own castle. Only a handful of others had joined him there. The garrison had unanimously declared itself in favor of Hamet, as had the civilian population of the city. All Derna awaited not only Hamet, their legitimate ruler, but Eaton the Deliverer. With him they would march on to Tripoli, release the three hundred officers and men of the American frigate, U.S.S. *Philadelphia*, who were being held as prisoners there, and would depose the enemy of the United States, Yusef.

Eaton, knowing the Arabs, heard the report with skepticism. It was a charming custom of the North Africans to tell a man what he wanted to hear, but that news was not necessarily accurate. Often, as the General had discovered during the years of his sojourn in the Barbary states, stories were made up out of whole cloth for no reason other than the pleasure they would give the recipient of the alleged news. So Eaton listened politely, but wanted confirmation of the fall of Derna before accepting the story. As it happened, he was right; the tale was completely false.

But the Greeks and some of the other Christian mercenaries were more gullible than their commander. Crowding forward to listen, they began a spontaneous celebration the moment the courier finished telling his story, and fired their rifles into the air.

The night was dark, with a layer of heavy clouds obscuring the moon and stars, and the Arabs on the opposite side of the castle ruins had no idea what was happening, but immediately assumed that the Americans and Europeans had been attacked by a band of Arabs. It did not occur to the hired Arab followers of Hamet that these attackers might be enemies; it was enough that they were fellow Arabs. The Americans and Europeans

10

owned splendid firearms and fine horses, their blankets were made of the best wool, and even their boots were expensive.

Therefore, without stopping to think, Eaton's Arabs raced toward the camp of the Christian mercenaries, intending to obtain their share of the booty. A Greek sentry heard them coming, and gave the alarm that sent the hard-bitten adventurers hurrying into a defense formation. A suicidal clash between the two elements of Eaton's army appeared inevitable. And Hamet Karamanli, who knew as well as any of the officers what was happening, ran into his own tent and threw himself, fully clothed, into bed.

General Eaton reacted with predictable valor. His horse had been unsaddled for the night, and was grazing nearby, so Eaton leaped onto the animal's bare back and galloped toward the scene of the impending conflict. Arabs and Greeks alike were shouting, taunting each other, but the General's deep voice rose above the clamor. "Stop!" he shouted, first in Arabic, then in Greek, then in the lingua franca of North Africa. "I will cut off the head of any man who dares to fire a shot!"

Emphasizing his words, he twirled his scimitar over his head with a skill displayed only by the Janissary Household Regiment of the Turkish Sultan in Constantinople. It was no accident that he could perform such a feat: the scimitar had fascinated him since he had first come to the Barbary states, and he had been practicing for years.

It was surprising that, in the darkness and confusion, he was not shot down by men on one side, or both. But he made such an imposing figure on the back of his nervous, prancing stallion that the Arabs and Greeks alike fell silent. William Eaton was too much of a realist to waste his breath telling the men of his two component units they were brothers working toward the same goal. They were natural enemies who would have enjoyed clawing at each other, and he knew that only his own authority prevented them from initiating an enthusiastic program of mutual extermination.

So he ordered them into parade formation, and sent them

marching in opposite directions. That ended the immediate crisis, at least for the moment. Neither the near-battle nor the false news that inadvertantly sparked it was important. The one significant fact to emerge from the incident was the ability of Eaton to force his men to obey him. Many had been in his employ for only four days, and none had known him for more than a week or two. No one in the area had any reason to respect Americans, who were a rare breed in the region. It was Eaton himself who commanded that respect through the sheer power of his personality.

He had literally spent a lifetime preparing for this brief campaign. Everything he had done since earliest childhood had helped to make him ready for the supreme test, and it was not accidental that he won overnight fame. What does astonish the modern student is that his glory should have faded so quickly. Six years after his fabled march to Derna he was dead, and the following year, when the War of 1812 broke out, he was forgotten by all but a few men, even though his deeds formed the basis for an enduring peace between the United States and the Barbary states of Morocco, Algiers, Tunis and Tripoli.

The inventive genius that Eaton displayed on his march of nearly seven hundred miles almost beggars description. At one point midway in the march, when his food supplies were almost exhausted, he literally replenished them overnight. First, he conferred separately with several of the Arabs he had come to trust slightly, and learned from them that a large oasis was located about eighteen miles inland.

This oasis, they told him, was too dangerous to visit, however, as it was a main headquarters of the area's most ferocious tribe of Bedouin. Eaton thanked them for the information, saddled his horse and rode alone across the desert to the oasis. There he addressed the tribesmen in his most persuasive Arabic, although he knew the Bedouin were realists who would demand a great deal in return for the sheep and melons and barley he wanted to buy from them.

He harangued them for more than an hour, working them

up to a pitch of emotional frenzy while he searched his own mind for an inspiration. He had no money to give the Bedouin, and owned literally nothing he could offer them in trade. Finally, in quiet desperation, he asked what they wanted.

The *khan*, or leader of the tribe, replied that his men had been observing the march from a distance for several days. The Bedouin horses were superior to those of the strangers, the *khan* declared, but his people owned few camels. In return for one hundred camels he would supply the great Bey Eaton with all of the food he wanted.

The price was outrageous, and Eaton began to bargain, notwithstanding the fact that his camels were merely rented and did not belong to him. But he was already so deeply in debt that the trivial detail of ownership did not bother him. He would sign a receipt for the camels, and Commodore Barron would have to dig into his reserves for the money.

At last Eaton and the *khan* reached an agreement. In return for fifty camels the expedition would be given as much food as fifty such camels could carry. He and the Bedouin set out at once, and shortly before dawn the astonished sentries at the overnight camp saw their General approach with a large company of Bedouin whose pack mules were laden with sacks of barley and melons. Bringing up the rear were Bedouin women driving scores of sheep.

The camel owners made no protest, since Eaton agreed that the United States would pay them the handsome sum of two hundred dollars for each of the fifty camels. The only people who objected were the Arab troops who were being dismounted, and would have to ride pack mules for the rest of the march. But even they could not protest too bitterly, since they would be riding on full stomachs.

The story of the camel sale has a postscript that illuminates still another facet of William Eaton's many-sided character. He would discover, after reaching his destination, that the United States Navy was unhappy with him. In fact, Commodore Barron and Commodore John Rodgers were furious with him for exceeding his orders. Only Captain Stephen Decatur, a young officer recently promoted from the rank of Lieutenant, sympathized with him.

After he satisfied himself in his own mind that the Navy would pay none of the many debts he had contracted, Eaton had two choices. Either he could write to President Jefferson in the hope that the Executive branch of the American Government would pay his bills, or he would have to do something immediate and drastic. Past experience had taught him that transatlantic correspondence was painfully slow. In fact, it had taken him almost a year to get a reply from President Jefferson to one letter he had sent to Washington, the nation's new capital.

His Arab creditors, he realized, had no intention of waiting even a month or two for payment. Once they found out the Navy had no intention of supporting General Eaton, they would exact payment in their own way, with scimitar, pistol and knife. But Eaton was ready to meet that emergency, too, and did. He ordered his most reliable subordinates to make out a list of the wealthy supporters of Bey Yusef in the territory he had conquered.

When they gave it to him, he issued an edict—in the name of Hamet, of course—confiscating their property. He then sold their houses, lands and goods to the befuddled Hamet, and used the proceeds to pay his debts. Subsequently, after his triumphant return to the United States, he proudly announced in an address to a joint session of the Senate and House of Representatives that his spectacular campaign had not cost the American taxpayers a penny. He had been supported, he declared, by the grateful people of Tripoli, whom he had liberated from the grip of a tyrant.

His statement was not the precise truth, of course, but there were elements of truth in it. Certainly the funds had been supplied in one way and another by Tripolitanians. But it is doubtful that the men whose property was confiscated felt grateful to him, and Hamet was said to have become very angry

14

when it belatedly occurred to him that he need not have paid Eaton anything at all.

In a later age William Eaton might have acquired a reputation as an operator—on a very large scale. Even in his own time his scale was stupendous. He fought and won a campaign almost single-handed, and his victories enabled the United States to conquer a foe who had resisted America successfully for years. It is small wonder that Congress voted him a Gold Medal, and that the legislature of Massachusetts made him a dazzling gift, a tract of ten thousand acres.

Of far greater significance, however, is something that happened almost a century and a half after General William H. Eaton made history in North Africa. During World War II, when the British and Germans clashed in the same area, operations and supply officers on both sides were ordered to study the campaign of Eaton in full detail. The fact that he had been remembered by professional soldiers for almost one hundred and fifty years would have pleased William Eaton.

Not until he had lived his life did his contemporaries, including those who had known him best, begin to understand this strange man who seemed to delight in defying convention. Eaton had no interest in acquiring riches, and declined several offers to run for high public office.

One clause in his will should have provided a clue. His relatives and friends misunderstood it, thinking it an outgrowth of his long feud with a wife he detested, and who loathed him. He asked to be buried with his horse. What he sought, even in death, was a place in history that was unique.

He died scarcely realizing he had already won that place, for all time. He alone, of all Americans, conquered a foreign land with a ragged army of mercenaries, and placed his hand-picked puppet on a throne in order to insure permanent peace in a part of the world where peace had been unknown for centuries.

15

CHAPTER TWO

LITTLE ACORNS AND SPINDLY OAKS

The birth of William Eaton on February 23, 1764, at Woodstock, Connecticut, was an occasion that gave joy to no one. His parents, who already had a large family to feed, clothe and educate, accepted the arrival of another child with the resigned calm of British colonials who suffered the curse of a huge brood as a normal hazard of living. Nathan Eaton was already extending himself in an attempt to support his clan, and now that he was able to put his older sons to work on the farm, spent several hours each day teaching school in an attempt to bring in enough money to meet the insatiable demands of his family.

William's early life was drab, although many years passed before the boy realized it. He suffered the usual inconveniences and hazards of a younger child in a large family engrossed in the all-absorbing task of earning a living. His mother was far too busy to pay much attention to him, and he grew up with an insatiable hunger for a woman's love, an appetite that would cause him far more pain than pleasure. His busy, remote father was his idol, and the boy's desire to emulate him unquestionably was responsible for William's dreams of glory.

Nathan Eaton had served as a captain in the Connecticut militia during the last of the French and Indian Wars, had seen two years of active service on the wilderness frontier north of Hartford, and had distinguished himself in several skirmishes with the Ottawa and Algonkin, two of the Indian tribes that had caused persistent trouble for the American settlers. Nathan was treated with respect by his friends and neighbors, and the family regarded him as a hero worthy of mention in the same breath with Lord Jeffrey Amherst, the British and colonial military commander in the war. William wanted men to doff their hats and pull off their stocking caps when they entered his house, too.

From the time he was entered as a student in his father's one-room school at the age of five, the boy proved himself an eager, apt pupil. He developed a prodigious memory, and according to a biography, *Life of the Late General William Eaton*, which was published in 1813, two years after his death, he had memorized all of John Milton's *Paradise Lost* by the time he was six. The author of the book remained anonymous, but was undoubtedly Eaton himself, since his innermost thoughts and the trivia of daily living were elucidated in such full detail that no one else could have known that much about him.

Whether he really memorized *Paradise Lost* is, therefore, open to question. In his anxiety to present himself in a favorable light, Eaton was somewhat inclined to exaggerate. It is probable, however, that he had memorized long passages from Shakespeare, as well as bits of Greek philosophy and Roman oratory by the time he was nine. For the rest of his days he had a tendency to quote from these sources on any occasion, appropriate or otherwise. He was reared in a devout Congregational family that took its Scriptures seriously, and he accepted the injunction in the Gospels to put his candle in a candlestick and not hide his light under a bed.

In 1774, on the eve of the American Revolution, the family moved to the town of Mansfield, Connecticut, where Nathan had purchased a somewhat larger farm and had found a position as headmaster of a school that would pay him a living wage.

17

The area was dominated by the thinking of political leaders in Hartford, and by the time the war broke out in 1775, eleven-year-old William was a confirmed, ardent patriot who could scarcely wait until he was old enough to take up arms against the tyrant King George III and the evil Prime Minister, Lord North.

Like so many others in a period of fierce war, he saw friends and foes in simple blacks and whites, and his feelings were so strong that it appears strange at first glance to find him becoming a strong Anglophile after growing to adulthood. Like so many Americans of the era, however, he remained ambivalent in his attitude toward Great Britain, admiring all things British and wanting to behave like an English gentleman, even while professing a violent hatred for the mother country.

By 1780 the Americans, who had been on the verge of losing the war, had rallied sufficiently to be holding their own. But the military situation was complicated. Major General George Washington, the American commander, needed more troops to stave off the threat of an attack in massive force by Sir Henry Clinton, who was making his headquarters in the occupied town of New York. An appeal was issued to New York and Connecticut, New Jersey and Pennsylvania to supply as many new regiments of militia as could be raised.

The glory-seeking William packed a few belongings in an old sheet, stole a musket that belonged to an older brother and ran away to Hartford, intending to enlist in the state militia. Instead he listened to a stirring appeal made by a recruiting sergeant in the Continentals, the regular army, and joined it instead. He was already very tall for his age, and fairly husky, so he lied about his age. And the sergeant, pressed by his superiors to fill recruiting quotas, did not ask too many questions.

The boy vanished from home early in January, and two weeks later found himself in an unheated barracks in New Haven. He spent his days drilling. The weather was bitterly cold, the recruits were issued no uniforms or other equipment, and the boy's clothing was inadequate to protect him. The toes on his left foot were frostbitten, he developed a case of the ague, the eighteenth-century name for influenza, and was promptly dismissed from service by officers who had too few facilities to care for the sick.

Penniless and knowing no one in New Haven, William was forced, for the first time in his life, to face harsh reality. He met the test well, finding work as a chair mender in the little factory of a New Haven furniture manufacturer who was having difficulty employing unskilled and semiskilled laborers. William spent a month working in the factory, and by living frugally managed to save the better part of his meager wages. In order to save rent he slept under a workbench in the factory. He lived almost exclusively on bread, cheese and weak beer during that month.

When he had saved enough to see him home, he started on the journey to Mansfield, but a return of the ague, brought on no doubt by his Spartan mode of life, ruined his calculations. This time he was fortunate. A farmer who lived near New Britain took the boy in, refused to accept any money from him and offered him a home until he recovered.

Farmer Isaiah Appleby might have been less generous had he realized the consequences of his kindness. The care of the invalid was the responsibility of his attractive daughter, Sophie, who was a few months younger than her patient, and William fell madly in love for the first and only time in his life. Sophie Appleby gave him the tender attention that had always been lacking at home, and his attachment to her was so deep that he never really cared for anyone else to the end of his days.

No portraits or miniatures of Sophie have survived the ravages of nearly two centuries, if, indeed, she was ever painted, so it is necessary to take William's word that she was lovely beyond compare. According to his ecstatic description she had "a perfect visage," with blonde curls and blue eyes, and was "the epitomy of feminine daintiness." Perhaps he wasn't exaggerating very much, since Sophie enjoyed great popularity in the neighborhood and was the object of the affections of a number of young men, soldiers and civilians alike.

William spent his sixteenth birthday at the Appleby home and, in all, stayed for about ten weeks. His convalescence was a torment; Sophie refused to take his protestations of love seriously, and from his sickbed he was forced to listen help- lessly as swarms of other swains called on her.

When the weather became warmer the boy, completely re- covered, could delay his departure no longer. Before he left he gave Sophie a poem which, he declared, he had written for her. It read:

> *Love is too young to know what conscience is,*
> *Yet who knows not conscience is born of love,*
> *Then gentle cheater urge not my amiss,*
> *Least guilty of my faults thy sweet self prove.*
> *For thou betraying me, I do betray*
> *My nobler part to my gross body's treason,*
> *My soul doth tell my body that he may,*
> *Triumph in love, flesh stays no farther reason,*
> *But rising at thy name doth point out thee,*
> *As his triumphant prize, proud of this pride,*
> *He is contented thy poor drudge to be*
> *To stand in thy affairs, fall by thy side.*
> *No want of conscience hold it that I call,*
> *Her love, for whose dear love I rise and fall.*

Sophie appears to have had little or no interest in literature, which was unfortunate, as William's taste in poetry was im- peccable, which is more than can be said for his scruples. The poem he "wrote" was a carelessly copied sonnet by William Shakespeare, and Sophie's failure to respond hurt him.

He was destined to be hurt many times by her. Whether she was incapable of returning the passionate devotion of any man, whether it was William himself to whom she was indifferent, or whether she was a simple country girl incapable of appre- ciating a young man who was already becoming a very complicated human being is impossible to determine. It is enough that William left Sophie cold. He wrote to her regularly for years and, even after her marriage and his, sent her an occasional letter.

Her few replies, which were brief, indicate a lack of sensitivity and imagination, as well as an inability to master the fundamentals of English grammar, spelling and punctuation. A single example, a letter sent to William soon after his return to the home of his parents in Mansfield, will suffice as an illustration.

> Mr. William Eaton.
> Sir:
> Papa sayes it will be a warm sumer. I have gone for maney walkes, with my dog; a visitor who is a freind of Papa and Mama is now sleeping in the room, that you sleeped in whilst you was here.
> > I am, sir,
> > Yr obt svt,
> > Sofie Appleby
> At New Britain,
> April the 12th, 1780.

It would seem that, among her other weaknesses, Sophie had not bothered to learn the correct spelling of her own name. But her suitor was not a demanding youth; he wanted Sophie and showed no interest in her mind.

But he was concerned about far more than his unrequited love. His father greeted him amiably and expressed pride in him. The whole family, with the notable exception of his mother, was pleased that William had enlisted in the Continentals, and joined him in bemoaning the bad fortune that led to his discharge. According to the anonymous *Life*, "Mrs. Eaton indicated neither her displeasure nor her pleasure at the events leading to her son's enlistment and subsequent discharge. She made no mention of his absence."

Encouraged by his father and other relatives, and perhaps spurred by his mother's indifference, William was determined to enlist again. This time Nathan came to his son's aid, and wrote a letter of introduction to an old friend and comrade-in-arms, Brigadier General John Waterbury, whose militia brigade had been incorporated in the Continental Army.

William set out from home under far different circumstances. In his wallet was the letter and three crowns, in silver, which his father had given him. Wrapped in oiled paper was enough meat and bread, cooked by one of his sisters, to enable him to eat heartily for several days. And, perhaps best of all, he carried his father's precious long rifle, an honorable weapon with several notches carved on its butt.

Waterbury's brigade was in bivouac on Long Island, and a place was found for the young recruit in the company of Captain James Dana. Most of the men were veterans who had seen at least two or three years of service, but William was in his element at last. He took to military life with such enthusiasm that, within three months of his enlistment in May, 1781, he was promoted to the rank of corporal.

A stroke of bad luck spoiled William's chance of taking part in the climactic confrontation of the American Revolution, the Battle of Yorktown, in Virginia, where Lord Cornwallis surrendered his entire corps of redcoats and Hessian mercenaries to General Washington. Waterbury's brigade had been scheduled to march south to join the main American body, but when the time came Captain Dana was indisposed and his company remained behind to await his recovery. Yorktown was fought and won before his physician pronounced him fit for travel.

For all practical purposes the United States had won her independence, but few Americans yet realized it. Charleston, the cultural and social capital of the South, was still in British hands, as were large portions of the South Carolina hinterland and parts of Georgia. The war in that part of the country continued to be waged with vicious fury, while men in the North waited for Sir Henry Clinton to retaliate.

A peace commission was sent from Philadelphia, the American capital, to London, and negotiations on terms of peace were instituted. Most militia battalions either formally disbanded or simply dissolved as the citizen-soldiers decided the time had come for them to return to their homes. But the Continentals remained on duty.

William's company was still serving in Connecticut, spending most of its days doing patrol duty on the shores of Long Island Sound. Many of the older men, particularly the few who had seen continuous service since the outbreak of war in 1775, won discharges, and the noncommissioned officers were replaced. William, already in a post that called him to the attention of Captain Dana, was promoted to the rank of platoon sergeant and, prior to his release in the spring of 1783, when hostilities formally came to an end, he served as company sergeant major, a rank that in a later era would be known as first sergeant.

The United States treasury was empty, the paper money being issued by the Continental Congress was worthless, and the possibility that the Government would achieve financial stability within the next few years was remote. The troops were given honorable discharges, the thanks of Congress and their own officers, and were issued inexpensively printed pledges, in which the Congress promised to pay them their back wages and the bonuses offered to those who had voluntarily remained in service.

Sergeant Major William Eaton returned to Mansfield on foot, his pockets empty, his uniform threadbare and his shoes thin. He had not seen action in a single engagement of the war, but at the age of nineteen was a bona fide veteran of a corps that, with justice, was proud of its achievements. Thereafter, for the rest of his life, William took care to tell strangers that he had served for two years in the Continentals.

Other veterans were drifting, taking whatever work they could find in an attempt to resume the patterns of civilian living, but William had no desire to follow their example. He thought long and hard about his future, in which Sophie Appleby figured prominently. He paid a visit to her and her family in New Britain, and when he went back to Mansfield

23

the groundwork had been laid for a complete misunderstanding.

William believed that Sophie intended to wait for him, and was prepared to be patient until such time as he could earn the kind of living to support her in the style she wanted. Her parents appear to have thought that the young couple had become betrothed, too. But Sophie, who had a mind of her own, had either agreed glibly with William's ideas in order to get rid of him, or perhaps suffered a genuine change of heart. Whatever her real feelings, she soon made it evident that she wanted no more to do with a young man whose future was dubious.

The eager, sentimental William bombarded her with letters, some of them, according to his anonymous *Life*, twenty-five to thirty pages long. Sophie burned or discarded most of the letters, but enough were preserved to indicate the main outlines of William's plans. He obtained a position as a schoolmaster in Mansfield, meanwhile returning to his own studies. He was determined to obtain a college degree, he wrote, but was vague as to his vocational intentions after he won it.

Sophie rarely answered his communications, and he complained incessantly that he was pining away for her. But his unhappy love life did not prevent him from carrying out his plans. Indeed, by 1785 he had moved into high gear. In addition to his teaching he obtained a position as a clerk in a store, and began the advanced study of Latin and Greek with a clergyman by the name of Nott.

In the following year he obtained a teaching position for higher pay in Windham, New Hampshire, and by 1787, the year the Constitutional Convention met to begin the formation of a new, strong Federal Government, he had saved enough money for his college education. He entered Dartmouth, New Hampshire's most prominent institute of higher learning, and in 1790 he was awarded a degree as a Bachelor of Arts.

He was graduated with honors, and seems to have been a good citizen as well as a good student. Unlike younger undergraduates, who enjoyed playing pranks and drinking heavily, he attended to his own affairs and remained sober for three years. He had acquired a reputation as a scholar, and careers in both the clergy and the academic world were open to him. He had been industrious, totally lacking in color, and nothing in either his military career or post-army life hinted at the eccentricities he would soon develop.

"I do not care for the ministry," he wrote to Sophie, "and the life of a professor does not appeal to me, either. Although I do not truly care if I ever become wealthy, I nevertheless want employment in some honorable profession. It will not be long now before we are married!"

William returned to Mansfield for a holiday, expecting to hear from Sophie there before he went on to New Britain to see her. But she did not write to him, and instead he received an embarrassed letter from her father, informing him that the girl of his dreams had been married the previous week to one Thomas Smith, a neighbor who owned a farm of one thousand acres.

A perspicacious young man would have realized that his semi-betrothed had succumbed to the lure of prosperity, and would have done his best to forget her as quickly as he could. But William was naive, and all his life would continue to display an inability to understand women. His first reaction was that Sophie had been tricked by her parents into marrying Smith. He sent Appleby a coldly furious reply.

Receiving no answer, he magnified his dream of Sophie, and wrote her a letter she carefully kept and handed down to her own children. By this time, perhaps, marriage had disillusioned her, and the romantic approach of her former suitor sounded good to her. Whatever her reason may have been, she took pains to preserve this communication, as she did future letters.

William, writing in flowery polysyllables he reserved for his one-way correspondence with Sophie, a language unlike any other he used in communications with anyone, declared his undying love for her. To the day of his death, he said, he would worship the ground on which she left her sweet, indelible footprints. The sound of rain would forever remind him of her voice. He had no portrait of her, but needed none; his vision of her was etched for all time in his mind.

The letter ran 36 closely-written pages, and Mrs. Smith put it away in a book with a sprig of spring flowers. Whether Mr. Smith also saw the letter, and what he thought of it if he did, are facts unknown.

It was at this juncture in William Eaton's life that he became eccentric in manner, dress and aims. Had he lived thirty or forty years later, when Romanticism was in full bloom, it would have been claimed that his disappointment in love had unhinged his mind. The truth of the matter is that he reveled in his jilting. The sheer drama of his discovery that Sophie had married someone else was delicious, and he never forgot it. Even when he had become a world-renowned man in his mature forties, he referred to his crushing blow as though it had taken place only a few days earlier.

He did not allow the disappointment to make him celibate, however. He had been enjoying an affair with a New Hampshire barmaid during his final year at Dartmouth, and on a number of occasions went back to see her. Thereafter there were women in his life as long as he lived, some in Philadelphia and New York, a number in North Africa, where he was no stranger to the brothels of the Barbary states.

The marriage of Sophie did one thing he was quick to recognize: he was under no compunction to find a position that would pay him enough to marry. Instead he could do what he pleased. Several of his classmates were natives of the Green Mountains of Vermont, and he accepted their offer to make his home in the place that, technically and in the firm opinion of its citizens, currently enjoyed a status unique in American history. Formerly a part of New Hampshire, Vermont was populated by the most rugged of individualists, men who insisted on following their own way of life. New Hampshire still claimed the district, but Vermont had firmly declared herself separate and, rather than bow to the will of her neighbor, had established herself an independent republic.

Great Britain, anxious to salvage something from the disaster of the American Revolution, had offered to recognize free and separate Vermont, and the legislature cannily used this diplomatic ploy as a weapon to obtain what she really wanted from the newly organized Federal Government of the United States. If she were granted statehood, she said, and the claims of New Hampshire were rejected, she would enter the Union. If not, she would go her own way and accept recognition by the British.

The Green Mountain Commonwealth, as Vermont called herself, seemed a natural place for an ambitious young man to win fame, and in the early autumn of 1790 William Eaton traveled to the little village of Windsor, which he believed to be the capital. On his arrival there, however, he learned that the House of Delegates had transferred itself to the somewhat larger town of Bennington, in the southwest corner of the district, near the boarders of Massachusetts and New York.

For the first time William showed a genuine flair for drama, and arrived in Bennington dressed in a suit, waistcoat, boots and hat of dark green. Even his saddle and saddlebags had been dyed green, and patriotic citizens cheered him as he rode through the streets searching for a place to stay.

Thanks to the intervention of his friends he found a home with one of the most prominent citizens of Vermont, Stephen R. Bradley, soon to become a senator. Bradley recognized something unusual in the young man, whom he called "extraordinary," and quickly decided to help advance his career. Through his influence William became Clerk of the House of Delegates, in effect chief of the Vermont civil service.

He was holding that post in March, 1791 when the drama of Vermont ended abruptly. Thanks in part to the vigorous efforts of Secretary of the Treasury Alexander Hamilton, and in part to the innate, rock-bound common sense of her own people, Vermont became the fourteenth state in the Union.

Clerk Eaton almost immediately lost his taste for local politics. He had no desire to spend his days laboring with mountains of papers, making friends in high places and, in due time, if he mended enough fences, being elected to the federal House of Representatives, then the Senate. For some, he said in a letter to his favorite sister, Mrs. Amos Paine of Woodstock, Connecticut, "fame is a slow journey through the labyrinth of politics. Such a lot is not for me. I must find glory more quickly, ere my candle sputters and dies. I know not why I am convinced that I will not live to old age, but I will not. Therefore I must find myself a path of glory more quickly than that course followed by those whose pace is slower and more gentle."

Uncertain what kind of career he wanted, Eaton finally decided on something he knew, the military. Senator Bradley was sorry to see him leave the political arena, in which he showed promise, but helped him by writing to the War Department on his behalf. Secretary of War Henry Knox responded by granting William a commission as a Captain of Infantry, his commission dating from March 1, 1792.

Captain Eaton was immediately ordered to take command of a new company just being formed at Bennington, where he was already living, and when recruiting was completed, to proceed into Massachusetts for purposes of intensive training.

The glory seeker had entered the regular army at precisely the right time. Ever since the end of the Revolution affairs in the Ohio Valley and the territories that extended to the Mississippi River had been in a sorry state. The area comprising the future states of Ohio, Indiana, Illinois, Michigan and Wisconsin was infested with Indians who resisted the advances of settlers into the wilderness. Border forts at Detroit, Erie, Niagara and other places that, under the terms of the Treaty of 1783, were to have been turned over to the United States, remained in the hands of the British.

Major General Arthur St. Clair, who had never distinguished himself in the Revolution, had been the commander of the Army in the Ohio Valley, and had been administered a smashing defeat by the Indians in a ferocious battle fought in November, 1791. The entire country was demanding that something be done.

28

President Washington responded by appointing the most dashing of Revolutionary War field commanders, Major General Anthony Wayne, to the post of commander in chief of the Army. Wayne, it was announced, would take personal command in the West, and a new military force was being organized to serve under him. Wayne himself promised action, and his record indicated that life for a soldier on the frontier would be far from dull.

New methods and techniques of training were being utilized, and inspectors sent out by Wayne made certain that the troops, who were being called the American Legion, learned the principles of guerilla fighting in the forests. Marksmanship and individual effort were stressed, and the men were taught how to live comfortably in the wilderness, eating roots and berries they were taught to recognize as edible and making shelters out of the raw materials at hand. They learned how to stalk an enemy in the deep woods, how to leave no traces when they marched and, above all, how to move swiftly.

Captain William Eaton proved himself exceptionally adept at his new trade. A report sent to Secretary of War Knox from Springfield, Massachusetts, by Major Carl Overton, one of Wayne's inspectors, declared, "Captain Eaton, who works very hard, is proving himself an adept field officer, and will be of inestimable value to the Legion."

Captain Eaton also found time to meet, woo and win himself the most unlikely of brides while his company was in training for the campaign in the West.

CHAPTER THREE

THE INDIAN FIGHTER

The Legion's battalions of New England recruits lived, trained and maneuvered in the deep forests of the rolling hill country east of Springfield, Massachusetts. The terrain was vaguely similar to that in which they would be operating when they went into action, and the men worked under conditions not unlike those they would encounter in the West.

Captain Eaton's company made rapid progress and the commander of the unit soon became known as a "slave driver." No member of the command ever made the same mistake twice; the punishment inflicted on him for a second violation of rules or an error of judgment was too unpleasant to be tolerated. But, at the same time, the Captain was scrupulously fair, protected his men from higher authority, and made no attempt to curb their activities when they were off duty. As a consequence the men gave him their unqualified loyalty, and the unit made better progress than any other in New England.

It was evident that William Eaton had found his true vocation. As General Wayne later remarked, he had an instinct for the art of war. He not only knew how to handle men, but showed such a talent for tactical improvisation in maneuvers that his company invariably won the war games that comprised the core of the training program.

He also displayed remarkable personal initiative. Knowing the company would be operating against the most ferocious of the Western tribes, the Miami, he made strenuous efforts to learn the language of the savages. A captain of scouts who had served under General St. Clair in the area known as the "Miami Slaughterhouse" was familiar with the tribe's tongue, and William persuaded the officer to give him lessons in it. They spent several evenings each week at the task, William rewarding his teacher with jugs of apple brandy in payment, and within a few months the pupil had mastered the difficult language. He had an almost uncanny ability to familiarize himself with alien speech, and apparently learned easily as well as quickly.

The troops trained in a vast tract of forest that stretched from Springfield to Worcester. Occasionally William and the other officers found quarters for themselves in small villages that had been carved out of the wilderness. One of these communities was a place called Brimfield, where the widow of Brigadier General Timothy Danielson, a militia leader during the Revolution, opened her home to them.

Eliza Danielson was in her forties, and had two teen-aged children, a son who wanted a military career and a daughter who was unpopular in the neighborhood because of her sharp tongue. Mrs. Danielson herself had acquired a reputation as a shrew, and there seems to be little doubt that the name was earned. A homely, dominating woman with a penetrating, shrill voice and a chip on her shoulder, she took delight in feuding with everyone who crossed her path.

One brief stay at the Widow Danielson's was enough for most of the Legion's officers. Life was too short, and the mistress of the house was too consistently unpleasant. Eaton was the exception, and not only stayed with her regularly, but began to visit her when he was off duty on Sundays and, sometimes, evenings during the week.

Eliza was no less a virago in her treatment of him, but her querulous abuse did not seem to bother him. There are no other indications in his life that he was a masochist, so it is

31

unlikely that he enjoyed the torrents of vitriol she poured over him. It may be stretching credulity to suggest that he had at least found a woman who paid attention to him. A personable young officer of 28 who was tall, had a far better mind than most of his colleagues and was the essence of gallantry in his treatment of ladies could have found any number of girls who would have been interested in him.

But, to the astonishment of everyone who knew William, he and Eliza announced in the summer of 1793 that they intended to be married in the immediate future. The widow's reasons are not hard to imagine: she had found a man, and perhaps realized this was her last chance to snare a new husband. It is difficult to imagine why William wanted to marry her, however, and nowhere in his correspondence, his *Life* or the Journal-Diary he began to keep at approximately this time does he give any clues. The *Life* confines itself to the prim statement that Mrs. Danielson and Captain Eaton were married late in August, 1793.

It is true that William was fond of his stepson, but this factor was balanced by a loathing for his stepdaughter, which he never concealed, and which was reciprocated. It is also true that Eliza owned her own home in Brimfield and that the farm left to her by her late first husband paid her a modest income. But had William been looking for an heiress, he could have done infinitely better for himself.

It may even be farfetched to speculate that he was striking back at Sophie, who rarely answered his letters. After all, he was long accustomed to a one-way correspondence with her, and she had been married for some time.

It is a fascinating if futile exercise to speculate on Eliza's magnetism if any. She must have attracted William in some way, for some reason. Perhaps, although this is no more than a guess, he was looking for an older woman who would become a mother substitute and give him the love that his harried mother was too busy to lavish on him. Or it might be that he had something of a masochistic streak, mixed with a romanticism demonstrated by his continued yearning for his lost love, that made him enjoy the unpleasantness, indifference and abuse that Eliza meted out to all men.

If he was motivated by either of these unconscious desires, he soon overcame them, and undoubtedly was desperately sorry for any momentary weakness he had shown. Even in an era before psychology and psychiatry were known, a man would have had to be very neurotic indeed to tolerate General Danielson's widow for more than a very brief time. For the rest of his life the naive young man had ample reason to regret his aberration.

Whatever his motives, William married Eliza Danielson, a rash act he must have regretted at once. Nothing in their subsequent, dutiful correspondence indicates that there was any love or affection that bound them together or, for that matter, that they had anything in common. Eliza invariably scolded her husband, berating him for imagined grievances. She knew, she wrote, that he was becoming intoxicated every night, a charge that she herself must have recognized as absurd, since he drank very little and had no real liking for liquor. She also accused him of infidelity, and certainly had grounds for her jealousies. She had no way of knowing that he had affairs from time to time, and may have based her charges on her knowledge of the basic nature of the male animal. It is also possible that her repeated accusations may have driven William into the arms of other women. Eliza was a woman who, when an idea had occurred to her, clenched it between her teeth and refused to release it.

William's letters to her were remote, stiff and impersonal. What he wrote, through the years, was little more than a series of semiformal reports, somewhat less detailed than those he sent to his superiors in the Government. He dutifully inquired after Eliza's health in each communication and informed her that he was in good health, even when he wasn't. Aside from this slight gesture to convention, he might have been writing to a stranger.

The fact of the matter is that he and Eliza were strangers, and never came to know one another well. At no time in the eighteen years of their marriage did they spend more than a few consecutive weeks under the same roof. William learned that what his friends had warned him was true: no man could live with Eliza for more than a very short period of time.

But their initial parting had been planned well in advance. William knew he was leaving Massachusetts early in September, 1793, with his company, yet the marriage took place only two weeks earlier. There was no valid reason he and Eliza had to wait so long; they could have been married in June or July had they wished. In any event, the facts are eloquent; fifteen days after their marriage the bride and groom ended their honeymoon, sleeping in the same bed in which General Danielson had died, and William marched off to war.

He and his company acted as the advance guard for the New England contingent, and went by way of Albany and New York to Philadelphia, the seat of the Federal Government. There the ambitious young man, who had learned something about the way governments operate during his term as clerk of the Vermont House of Delegates, saw to it that men in positions of power became aware of him. He spent most of his time at the War Department, making the acquaintance of Secretary Knox and his civilian and military subordinates, and he also went out of his way to cultivate the friendship of influential members of the Senate and House of Representatives.

This was a practice he followed for the rest of his life, and it always paid handsome dividends. Eaton always had friends in Congress who were ready to support him in whatever venture he chose to undertake. He was one of the first lobbyists in America, and his principal aim was to promote himself. He succeeded admirably.

After spending a pleasant and profitable two months in Philadelphia, during which time the rest of the New England contingent went West without him, William and his company marched to Pittsburgh, where the Legion had established its headquarters. The flamboyant young officer and the even more flamboyant Anthony Wayne immediately took a liking to each other, much to the annoyance of senior officers who had been trying in vain to win the confidence of the commander in chief.

Lieutenant William Henry Harrison, Wayne's aide-de-camp, who was destined to become a renowned Indian fighter, administrator and eventually President of the United States, recorded his own impressions of this rapport in a letter to a colleague who would soon join the Legion. "The General," he wrote, "has found a kindred spirit in Captain Eaton of Massachusetts. They dine together frequently at the General's quarters, Fort Pitt, and spend their evenings speaking to each other in the language of the savage Miami, which they practice assiduously. I do not know what they say, even when I am present, since the language falls strangely on my ears, but they laugh and whoop and find great merriment together.

"Their friendship is odd, since most of the gentlemen close to the General are, like him, capable of drinking several quarts of ale with their dinner and finishing their meal with a bottle of port or brandywine. When Eaton is with him, however, the General does not seem to mind drinking alone, Eaton being most abstemious.

"Captain Eaton wears his cloak with a great flair, and he has demonstrated to the General that he is a fine rider and an even better marksman. Some members of the staff are annoyed because the General so frequently tells them to emulate Eaton in order to become better soldiers, since Eaton served in the War with Great Britain, and is no novice in military life."

William made only one mistake during this period, although he did not regard it as such, and good fortune not of his own doing put him on the right side of the fence. His self-assurance, combined with his quickly-won friendship with Anthony Wayne, made him a powerful enemy. Brigadier General James Wilkinson, deputy commander of the Legion, had little use for him, and wrote to his own aide: "We will never conquer the savages so long as men like Capt. Eaton serve in the Legion.

Eaton talks of his ability to withstand the hardships of wilderness living, but I will wager a large sum that his resolve will crumble when he is forced to sleep on the ground and eats meals less lavish than those prepared by Wayne's cook."

Wilkinson proved to be completely wrong. When the time came to march into the forest, William conducted himself with the cheerful aplomb of a born frontiersman, and the scouts, most of whom had spent the better part of their lives in the forests, assumed that he was one of their own number.

The quarrels that Wilkinson deliberately picked with William did him no harm, however, and, on the contrary, actually solidified his position with Wayne. The ambitious, scheming Wilkinson, who a few years later became involved in a conspiracy to turn a large part of the West over to Spain, was trying, in a surreptitiously conducted campaign, to persuade the War Department to retire Wayne on the grounds of incompetence. Then, he hoped, he would be promoted to Major General and given the command of the Legion.

As it happened, Anthony Wayne knew of his deputy's activities, and with the wisdom of a seasoned veteran made no attempt to halt them. He knew that Wilkinson would destroy himself and, in spite of Lieutenant Harrison's agitated warnings, ignored Wilkinson's conniving. He knew who the Brigadier General's friends were, however, and none of them won his own favor; similarly, he took a friendly interest in the men Wilkinson obviously disliked, so the more harshly Eaton was attacked the more firmly the commander in chief defended him.

In the late autumn of 1793 the Legion left Fort Pitt and moved into the wilderness of the Ohio Valley. There, at the site of St. Clair's defeat, Wayne built a strong post which he called Fort Recovery, and his troops went into winter quarters. His scouts remained active, some of them checking on the preparations for hostilities being made by the Miami and other tribes, while others posing as peddlers visited the trading posts and forts of the British, who were secretly encouraging the Indians.

William Eaton quickly tired of garrison life. Once the con-

struction work on the palisades and buildings of Fort Recovery
was completed, he had literally nothing to occupy his time
until spring came, and a young man whose appetite for glory
was unappeased felt bored and restless. Deciding his company
didn't need him until the campaign in the field began, he
applied for permission to scout the Miami.

General Wayne sensibly rejected the request. There was no
more dangerously treacherous tribe of savages on the North
American continent than the Miami, and William, who had
spent his entire life in New England prior to joining the
Legon, had literally no experience as a scout. The young officer
refused to accept the commander in chief's answer as final,
however, and opened a bombardment of pleas and arguments
so intense that the staff officers thought he would be court-
martialled.

Under the best of circumstances Anthony Wayne was short-
tempered and became irritated when his orders were questioned. At the moment his mood was particularly sour, partly
because he was suffering from a severe attack of gout, partly
because two regiments of Kentucky riflemen the War Department had promised him had not yet arrived. Most officers spoke
cautiously in his presence. Even General Wilkinson took care
not to cross him openly.

But Eaton believed he could handle the General, and quietly
proved his contention. On each of four successive days he went
to the commander in chief's headquarters to renew his request,
and the stubborn Wayne finally capitulated. Within an hour of
the time he gave his approval William left Fort Recovery on
foot, dressed in buckskins.

The month that followed is one of the most tantalizing,
mysterious periods in the life of William Eaton. Only the bare
outlines of what he did, and where, are known. He submitted
only one written report to Wayne, at the end of the month,
and it listed his accomplishments, not his activities. His *Life*
is reticent on the subject, too, and reveals one of the more
attractive facets of his basic philosophy.

Unlike most glory seekers, he wanted to be known only for

the actual good he accomplished, and he felt that his methods of achieving his ends were his own affair. His *Life* quietly lists the results of his scouting trip and his report to General Wayne does the same, sometimes in identical language, but he says literally nothing about the means he employed.

He penetrated deep into the forest homeland of the Miami, and apparently visited two of their major towns, where he saw their braves and the warriors of their allies congregating. Presumably he disguised himself as an Indian and was sufficiently clever to avoid detection; the correspondence of Harrison and that of several other officers flatly asserts that he completely fooled the savages by pretending to be one of their number.

The desire to transform himself into something new, something that he was not, was an element in the character of William Eaton that was to be repeated later in his life with far-reaching results. Why did he want to be taken for an Indian? Why, later, did he go to such lengths to disguise himself as an Arab, to submerge his own personality into that of a semibarbarian from a distant land?

The modern reader can do no more than stab in the dark. Was he something of a "mystic"? Perhaps. Was he so dissatisfied with what he may have considered a prosaic and dull existence that he sought excitement by assuming new roles? These, or a score of other interpretations might explain his "Indian phase" and his later "Arab phase." Since there is nothing in his own writing or in the observations of those who were close to him that might pin down what he actually felt, it is useless to speculate at random.

It is enough to note that there was a streak in his character that made him unlike his contemporaries or, for that matter, most men of most ages. He was one of those extraordinary human beings who, for lack of more information, defies precise definition. Let the reader merely realize that he was unique, by any standard in any era.

Many eyewitnesses report that, four and one-half weeks after Captain Eaton left Fort Recovery he returned wearing Indian leggings and moccasins, his head shaved on either side of a scalp lock, and with several dyed porcupine quills in his berry-darkened hair. He looked so much like a Miami warrior, in fact, that one of the sentries at Fort Recovery was about to shoot him when he managed to identify himself.

The news he brought with him was as accurate as it was full. He gave General Wayne the complete details of the Miami war plans, facts that were subsequently substantiated by three experienced scouts, each of them operating independently of the others. General Wayne took William at his word and, making his own plans accordingly, soon left Fort Recovery with the bulk of the Legion.

Captain Eaton had been too successful for his own good. General Wayne sent a special message to the War Department commending him for his efficiency, and then ordered him to remain at Fort Recovery as deputy commander of the post. The rest of the Legion marched off to do battle with the foe. William, whose company stayed behind with him, was condemned to a dull garrison existence.

William was so discouraged he wrote a gloomy letter to his brother-in-law, Amos Paine, and spoke of resigning his commission. He also sent a note to his stepson, Eli Danielson, urging the boy to abandon his hopes of seeking a military career. "You will do better," he declared, "to enter one of the more staid professions. There is more glory in the law than in the Army."

But the Eaton luck remained good. While General Wayne ruthlessly pursued his foes, maneuvering incessantly and hoping to force the enemy into a climactic battle, the Indians employed some clever tactics of their own. They could best disrupt Wayne, they believed, by attacking the strongholds he had established as his bases, and the most obvious of these was Fort Recovery.

At dawn on June 14, 1794, a war party of approximately five hundred braves launched a ferocious assault on the palisades of Fort Recovery, which was ordinarily defended by a force of only 105 men. Although the Indians did not know it, a convoy of mules and pack horses had arrived the previous day, escorted by fifty mounted dragoons and ninety riflemen. These reinforcements gave the defenders the strength to hold their own.

The commander of Fort Recovery, a major, suffered a painful wound early in the action, and was carried off to the interior of the compound to be treated by a surgeon. This left Captain Eaton in charge, and he quickly proved himself worthy of the responsibility. "The Captain," Third Lieutenant John Hyde of Bennington, a member of William's own company, wrote to his parents, "was like a gale that blows in from the sea. He was everywhere, directing our operations, rallying the defenders, posting men to the weak places and rallying those who faltered."

The initial attack caught the defenders off guard, and the Miami almost succeeded in storming the palisades. The confusion became worse when the Major was felled by an arrow, and a score of braves actually reached the top of the north palisade, a wall of saplings, the tops of which had been sharpened. William promptly set an example for his sharpshooters by calmly aiming his rifle at the intruders and killing two of them. The Legion marksmen cut down all but four who managed to escape.

By then the entire garrison was alert and William ordered the rifle platforms on all four sides of his perimeter manned, but kept the better part of his little force in the center of the compound as a reserve. As the need arose he sent these troops from place to place, in order to bolster the defenses. And he repeatedly issued the same order to his men: "Don't fire too soon," he told them. "Wait until the warriors are only a few paces from the walls. Then, when you shoot, don't miss!"

Again and again the Indians stormed the ramparts, but were thrown back. Growing desperate, they sent flaming arrows over the palisades, hoping to start a fire that would drive the troops into the open. But William met that emergency too. He used his reserves as a bucket brigade, under the direction of the

40

officer who had commanded the pack convoy. Every available receptacle in the fort was filled with water at one of the two wells and whenever a building caught fire men were on hand to throw water on it and put it out. Meanwhile the rifle platforms were still manned.

After more than seven hours of almost continuous fighting, the Miami made a last, frenzied attempt to capture the post. Some of the braves, William said in his official report to General Wayne, were frothing at the mouth, and he believed they had been crazed by cheap liquor the British had given them.

William cooly ordered his troops to hold their fire until the savages literally reached the base of the palisades. Then every man was told to fire at will. It was impossible to miss at such close range, but the defenders were protected by the walls of the palisades, and their own losses were slight. In the final assault alone, more than one hundred warriors were either killed or severely wounded, and the Miami withdrew, badly battered.

The Legion's casualties in the affair were miraculously low. One soldier was killed and six were injured; the only officer hurt was the commandant. And the American flag continued to fly over the inviolate fort.

William sent off a special courier with a full report to General Wayne, and a few days later received a letter of congratulations in return. Wayne informed him that he was being commended in another message to the War Department, and as a "reward" for his valor and success, was being given command of Fort Recovery. He had no choice, and accepted the "honor."

For the rest of the summer he and his men saw no significant action and took no part in the climactic Battle of Fallen Timbers, in which General Wayne destroyed the capacity of the savages to wage war and forced them to sue for peace. The campaign in the West at an end, new garrison troops were dispatched from the East, and the victorious Wayne sat down with representatives of eight Indian tribes to draw up peace treaty terms.

Captain Eaton, who had no intention of twiddling his thumbs at Fort Recovery, applied for a leave of absence and subsequent transfer. Wayne approved his application, and he set out for Massachusetts by way of Philadelphia and New York. One of the first conquerors of the West to arrive in the nation's capital, his exploits as a scout and his spirited defense of Fort Recovery made him a genuine war hero. Members of Congress reacted accordingly, as did other government officials.

It was during this period that William's interest in North Africa first became evident. He had read the Koran, the holy book of Mohammedanism, during his stay at Fort Recovery, and had also steeped himself in the history of the Turks' far-flung Ottoman Empire, which was still powerful, although growing weaker. At the age of thirty William was thinking in long-range terms, and apparently was developing a desire to visit either Turkey, where no Americans were admitted, or the Barbary nations of North Africa, which were nominally a part of the Ottoman Empire, but for all practical purposes ruled themselves.

In order to further his new goal the canny Captain Eaton made it his business to meet every official of the State Department who might be useful to him. Senators and congressmen were his patrons, so it was easy to arrange introductions. William lingered for a month, dining with men from the State Department who were flattered that the war hero had sought them out. Reaching high, William even managed to become friendly with Secretary of State Timothy Pickering.

Finally, unable to delay any longer, William traveled north to Brimfield where a blistering welcome awaited him from his wife, who accused him of living riotously with fallen women in Philadelphia and New York instead of coming home to her. For once, apparently, William was innocent; if he enjoyed any escapades in his travels they are unrecorded.

He and Eliza fought incessantly from the day of his arrival, and he was so miserable that he sent a letter to the nearest Army headquarters, in Boston, asking that his leave be cut

42

short and that he be posted at once to active duty. His request was granted, and he was sent to familiar, nearby Springfield, as officer in charge of recruiting. Thereafter, for the remaining months of 1794, he returned to Brimfield only on weekends to renew his battle with Eliza.

His stepson could not get along with Eliza either, and the boy came to Springfield to live with William. Eli Danielson appears to have been closer to Eaton than anyone he had ever known, and before leaving Springfield William arranged to have him admitted to Dartmouth College. Eliza was opposed to the idea for reasons of her own—if she needed reasons—so William paid for Eli's education himself.

New orders came from the War Department in mid-December, 1794, and William was so anxious to escape from his wife that he left Massachusets the week before Christmas for his new post. His company had already been transferred to the Third Infantry Regiment, which was stationed in Georgia and commanded by Colonel Henry B. Gaither. William was ordered to join the regiment and retake command of his unit.

He entered Eli at Dartmouth, then returned to Brimfield for a token visit of two days before starting out again. If he had not known before coming home from the West that his marriage had been a terrible mistake, he undoubtedly knew it now. But he never complained about Liza, and in his own way was loyal to her. Others wrote at great length that she was bad-tempered and treated him nastily, but he suffered her abuse in public silence. It is significant to observe, however, that never during all the years of their marriage did he see her anywhere but in Brimfield. Even when he was enjoying the fame he had always craved and made triumphant appearances in Philadelphia and Baltimore and New York, in Hartford and Boston and Providence, Eliza stayed at home. Her son's correspondence makes it clear that she wanted to accompany her husband and share in his glory, but William refused to take her with him.

Their pattern was formed when he left Brimfield in December of 1794. He traveled by way of Connecticut, stopping to see his relatives in Mansfield. His most recent encounter with his wife had left him with a desire, stronger than ever, to see Sophie Smith, and he sent a relatively brief letter to her in New Britain indicating he "might" be in the vicinity shortly. But Sophie did not reply, and he went straight to New York and then to Philadelphia, again renewing his friendships with senators, congressmen, his superiors in the War Department and his new acquaintances in the State Department.

While in Philadelphia he also spent considerable time in the city's bookshops, and purchased a number of volumes on Islam. It is impossible to determine what had sparked his interest in the Mohammedan lands, and it can only be reported that they fascinated him. He had studied philosophy at Dartmouth, and perhaps had been introduced to the writing of the Prophet Mohammed there. He himself offers no explanation of his reading at Fort Recovery, but one fact is plain. He must have taken the *Koran* and the history of the Ottoman Empire into the West with him.

He always carried books no matter where he went, and attributes no special importance to his choice of reading matter in the Ohio Valley wilderness. By now, however, a new goal had crystallized within him, and a notation in his Journal-Diary, written on January 5, 1795, in Philadelphia, is very clear.

"I wish to learn Arabic," he wrote, "and to find out all I can about the Ottomans. Some day I shall visit that far-off part of the world, and if the Almighty wishes it for me, may even live there for a time. Therefore all I can discover and learn now will be of use to me later."

None of his friends or relatives were engaged in trade with any of the Mediterranean countries, and neither members of his own family nor his wife's were seamen. The Barbary states were not yet prominent in the news, having just begun their raids on American merchant shipping, and no mention of Tunis and Algiers, Morocco and Tripoli can be found in American newspapers prior to 1796 and 1797.

Hence there is no logical reason why William should have

felt impelled to learn the language of that remote region, or why he should have wanted to find out all he could about the religious beliefs and customs of Mohammedans. In later years he sometimes mentioned his belief that he had been brought to North Africa by his kismet, the Arabic term for a predetermined fate willed by God, but if he really held such a view it was not accurate.

He himself was responsible for his kismet, first having developed an interest in the region, then cultivating the friendship of men who had the power to send him there, and, finally, asking them to use that power on his behalf.

Perhaps it is enough to note that Islam became his hobby, and that he carried a trunk filled with books on the Ottoman Empire with him when he left Philadelphia for Georgia. Inasmuch as a number of these volumes were written in Arabic, it was obvious that he was serious in his desire to learn the language.

Apparently he made no mention of his long-term thinking to anyone, however. He regarded young Eli Danielson, now something of an alter ego, as worthy of every confidence, but said nothing to the boy about his plans in any of the long letters he sent to Dartmouth. Like the Mohammedan rulers he was coming to admire, William knew when it served his best interests to keep his mouth shut.

Meanwhile he had every reason to believe he could advance his military career and win additional renown in his Georgia assignment. The Creek Indians were stirring, threatening to exterminate Americans, the Spaniards in the Floridas were casting covetous eyes across the borders of the weak young United States, and British agents were reputedly active in the area. Georgia was fertile ground for a glory seeker.

CHAPTER FOUR

THE ADVENTURER

William booked passage on a coastal schooner, the *Doodilian*, and sailed from Philadelphia on January 9, 1795. This was his first experience at sea, and like so many before and after him, he discovered that a voyage parallel to the shores of the United States could be a harrowing experience. He became violently ill, conceiving a dislike for the sea that he felt for the rest of his life, and spent the first few days in his bunk, too ill to care whether the schooner capsized or reached her destination.

Eventually he recovered and began to enjoy himself. There were only three passengers on board the cargo ship, which had accommodations for eight, so he slept in a cabin of his own, a luxury that few travelers were ever granted, and to his surprise found the food delicious. He quickly developed a taste for roasted oysters and fried crabs and also dined on such delicacies as beef and ham pie, wild turkey and, one evening, a suckling pig. The master of the *Doodilian* obviously relished gourmet meals.

This was William's first taste, literally and figuratively, of high living. Money had been scarce since his earliest childhood, and although he had not gone hungry he had never been able to spend recklessly either. The government was paying for his passage and expenses, so he took a holiday on the high seas. There is a line in his Journal-Diary, written on board the schooner, strongly hinting that for the first time in his life he began to recognize the comforts money could buy.

"This voyage," he scribbled, "was a nightmare in its first days, but I now find it comfortably salubrious. Would that I could afford the joys of the table that here are commonplace."

He returned to the mundane when the *Doodilian* put into Savannah, the principal town of Georgia, and he disembarked. Little more than a village at the close of the American Revolution, it was still a raw frontier town. Most of its houses, offices and stores were log cabins, the building in which the state legislature met resembled a dilapidated barn, and no self-respecting New England farmer would have lived in the governor's official mansion. The army barracks were shabby, and the officers' quarters were approximately on a par with the crude lodges of the Miami Indians in the Ohio Valley, William noted in his Journal-Diary.

But the citizens of Georgia were friendlier than any people he had ever known. "There is much dining in this place at the homes of the wealthy and of the gentlemen of the state government," he wrote. "The company of Army officers is sought by all, and scarce a night passes that I fail to dine as the guest of some worthy and his wife. Only rarely am I forced to endure the gastronomical tortures of the officers' mess hall."

It was something of a novelty to be a social lion, and William enjoyed himself thoroughly. Since his meals cost him so little he was able to save nearly all of his wages as a Captain, which amounted to approximately $42 per month. He had already paid for Eli Danielson's tuition, room and board at Dartmouth College out of funds previously saved, and had nothing else on which to spend his income. Apparently he contributed nothing to the support of his wife and stepdaughter, who continued to live on the income from the property that Eliza's first husband had left her.

Ten weeks of Savannah's social whirl satiated William, and

he was relieved when Colonel Gaither received orders from the War Department transferring the regiment to a village outpost, St. Mary, which was located near the border of the Spanish Floridas. The unit was given a twofold mission: it was directed to overawe the Creeks, then establish friendly relations with them, while at the same time halting the flow of British and Spanish agents across the border. At least there was important work to be done.

Colonel Gaither began the construction of a trading post at St. Mary, hoping that the offer of inexpensive blankets, cooking utensils and trinkets might make the Creek more amenable. At the same time, however, he had to bolster his defenses, and sent William off to the border to build a new fort and observation post on the American bank of the St. Mary's River, the dividing line. William was given two platoons in addition to his own company for the purpose.

The assignment rapidly proved to be far more difficult than it appeared on the surface. Most of the vegetation in the vicinity of the river consisted of grass, swamp reeds and bushes. There were no trees of consequence within several miles in any direction, so the troops put aside their axes and reached instead for their spades.

The fort was made of mud, reinforced with long strands of grass, and in order to make it as strong as possible, the walls were five feet thick. The main building was only one story high, since anything bigger might have collapsed, and even the outer wall, which stood eleven feet high, was made of mud.

William privately called the place "the Monument of Mud," and referred to it by that name in his correspondence with Colonel Gaither. He was disgusted and declared that he, his officers and men were filthy, unable to clean themselves or their uniforms in the muddy waters of the St. Mary's River. Gaither, who had been associated with General Wilkinson and had been influenced by his friend, strongly disliked William and promptly assigned him to permanent duty at the place.

An army officer had to make the best of any given situation, and William tried. Although it was customary to give small border forts and similar outposts the formal names of their builders, William wanted no such honor for himself. Hoping to do himself as much good as he could, he called the bastion Fort Pickering and sent the Secretary of State a letter telling him what he had done. Pickering, who would have been less happy had he seen the post, was overwhelmed, and wrote William a warm letter of thanks.

The garrison settled down to keep the border clear and when possible prevent the Creeks from causing mischief. William, with little else to occupy him, immediately decided to learn all he could about these savages. Replacing his uniform with buckskins he had brought with him from the Ohio Valley campaign, he left a lieutenant in temporary command of the fort, and went alone into the wilderness, seeking the Creeks.

After two or three days he encountered a small party of braves, and managed to make himself understood by speaking the tongue of the Miamis. Once the Creeks realized that he had no hostile intentions, they accepted him, and took him with them to their village. Once again William Eaton demonstrated his extraordinary ability to establish a rapport with an alien people, to win their friendship and ultimately to be accepted as one of their own number.

His visit to the Creeks was marked by exhibitions of good will on both sides, a remarkable feat. The savages would have nothing to do with other Americans, and Colonel Gaither's trading post was a desolate failure. In the seven months of its miserable existence, not one Creek went near it and it was forced to close. By the end of that same period, William was adopted by the Creeks, who made him a blood brother in a formal ceremony.

Showing his usual aptitude for languages, he became thoroughly familiar with the tongue of the Indians. He also showed a sympathetic understanding of their tribal customs, and was offered the daughter of a chief as a bride. Notwithstanding the fact that he was already married, he took the girl back to Fort

Pickering and she lived there with him for the better part of a year before returning to her own people.

From the time Fort Pickering was built until William's retirement from the Army in December, 1796, relations between the Creeks and the United States were peaceful. The savages conducted no raids on wilderness settlements or remote plantations. Not one settler was molested or threatened, and nothing was stolen. Even though British agents continued to roam through the area, bribing the Indians and trying to stir up trouble, the friendship of one man was a force strong enough to insure tranquility.

Colonel Gaither should have recognized William's achievement, but apparently took the unexpected peace with the Creeks for granted. So did his immediate subordinates, and nothing in their official dispatches to the War Department even hinted at Captain Eaton's accomplishment. The citizens of Georgia were aware of what William had done, however, and the state legislature voted him a purse of five hundred dollars.

He could have used the money, but instead graciously rejected the gift. Georgians were poor, he said in a letter to the legislature, and he preferred to see the money used to improve roads. The stunned assemblymen, who had never heard of anyone turning down hard cash, made him an honorary citizen of the state and offered him a tract of land any time he decided to settle there.

The relations William established and maintained with the Creeks took only a small part of his time, and he continued his studies of Islam. He became proficient in the reading of Arabic, although there was no one with whom he could speak the language. He also became something of an expert in the history of Islam and the philosophy of Mohammedanism. A few casual references in his letters to Eli Danielson indicated the pleasure he felt as he made progress, but as yet he had no concrete future plans. He still did not know how he might use his newly acquired knowledge.

But Arabic and the Creeks were side issues. Most of William's attention and time were being devoted to an activity that had become a mania for thousands of Americans. Virtually every man who had money—and many who did not—speculated in Western lands. Even President Washington caught the fever. Robert Morris, the prominent Philadelphia banker who had been one of the principal financiers of the Revolution, went bankrupt and was sent to debtors' prison. The same fate awaited Major General Henry Lee, who had achieved fame as Light-Horse Harry Lee, and scores of others were similarly afflicted.

Land companies were springing up everywhere, establishing dubious claims to vast tracts in Tennessee, Mississippi and Alabama. Some men invested their life savings in these ventures, while others, gambling still more recklessly, wrote promises to pay for their purchases. Occasionally investors received dazzling returns, sometimes earning as much as $200 for every dollar pledged, but in most instances disaster crushed the optimists who were trying to get something for nothing. Nine out of ten land companies failed, and when they did thousands of investors went bankrupt.

Colonel Gaither, who had first invested in Western lands in 1794, was either shrewd or lucky; perhaps he was both. In any event, he had become wealthy by the time William Eaton arrived in Georgia, and the regimental commander's good fortune was the envy of all his officers. William, who had never in his life gambled a penny on anything, decided to take a fling in land speculation, and invested $200 in a new company just formed in Mississippi.

Two older, larger companies were interested in the same tract, but apparently the new concern had the best claim to it. The others began spirited bidding to buy out the newcomers. The results were electrifying, and created newspaper headlines throughout the United States. Only nine weeks after William invested his $200, he received $15,000 in return, a fortune in a day when an officer of his rank earned only $500 in a year.

The company decided to try again, and the original investors were given the first opportunity to put money into the new venture. William cautiously kept aside $3,000 in cash and returned $12,000 to the company. This time he had to wait longer for results. As the months dragged he began to think that his money, like that of so many others before him, would vanish.

But his luck remained good, and his $12,000 became $54,000, which made him wealthy. He wisely decided to withdraw before he was burned, and had the funds deposited in his name in three banks, two in Philadelphia and one in New York. Suddenly and unexpectedly, in early October, 1796, he found himself a wealthy man.

Meanwhile Colonel Gaither's luck had turned sour. His own land speculations were turning to dross, and he not only lost his profits but his original investments as well. At the same time William was becoming rich, Gaither went bankrupt overnight.

The jealous Colonel immediately turned on his subordinate. William had spent official Army time on his private business, he said, and therefore was guilty of malpractice. He also accused Captain Eaton of selling government supplies to the Creeks for private profit and added charges of insubordination and disobedience for good measure. The first William learned of his superior's accusations was an official notice from St. Mary's telling him he had been court-martialled in absentia and found guilty. He was ordered to remain at his post pending a review of the case by the War Department, but in the meantime would receive no wages.

It was true, of course, that land speculations had kept William occupied on army time, which was technically a violation of regulations. It was also true that he was no guiltier than Gaither and dozens of other officers, although this, naturally, was no defense. The other charges were groundless, however, and he was furiously angry. Ordered to remain at Fort Pickering, he could not go to Philadelphia to defend himself. He therefore did the next best thing, writing a long, clear statement of self-defense that any military lawyer would have been proud to have composed.

Having sent the communication to the War Department,

William could do nothing but wait. His honor and reputation were at stake, but he could not help himself, and life at Fort Pickering became a nightmare of suspense. Gaither was no longer communicating with his subordinate, William wanted nothing to do with the Colonel, and, with the Creeks at peace and no British or Spanish agents trying to cross the St. Mary's River in the vicinity, the doldrums set in.

On December 2, 1796, a court-martial review board reversed the findings of the 3rd Infantry Regiment court-martial. Captain William H. Eaton was declared innocent, and was exonerated. The War Department restored his pay, privileges and rank on the Captain's list. A mild rebuke was issued to Colonel Gaither, who was informed he had been too zealous in his prosecution of his Captain.

William received the good news on December 17, 1796, but was dismayed to learn that neither he nor Gaither was being transferred. Relations were so strained that the two men could no longer work together amicably, yet both were being retained in their present posts. Since the official rebuke to Gaither made it unlikely that he would ever be promoted to the rank of Brigadier General, it was obvious that he would make life as miserable as he could for William, who saw no future for himself in the Army.

With the United States at peace, officer promotions had been slowed to the proverbial snail's pace, and under the best of circumstances William would have to wait at least ten more years before he could be made a major. And if Gaither gave him a bad report before he could be transferred elsewhere, which seemed likely, he might never be promoted.

Probably the decision to leave the Army had been building in William for some time. The path to glory he had chosen for himself was tortuous and strewn with obstacles. Certainly the realization that he would have to continue to serve under Gaither spurred him to take immediate action. Never one to dally when he had made up his mind, he resigned his commission, effective December 31st, 1796.

He remained at Fort Pickering until midnight on that date. Then, turning over Fort Pickering to a captain sent from St. Mary to replace him, he set out at once for Savannah, not bothering to pause at regimental headquarters. Members of the Georgia legislature sympathized with him, and several urged him to settle in the state, but he had less desire than ever to live the quiet existence of a back-country farmer, be it in Connecticut, Massachusetts or Georgia.

No transportation by sea being available, William made his journey north by land. He traveled rapidly, using rented post horses, and did not tarry anywhere. As yet, from what he wrote to Eli, he had no definite plans in mind, but his obvious immediate goal was Philadelphia, where he hoped to utilize the friendships he had been cultivating for several years.

A shock awaited him when, in February, 1797, he reached the capital. He went first to the War Department, intending to pay courtesy calls on several of his former superiors, and learned that, although his resignation had been accepted, it would not become effective until June 30th. He was still in the Army.

But the War Department had no assignment for him. He faced the dreary prospect of spending almost five months in Philadelphia doing nothing. He appealed for an immediate release, but his request was rejected; under a new policy, officers were required to wait six months from the dates of their resignation before being released.

Then, unexpectedly, Secretary of State Pickering, still glowing because a fort had been named for him, came to William's rescue. He had confidential work for a trustworthy, able man, and asked the War Department to send him Captain Eaton on loan. Everyone's problem was solved.

William's first assignment for Pickering was delicate and important. A special congressional committee of two senators and two representatives was cooperating with the State Department in the secret investigation of an espionage-treason case involving both the British and French legations. As yet no concrete evidence had been gathered, and no formal accusations could be made against anyone. The most difficult aspect of the case was that, if mishandled, it might cause both Great Britain and France to terminate diplomatic relations with the United States.

According to the little that had been gleaned, a physician in New York, Dr. Nicholas Romayne, had been used by the two legations as an intermediary. Espionage agents had reported their findings to him and he, in return, had paid them with funds obtained from the legations. A cautious man, Romayne had worked so discreetly that the American Government could prove nothing against him.

William was given the task of going to New York and finding out what he could about the physician. He chose the direct approach. Dressing in old clothes, he went straight to Romayne and introduced himself under his real name. The story he told contained elements of the truth and sounded convincing. He had been a Captain in the Army, he said, had lost all his money in land speculation and, having been found guilty on many charges by a court-martial board, had been dismissed from the service.

As proof of his contention, he showed Dr. Romayne the findings of Colonel Gaither's board at St. Mary. He had no money now, William said, and also wanted revenge against the men who had disgraced him. He indicated that he knew the precise location and strength of every border fort in Georgia, and hinted that he would be willing to sell this information if the price was right.

Romayne, while carefully refraining from admitting that he might find a purchaser, merely sounded sympathetic, gave William enough money to pay his expenses at a cheap inn for a few days, and asked him to come back within a week.

William, still living his part, went to an inn near the old British military post, Fort George, near the lower tip of Manhattan Island. He wrote a brief letter to Secretary Pickering, saying only that if any inquiries were made about him, it would be well to indicate that he had been discharged from the Army.

Romayne kept William waiting for eleven days, during which

time the chargé d'affaires of the British legation found it convenient to bring up the subject of a Captain Eaton at a dinner party. He was informed by a brigadier general on the War Department staff that Captain Eaton had been dismissed from the service. The case was a painful one, the general said, and he didn't want to discuss it. The chargé d'affaires, of course, had learned all he wanted to know.

Dr. Romayne sent for William and told him that, if he proved he could deliver detailed information about the border forts, he would be given the sum of one hundred dollars. Feigning indignation, William threatened to go to the Spanish legation where, he claimed, he would be given $1,000 in gold at once.

Romayne capitulated, and offered to match the sum in return for the information. The offer was all that William needed: he had trapped the intermediary. Drawing a pistol from an inner pocket of his coat, he forced the physician to stand aside while he went through the drawers of Romayne's desk. There he found a number of incriminating documents, which he kept.

Had he walked out at that point and returned to Philadelphia, his mission would have been successful enough to win him a commendation. But he saw no reason to give Romayne an opportunity to escape. So, in a daring move, he forced the physician to accompany him to the local Army headquarters. There he identified himself, but without explaining anything about the case on which he was working requested that two sergeants and a junior officer be assigned to him, together with transportation, to escort his prisoner to Philadelphia.

Three days later a triumphant William delivered the person of Dr. Romayne and the incriminating evidence to the State Department. Immediately thereafter two officials on the staff of the British legation and the French military attaché quietly left for home at the request of the United States Government. The members of the congressional committee added their congratulations to the thanks of the State Department, and William solidified his position.

Within a few days of the incident, on March 4, 1797, John Adams of Massachusetts was inaugurated as the second President of the United States, which was fortuitous for William Eaton. President Adams was informed of the recent incident and, with the threat of war with both Great Britain and France hanging over his head, he sent for the competent Captain Eaton. There was a task the President wanted him to perform, that of informally neutralizing the Spaniards, who could add to the miseries of the United States if they attacked Georgia or sent gunboats up the Mississippi River from their great base at New Orleans.

A presidential assignment was of the utmost importance, and William knew that if he succeeded President Adams would be inclined to give him anything he wanted. He made his plans with care, and saw to it that he was invited to a dinner party attended by Don Diego de Rivera-Sanchez, the deputy minister of the Spanish legation. Don Diego was an ambitious man, anxious to rise higher in the service of his country, and William saw him as the perfect instrument for carrying out President Adams' wishes.

Captain Eaton appeared at the dinner party in dress uniform, which he was still entitled to wear. He made it his business to charm Don Diego. By the time the evening ended, they had made an appointment to dine together a few days later.

William developed the friendship slowly and refused to become flustered when President Adams summoned him to find out what progress he had made. Refusing to be hurried, he insisted that all would be well.

Gradually, as he and Don Diego saw one another frequently in April and May, William allowed it to slip out that he had been stationed in Georgia. In fact, his position had been a confidential one, that of chief military inspector of the border posts. Don Diego was very much interested, but he too took his time.

Late in May William confessed to his new friend one evening that he was worried about his future. He was leaving the

Army in a few weeks, a fact that Rivera-Sanchez probably knew, and he had no plans. He was uncertain how he would live and didn't know what he would do to support his wife and step-children. But, he insisted, he didn't want to burden a friend with his troubles, and promptly dropped the subject. The hook was baited.

A few days later Don Diego swallowed the hook, inviting William to call on him at the Spanish legation. Only because of the great friendship he felt, the deputy minister declared, was he going to tread on delicate ground. If William cared to tell him all he knew about the border forts, Don Diego would be grateful, so appreciative, in fact, that he could guarantee the ex-officer good employment in New Orleans, a growing city with a wonderful future.

William was ready for just such an offer. He talked at great length, painting a picture of defense preparations on the American-Spanish border along the St. Mary's River that left the Spaniard gasping for breath. Embroidering on facts and using his fertile imagination, William spoke of secret forts located in the wilderness, of mobile reserve forces ready to pounce if Spain should launch an invasion from the Floridas.

Don Diego took careful notes, and when his guest was finished, he was prepared to keep his end of the bargain. But William feigned deep regret, saying he could not go to New Orleans. If he accepted payment for the information, he would be a paid spy and no one would ever trust him again. He had spoken in detail of his country's defense preparations, he declared, because he felt it in the best interests of both the United States and Spain to reveal them. As for his own future, he would find gainful, honorable employment somewhere in his own country.

When he and the deputy minister parted, he knew he still had the respect of Don Diego, which was essential to his scheme. Now, having done all he could, he reported to President Adams that he had completed his mission and that results should be forthcoming shortly.

Literally nothing happened. May became June, weeks passed, and at the end of the month William formally retired from the Army. He had no financial worries, thanks to his successful land speculations, and stayed on in Philadelphia, even though Eliza was writing him brusque letters demanding that he come to Brimfield.

Finally, in late July, the Spaniards responded. Don Diego paid a formal call at the State Department, and said that his Government was interested in arranging a new treaty of friendship with the United States. Negotiations were scheduled, President Adams appointed a special commission to travel to Madrid, and the American-Spanish borders were secure for the present, giving the United States time to deal as best she could with England and France.

William Eaton had been completely successful. As he had anticipated, President Adams asked if there was anything he could do in return. There was. William requested that he be appointed United States Consular Agent at Tunis on the Barbary Coast, a post that had fortuitously fallen vacant three months earlier.

The President checked with the State Department, which enthusiastically endorsed the idea, as did the War Department. Key members of both Houses of Congress also favored the appointment, and Adams was assured that the Senate would give its necessary confirmation. Only the new Navy Department, which the President had just created, was somewhat dubious and would have preferred someone who had closer ties with seafaring men.

However, since a Navy as such did not yet exist, and the President was just beginning to receive recommendations for his Navy's officer corps, the protest carried little weight. The appointment was made and the Senate confirmed it within forty-eight hours. William, now a high-ranking official of the State Department, was free to visit his wife in Brimfield, a questionable privilege, before going off to the world of the Barbary pirate states.

CHAPTER FIVE

RENDEZVOUS WITH DESTINY

The new Consular Agent had been given one of the most difficult diplomatic assignments in his country's short history, for
the United States was in deep trouble in the Barbary states.
The survival of the United States as an independent nation
depended on her ability to trade freely with the rest of the
world, and, if unable to develop her new industries and sell
her products beyond her borders, there was a strong possibility
that she might revert to a colonial status under either British
or French rule.

No area offered more lucrative profits than the nations on the
Mediterranean Sea, where there was a heavy demand for American lumber, furs and the cloth being produced by the rapidly
growing textile industry. But a state of near-anarchy existed in
the Mediterranean and the master of a merchant ship who ventured into those waters was risking his own life and those of his
men, as well as the possible loss of his ship and its cargo.

On the northern shore of Africa, known as the Barbary Coast,
were four nations, all of them part of the sprawling Ottoman
Empire of the Turks but for all practical purposes independent
nations that paid only token allegiance to Constantinople.
Strongly anti-Christian on religious grounds, Morocco and Al-

giers, Tunis and Tripoli were literally pirate nations whose rulers supported themselves, their courts and their harems by payments of tribute from any country that wanted to send its merchantmen into the Mediterranean, a body of water the Barbary Coast masters considered their private sea.

There were no subtleties in the arrangements. The governments of Great Britain, France, Holland, Denmark and Sweden, all of which had large merchant fleets, paid the rulers of Barbary large sums of money each year in blackmail. When one of them was late in making a payment, or when a Dey or Bey wanted an extra "contribution," a pirate fleet sailed into the Mediterranean and captured a merchant ship. The vessel was impounded and sometimes kept, its cargo was confiscated, often its sailors were enslaved. There were former seamen who were spending the rest of their miserable lives in bondage.

All of the European nations had navies, those of the British and French being the largest and most powerful on earth. Had London and Paris wished, their warships could have blown the pirate fleets out of the sea and bombarded the capitals of Barbary. But they refrained, in part because it was easier and cheaper to pay tribute, in part because England and France were on the verge of war with each other and did not want to be distracted by minor campaigns.

The United States suffered several major disadvantages when American ships entered the Mediterranean. The new nation had no navy, and her homeland was located more than three thousand miles away. A proud young nation that had just won her independence by force of arms resented bullying by anyone, and the very principle of paying tribute was contrary to the principles on which the new republic was founded.

In spite of handicaps and scruples, however, the United States found herself being drawn into the European pattern. The first American vessel to run afoul of the Barbary pirates was a brig, the *Betsey*, which was captured by the Moroccans in 1784. The Confederation Congress authorized John Adams, the American minister in London, and Thomas Jefferson, her minister in

Paris, to negotiate for the release of the ship, her cargo and her crew.

The Moroccan minister in London represented his Emperor in the talks, and his demands were so outrageous that the reasonable Jefferson, who hated war and was dedicated to the idea of seeking peaceful solutions to international problems whenever possible, wanted to build a navy and teach the Moroccans a lesson. Adams, who was more realistic, knew it would be impossible to build ships and train a fleet. During the period of the Confederation, before the Constitution was prepared and adopted, the thirteen states of the American Union could agree on few problems. Not until the new Federal Government came into being in 1789 did the nation begin to grow strong.

Adams recommended that, in order to prevent the crew of the *Betsey* from being enslaved, the United States should treat with the Emperor as the nations of Europe were doing. The Confederation Congress agreed because it had no choice. The talks dragged, in part because it took so long for each new set of proposals and demands to be sent across the Atlantic for approval. Finally, in 1786, the American Consul at Gibraltar, Thomas Barclay, signed an agreement; the United States paid the Emperor of Morocco $10,000 in cash and the master and crew of the *Betsey* were allowed to sail for home in the brig. Her cargo had long since been confiscated by the Moroccans, but the men and ship were safe, so no American objected too strenuously.

American shipping in the Mediterranean increased, and in 1792 several American merchantmen were captured by Algerian pirates. President Washington, unable to deal with the situation forcibly, sent a recommendation to the Senate in his own handwriting, asking that funds be appropriated to secure the release of the enslaved American seamen and prevent such incidents in the future. The Senate, equally unhappy, voted the sum of $40,000 as ransom, and authorized the payment of an additional $25,000 per year to the Dey of Algiers in return for his promise that his ships would not molest American shipping.

Unfortunately, that was merely the beginning of America's troubles. In 1793 Portugal concluded a new treaty with Algiers, by which Portuguese ships were allowed to sail where they pleased in the Mediterranean. In return Algerian ships were permitted to leave the inland sea and cruise in the open Atlantic. American ships were captured in the Atlantic, and the Dey of Algiers blithely insisted the tribute he was receiving covered only the Mediterranean. The freedom of each ship captured in the Atlantic had to be purchased with fresh tribute.

The Algerians proved themselves exceptionally adept in the art of extracting money from the United States. As the largest and most powerful of the Barbary pirate states, Algiers found herself in a position to call the tunes, and did. The United States was forced to promise the Dey that a thirty-six-gun frigate would be built in American shipyards and presented to him; whenever a new American Consul was appointed, the United States was required to give the Dey $20,000 in silver and $21,000 in naval stores. "Gifts" of $17,000 were expected annually on the birthday of the Dey, that of his eldest son and for each of several Mohammedan holidays.

By the time William Eaton joined the consular staff in the Barbary states, the United States had already paid more than $1,150,000 in blackmail to the Dey of Algiers. The efficient, hard pressed American consul in Algiers, Joel Barlow, was required to work out similar agreements with Tunis and Tripoli. The latter was concluded and signed in November, 1796, the former in January, 1797. Both of these "treaties of peace and friendship" were humiliating, guaranteeing that in return for regular cash payments and naval stores, the pirate navies of Tunis and Tripoli would not molest American shipping. American Consular Agents would represent the United States in both states, reporting to the Consul at Algiers, who would be their superior, and the Dey of Algiers guaranteed the good faith of the two lesser Barbary nations.

Feeling in the United States ran high, and there were daily denunciations of the pirates in both the Senate and the House.

63

In 1797 President Adams authorized the construction of six powerful frigates, as well as the building of a large number of sloops-of-war, schooners and ketches. Ambitious young officers in the merchant marine were being recruited and interviewed by the new Navy Department, and American newspapers freely predicted that the payment of blackmail would stop when the United States Navy took to the high seas.

In the meantime Barlow and his associates had the ticklish task of maintaining peaceful, if not cordial, relations with the Barbary rulers and above all trying to hold the demands for fresh payments of tribute to a minimum. American lives and American shipping were at stake, and American diplomats were required to speak softly and placatingly. The Bey of Tunis received an outright gift of $100,000 in return for signing his treaty, and the Bey Yusef Karamanli Pasha of Tripoli was given $50,000. Everyone knew these payments were merely the start, not the end, but, until the United States became stronger there was no alternative.

William Eaton received his State Department appointment in July, 1797, and expected to sail soon after paying a token visit to his wife. He spent a few days in Brimfield, but they seemed endless. He and Eliza were barely on speaking terms when he returned to Philadelphia, eager to set out for Islam. In the capital he met James L. Cathcart, the newly appointed Consular Agent to Tripoli, and together they waited for official transportation.

It was a painfully long wait, one that would have tried the patience of a much milder man than William. Relations between the United States and France were becoming increasingly strained, and as the ships and crews of the new Navy were ready for sea duty, they were used to protect American shipping from the powerful French Navy. For all practical purposes an undeclared naval war between the United States and France was being waged, while both nations pretended, on the surface, that all was well.

The United States literally lacked the strength to declare war on one of the world's most powerful nations, and France, knowing she would be engaged in a life-or-death struggle with Great Britain in the immediate future, refrained from making a declaration of war against the Americans. Warships maneuvered, American merchantmen traveled to Europe and the Caribbean escorted by Navy ships that were on constant sea patrol duty, and a war fever gripped the American people.

Meanwhile William Eaton and James Cathcart lingered in Philadelphia, waiting in vain for a ship that would carry them to their new posts. Months passed, and William had literally nothing to do but dine with senators and congressmen, become friendly with new officials in the State and War Departments —and write long, passionate letters to Sophie Smith. He read more Turkish histories, studied the few, incomplete maps of the Barbary Coast that were available, and was overjoyed when Eli Danielson sent him two books in Arabic purchased from a bookstore in Boston. Unfortunately, there was no one with whom he could speak Arabic, and he was longing for the day when he could converse in it.

There were periods when he thought that day would never come. Plans were being made to move the nation's capital to a new town being built for the purpose, Washington, and in one letter he wrote despairingly to Eli, who was completing his education at Dartmouth, that he was afraid "Washington City will be completed and its buildings moss-covered ere my ship sails!"

On three different occasions he made brief visits to Eliza in Brimfield, but she quickly drove him back to Philadelphia. Apparently the thought of taking Eliza along to Tunis occurred to neither husband nor wife. It is true that few wives traveled abroad with men assigned to diplomatic posts in the late eighteenth and early nineteenth centuries, but the majority of husbands expressed their regrets in letters to their spouses, wishing it were possible for them to go together. William did not bother to observe the amenities in his crisp correspondence with Eliza, nor was she sorry she wasn't going with him.

Eli was granted his Bachelor of Arts degree at Dartmouth, and immediately joined his stepfather in Philadelphia. By now William was a familiar figure in the crowded corridors of the State Department, and it was easy for him to obtain a post, at $300 per year, for Eli to accompany him as his personal secretary. The consular staff-designate for Tunis now consisted of two persons. Eliza wrote William a letter of bitter complaint. She felt certain her son would die on foreign soil and was already blaming her husband for his murder. Neither William nor Eli bothered to reply on the subject.

Finally, almost a year and a half after William's appointment, the undeclared naval war with France subsided. On December 4, 1798, William, Eli Danielson and James Cathcart embarked for the Barbary Coast on board the United States brig *Sophia*. There were four other ships in the convoy, all of them symbols of America's degradation.

The *Hero*, a brig of 350 tons, carried naval stores which were being sent as a "gift" to the ruler of Algiers, and was so heavily laden she rode low in the water. The *Hassan Baschaw* was a refitted brig of 275 tons; she carried eight cannon, all of them 6-pounders, and had been converted into a warship. She would join the Algerian navy and in due time would menace American shipping. The *Skjoldabrand* was a sleek schooner of 250 tons that the embarrassed American Government had purchased from her Swedish owner and had fitted out with sixteen 4-pounder cannon. She, too, was a "gift" for the Algerian navy, as was the *El Eisha*, a 150-ton schooner which mounted fourteen 4-pounders.

The Dey had demanded these ships and stores because, he claimed, the United States had not met its treaty obligations, was in default and tardy in its treaty payments. The officers and sailors taking part in the cruise were unhappy and William Eaton was miserable. "It is sad to reflect," he wrote in his Journal-Diary, "that our beloved nation could sink so low in her self-esteem. I pray that I will have an opportunity to cause the rulers of Barbary to think more highly of us in years to come."

The voyage was a long one. Storms delayed the convoy. William, still a poor sailor, spent much of his time in his bunk trying in vain to recover from seasickness. The *Hero* lost a mast in a gale and the squadron put into Gibraltar for repairs. The British authorities were friendly and willing to cooperate, but a recent plague scare had driven most laborers across the border into neighboring Spain. It took the better part of a month to obtain a new mast. American carpenters then fitted it in less than an afternoon and the ships set sail again.

On February 9, 1799, the ships reached Algiers, and William Eaton caught his first glimpse of the Islam he had been studying for so long. Cliffs came down to meet the sea, and the city itself was built on hills, rising sharply behind the harbor in a rough triangular shape. At the top of the highest hill was the *Kasba,* or palace of the Dey, crowded with minarets. The harbor itself was man-made, a long jetty having been built from the mainland to an outer island where a garrison was stationed. Ships were at anchor, and the newcomers saw their first galleys, the notorious warships manned by naked slaves chained to rowing benches.

Richard O'Brien, the new American Consul to Algiers, was on hand to meet the squadron. He himself had arrived in the city a few weeks earlier, and had a tale of woe to tell William and Cathcart. The Dey, Hussein, was angry because of the delay on the part of the United States in sending him the money due him under the treaty terms, and had refused to see him. It had been impossible for O'Brien to hire Algerian servants, and his one employee, a Frenchman who cooked and kept house for him, was forced to pay outrageous prices in the markets for meat, fish and vegetables.

William quickly discovered that it was not easy to be an American in Islam. O'Brien had been unable to provide him and Cathcart with transportation, so the entire party was forced to walk to the Consul's house, high in the hills, with several American sailors carrying their luggage. Algerian men spat at them and cursed them, and although the accents were unfamiliar, William understood what they were saying, and had a

67

hard time controlling his temper. "We have been called every vile name known to man and threatened with extermination, as thought we were vile insects. Our welcome," he added unnecessarily, "was somewhat less than friendly."

William, Cathcart and Eli met other members of the diplomatic community. They found the Danish Consul particularly amiable. The Europeans were unanimous in their opinion of the Dey: Hussein, they said, was a half-educated savage, and even the commander of the Turkish regiment stationed in the city for ceremonial purposes was afraid of him. They hastened to add, however, that he was far more civilized and subtle than his counterparts in Tunis and Tripoli, an opinion that William and Cathcart did not find encouraging.

Hussein could see the anchored ships of the American squadron from his windows in the *Kasba,* and the sight did a great deal to assuage his wrath. Seventy-two hours after the arrival of the ships he sent word that he would receive O'Brien and the two Consular Agents in an audience that afternoon.

The Americans were required to relinquish their swords at the palace entrance, and were submitted to the indignity of being searched for pistols and other hidden arms. Only when the commander of the guard was satisfied that they were harmless were they taken to the throne room, where the Dey Hussein Pasha awaited them. An interpreter was on hand, but to the astonishment of everyone present, William addressed the ruler in Arabic. Even O'Brien and Cathcart were surprised, William having told no one that he had become proficient in the language. His accent was abominable, but he made himself understood and found it easy to make out everything the Dey said.

A notation in the Journal-Diary indicates William's impression of the first Barbary sovereign he had met. "He was like a huge, shaggy beast, sitting on a low bench, with his hind legs gathered up like a tailor or a bear. On our approach, he reached out his forepaw, which Consul O'Brien was compelled to kiss, and we—including four American ship captains—followed his example. The animal at that time seemed to be in a harmless mood. He grinned several times, but made very little noise."

The Dey generously accepted the offerings of the American Government and declared that, reparations having been made, the treaty was in effect again. He ordered food served, and William promptly picked up a sticky honey cake with the fingers of his left hand and ate it, which is precisely what Hussein did. Both drank their strong coffee in cups held in their left hands, too, and the Dey found it difficult to believe that the newcomer had not spent a great deal of time in Islam. He questioned William rather closely and, although the visitor did not know it until much later, sent a report on the new Consular Agent to the Bey Ahmed Pasha of Tunis.

For inexplicable reasons of his own, Hussein did not grant permission for the *Sophia* to leave until March 2. William and Cathcart were beginning to understand what it was like to live in the realm of an absolute monarch whose every whim was the law of the land. Each day O'Brien went to the *Kasba*, hoping to gain permission for the brig's departure, but each day he was turned away without explanation. But the *Sophie* remained ready to sail on short notice and when Hussein suddenly gave the affirmative word on March 2, the travelers immediately went on board. Two Algerian warships escorted the brig out of the harbor.

The voyage to Tunis was a long one. A storm forced the brig to seek shelter for several days at Bizerta, and she did not reach her destination until March 14. The city, the site of ancient Carthage, was located on a shallow lagoon almost surrounded by high mountains. Ships were required to anchor in her port town, Goletta. On hand to meet the new Consular Agent and his companions was a Frenchman who enjoyed the protection of the Bey Ahmed Pasha, Joseph Etienne Famin. He had been employed as an assistant by Joel Barlow during the treaty negotiations and, pending William's arrival, had been performing the duties of consular agent. The other members of the diplomatic corps were also on hand, all of them seemingly delighted to greet their new colleague, and their houses, all located in

69

the same district, were decorated with bunting for the occasion.

The newcomers were escorted to Famin's house, where the American flag was flying and where the British Consular Agent managed to get in a private word with William. Famin, he said, was dangerous. The Frenchman had enjoyed a position of power for months and had made a small fortune by selling "rights" to the captains of American merchantmen. William's arrival deprived him of both influence and income and he would do everything he could to have the American discredited and sent home.

William was grateful for the information and immediately let Famin see that he was no "stranger" to Tunis. He "recognized" the Djama Zitouna, or mosque of the olive tree, from his reading, and indicated that he knew it to be one of the most important universities in Islam. He also "recognized" a number of other mosques, the *Kasba*, or palace of the Bey Ahmed Pasha, and various other buildings. He applied for an audience with the Bey as soon as he reached Famin's house.

It quickly became plain that the British Consular Agent had given good advice. Famin seemed determined to dog William's footsteps and tried, although in vain, to be present at a meeting that William and Cathcart had with the fourteen Americans permanently residing in the city. The French Consul, Maurice Herculais, was openly hostile to his new colleague, and William discovered that Famin and Herculais were close friends. It would be wise, the American decided, to find his own house as soon as he could.

Twenty-four hours after William's arrival he received word that he and Cathcart would be received by the Bey at once. He firmly declined Famin's insistent offer to act as his interpreter, saying he needed none. Famin responded with a vaguely worded threat, which William ignored.

Having prepared for his initial audience with care, William carried a sack containing ten thousand dollars in silver, part of the annual tribute demanded by the Bey. It was so heavy that, when unloaded from a wheelbarrow, three soldiers had to carry it into the *Kasba*. The Bey was very pleased, and his greeting was cordial. Unlike his fellow ruler of Algiers, he was tall, slender and elegant. He was also an educated man, and when he discovered that the new American Consular Agent knew Arabic, showed off his Greek. William replied in that tongue, and their relationship appeared to be established on firm ground.

Since Cathcart was anxious to reach his own post at Tripoli, he sailed at once on board the *Sophia*, and William was left to cope with his own problems. He first went house hunting, and found a suitable dwelling in the district where foreigners were permitted to rent. Famin was disturbed when he learned that his guest was leaving his home and became angry when William pleasantly rejected an offer to provide him with servants.

Instead, the American hired his own. His major domo, a man named Aletti, he described in a letter to O'Brien as "a tarnished jewel. He was born in Gibraltar, is free of London, a convict in Ireland, a burgomaster in Holland, was circumcised in Barbary, was a spy for the devil among the Apostles at the Feast of Pentecost, has the gift of tongues and has traveled everywhere in Europe and Barbary. And he will undoubtedly be hanged in America, for I intend to take him there."

The relationship was as permanent as William envisaged. Aletti remained with him to the end of his days, sharing all of his adventures, and after William's death became the butler in Eli Danielson's Boston home. There he comported himself with such dignity that he was known to everyone as "Mr. Aletti" and founded a line of scholars, his son becoming a professor of Latin at Harvard College.

Comfortably ensconced in his own house, William left the minor details of day-to-day consular work to the faithful and talented Eli, while he himself opened delicate negotiations with Ahmed. The United States wanted several cumbersome articles in its treaty with Tunis revised and, equally important, wanted to pay tribute in cash rather than in naval stores. Such supplies were difficult to obtain and were badly needed by the new,

71

rapidly growing United States Navy. So, instead of paying $35,000 in supplies, he was authorized to offer the Bey $100,000 in cash. The offer was not as generous as it appeared on the surface, since Ahmed also needed naval stores and, with Great Britain and France now waging war with each other, would have to pay at least $100,000 for supplies worth one third that amount.

Ahmed and his principal minister, Sahibtappa, who held the title of Keeper of the Seals, were very angry, and the failure of the new Consular Agent to provide Tunis with the naval stores was regarded as a flagrant treaty violation. Famin, who had been boasting that he alone could persuade the Tunisians to behave reasonably, quickly demonstrated that he had no real influence at court. In spite of his representations, the Bey refused to receive William in another audience.

So Famin was permanently discarded, and William opened a new channel by quietly presenting Sahibtappa with a bribe of $20,000. Immediately thereafter it occurred to the Bey that new treaty negotiations would mean that the United States would be compelled to make him additional gifts. He consented to negotiate, provided he was given $25,000 in cash for the privilege. William had no choice, and paid. Thereafter, for months, he and the Bey sat down to talk, bargain and wrangle every Tuesday afternoon.

Ahmed's demands were endless and occasionally both he and Sahibtappa required fresh proof of America's good faith—in the form of cash. By autumn the treaty renegotiations had ground to a standstill. William's reserves of cash were exhausted. But he still had patience, a paramount qualification in dealing with Barbary Coast rulers.

One of the minor but significant treaty clauses that the United States wanted to change demanded elaborate salutes by American ships coming to Tunis. Instead of listening reasonably, Ahmed made further demands, and insisted that he be paid one barrel of gunpowder for each shot fired by his shore batteries returning the salutes of American vessels.

William finally lost his temper and shouted that the request was too humiliating to be discussed.

The Bey replied, "You consult your honor, I my interest."

Adding insult to insult, the Tunisians concluded new agreements with the Ministers of Portugal and Sicily. The United States remained in the position of a humble suitor too shabby to be treated seriously.

The pressures increased. The Dey Hussein Pasha of Algiers boasted to his neighbor that he had received both naval stores and ships from the United States, and this, of course, made Ahmed all the more determined to extract what he could from America. The President of the United States was a man of bad faith, he declared, and could convince him of a genuine will to negotiate only by presenting him with an emerald ring the size of a seagull's egg.

He made the demand so repeatedly that William, forced to take it seriously, wrote to O'Brien for advice. The Consul at Algiers was stunned, too, so William finally wrote to the United States Minister in London, Rufus King. "I have found my *kismet* in Barbary," he said ruefully, "but I am not so certain I like it. If I had my own will, here, I would use American arms to force these brigand-kings to respect our nation. I am convinced that only gunshot and powder will compel the Beys and Deys of Barbary to treat with us in a civilized manner, honor the lives and property of American citizens and behave like gentlemen.

"I am tempted to believe it is my *kismet* to treat these thieves with the contempt they deserve. Their present attitude is insulting not only to every American citizen, but to every man, everywhere, who considers himself more than a savage barbarian. Pray convey to the President, the State Department, the War Department and the Navy Department my earnest request that a fleet of American warships be sent to the Mediterranean. With them should be transported five thousand trained, armed and well-supplied American infantrymen and cavalrymen.

"With these troops and warships at my disposal, I can guarantee the President and the Congress that the rulers of the Barbary Coast will sing a new song, more to our liking."

CHAPTER SIX

THE RELUCTANT DIPLOMAT

Consular Agent Eaton's Tuesday afternoon talks with the Bey Ahmed Pasha and Monday conferences with Sahibtappa occupied only a small part of his time. His actual consular duties were undemanding, and Eli Danielson was proving adept and forceful in dealing with minor matters. So William had the better part of his time to do what he pleased, and was fortunate that the Bey, who liked him personally, had granted him permission to travel wherever he wanted to go in the realm, an unusual privilege.

He took full advantage of his opportunities and soon became a familiar figure in every quarter of Tunis. He attended lectures at the university and debated fine points of Mohammedan philosophy with distinguished professors. He wandered into meat, fish and vegetable markets, where he enjoyed haggling with foodsellers, who learned that he drove a sharp bargain. Occasionally he went fishing with men who earned their living from the sea, sometimes he was a silent witness at court trials, which he found absorbing, and on holy days he enjoyed attending Moslem religious services. Only two mosques, which Christians were not allowed to enter, were closed to him.

He made frequent trips into the interior, too, visiting large

74

and small farms, and often riding across the desert to a distant oasis. Gradually he came to know the Bedouin and after the tribesmen learned to trust him he made it a habit to remain overnight with them, dressing as they did, helping them guard their flocks and sharing their communal life. His spoken Arabic improved immeasurably. He became fluent in the dialects of the aristocracy and lower class city people, the country folk and the wandering nomads. He also became thoroughly familiar with the part-Italian, part-Arabic lingua franca of North Africa.

Eli jokingly accused him of transforming himself into an Arab, a charge which William freely admitted. "I am like the little lizards one sees in one's garden here," he wrote in his Journal-Diary. "I change my colors to match those of the land in which I reside. Once I was a Miami, then a Creek, and now I am something of an Arab. But there are differences between my status and those of the real Arab. He professes loyalty to Constantinople, accepts the sovereignty of his local ruler because he has no choice, yet is, in truth, faithful only to himself. I, however, am passionately devoted to the interests of my own land, and will always place my devotion to the United States above personal considerations."

He was not indulging in loose, meaningless talk. Ahmed was so insistent in his demands for an emerald the size of a bird's egg that William quietly began to price gems, and thought seriously of buying the Bey an expensive bauble out of his own pocket if the State Department refused to grant him funds for the purpose. He had been given a specific mission and was determined to succeed, to the satisfaction of his Government, if it was possible.

As the months passed it became increasingly clear to him that a major stumbling block in his path was Joseph Famin. The Frenchman no longer had any right to concern himself with American business in Tunis, but William discovered that he was acting as an unofficial advisor to Sahibtappa. Famin, it seemed, was clever in thinking of new ways to extract money from the United States, and whenever the Keeper of the Seals received a payment, Famin got his share.

The deteriorating relations between William and Famin reached a new low when an American merchant ship, the *Lizzie*, put into Tunis for supplies. Although she was discharging no cargo, she was required, under the terms of the treaty between the Bey and the United States, to pay a tax on everything she carried in her hold. Most ships' captains were evasive, of course, and placed as low a value as they dared on their cargoes when the tax collector visited them.

Famin went to the master of the *Lizzie* and told him he could avoid paying the tax altogether if, instead, he paid the obliging Frenchman the sum of $1,000. The mariner agreed, then had second thoughts and went to the Consular Agent with the problem. William was horrified. Famin, who had no power to prevent the collection of the tax, was merely trying to swindle the man, who would have been liable to a court conviction, stiff fines and a possible prison sentence had he so blatantly broken the agreement made by the American Government.

The two Americans were walking down the *Marina*, the main street of Tunis, as they discussed the matter, and by sheer accident saw Famin approaching from the opposite direction. William halted him, and accused him of trying to obtain money from the ship's master under false and illegal pretenses.

Famin insultingly told him to mind his own business.

The combustible Eaton temper, which William had lost only once since coming to Barbary, soared to the boiling point. He would show Famin what an American thought of him, he said, and the Frenchman would remember the day as long as he lived.

Snatching a whip from the driver of a mule cart, William gave Famin a thorough beating witnessed by hundreds of ogling Tunisians. His clothes slashed to ribbons, Famin literally crawled away from the scene on all fours after being subjected to the most painful and humiliating thrashing ever experienced by a man who enjoyed the personal protection of the Bey.

Famin went at once to Sahibtappa to lodge a complaint, and it was believed in the diplomatic community that William would be expelled from the country. Herculais, the French Consul, even predicted that the American's immunity would be withdrawn, and that he would be cast into prison.

The following day Ahmed summoned William and Famin to the *Kasba*; he already knew all the details of the affair, but asked them to tell him what had happened. Famin spoke first, and said that William, who had been "very heated," had attacked him without provocation.

William interrupted to say that Famin was a liar, and gave his version of the incident.

The Bey turned back to Famin and said, "If the American was angry, he truly had good reason. I have always found him a very plain, candid man, and his concern for his citizens is no crime."

Famin immediately reminded Ahmed that the official protection of the Bey would become a meaningless symbol if attacks that went unpunished were permitted.

Ahmed asked the American his reaction.

William said, "I'd have disciplined him in the same way in the Kingdom of Heaven. And if he as much as speaks to an American again, I'll give him another whipping."

The Bey was amused, and after dismissing Famin from his presence, invited William to dine with him. No matter what their official relations, they were becoming good friends on an informal level.

William needed all the goodwill and friendship he could muster in the winter of 1799-1800. He received word from O'Brien to the effect that naval stores, painfully accumulated in the United States, were en route to the Bey and would arrive shortly. In the meantime, O'Brien forwarded a letter from President Adams to Ahmed, "apologizing" for the delay, which had caused a lapse under the terms of the treaty.

It appeared that smooth sailing was ahead. Unfortunately, however, although the original communication arrived on

December 27, 1799, the ships carrying the stores put into Leghorn, Italy, instead of sailing direct to Tunis. By the end of March, 1800, William was afraid that the entire, tenuous relationship between the United States and Tunis was on the verge of being terminated.

Sahibtappa, who was no longer receiving bribes of any sort, lost no opportunity to urge his master to break off relations with the Americans. He also threatened William, saying that the Tunisian navy intended to seize American merchantmen and apply their sale price to the American debt. William courageously replied that the vessels were armed and would defend themselves; if hostilities broke out, the fault would be that of Tunis. Sahibtappa insisted he did not care, that the American ships were weak, and that he was sending out a fleet for the express purpose of capturing Yankee ships.

William went to the Bey, and after several long, earnest discussions managed to convince him that President Adams' letter had been forthright and honest. Rarely had a diplomat done better work under more difficult circumstances, and the Bey agreed to wait a "reasonable" length of time for the ships carrying the naval stores to arrive. Meanwhile, in spite of Sahibtappa's pressure, Ahmed promised to take no overt action that would endanger the fragile state of peace that existed between the two nations.

Before the arrival of the stores, William managed to bring off a brilliant coup. He told the Bey repeatedly that the United States Government could not give supplies to a nation that failed to respect the American flag. The most objectionable feature of the existing treaty was a clause permitting the Tunisians to board American ships at will. William had been demanding the cancellation of this clause as well as that dealing with the objectionable exchange of salutes when American ships came to Tunis.

Well aware that the Bey was very anxious to get his hands on the naval stores, William made him an offer. A Tunisian warship could sail to Leghorn, with Eli Danielson as an official passenger, and a representative appointed by the Bey could go on board the American vessels and see for himself that they carried naval provisions being sent to Tunis.

The Bey agreed, the voyage was made, and the representative returned to Tunis, fully satisfied. The merchant ships, Eli Danielson told his stepfather, had remained at anchor because the commodore of the squadron had been informed that the Mediterranean was unsafe for travel. But Eli had done William —and the United States—a great service by insisting that the ships sail for Tunis as quickly as possible.

Pending their arrival, William had a powerful weapon and maneuvered it deftly. By using subtle threats he managed to persuade the Bey to eliminate from the treaty the two clauses that the United States found so objectionable. The new agreement was concluded, and was signed by both William and the Bey on April 26, the day that the squadron of three American ships actually arrived with the supplies.

As a "bonus" for these concessions, William promised the Bey, on his own authority, that another load of naval stores would be forthcoming. He sent his formal request to Washington for these supplies in the same packet that contained the new, revised treaty. President Adams and the State Department were delighted, Congress quickly appropriated the funds for the supplies, and they arrived at Tunis in record time, the brig *Anna Maria* reaching her destination in November, 1800.

Congress voted Consular Agent Eaton an official commendation for his success in revising the treaty with the Bey, and attached to the notice William received was a personal letter from President Adams, congratulating him on his achievement of what everyone in the Government had considered an impossible task. Never had William enjoyed greater favor.

His stock was high in Tunis, too. He had delivered so handsomely for the Bey, who had received large sums of cash as well as the naval stores, that the demands for the emerald ring were dropped, at least for the present. The belligerent policies of Sahibtappa had been discarded, and the Keeper of the Seals,

79

who had been so insistent in his statements that the United States would not live up to its obligations, was in eclipse. He had virtually no influence at court, where the American Consular Agent had become the Bey's favorite dinner guest.

William found success boring. He had little other than routine activities to occupy him, there were no challenges to make life exciting, and he toyed with the idea of requesting a leave of absence to visit his wife. Eli quickly disabused him of the alarming idea and he subsided, but not for long.

In December, 1800, he received a letter from his colleague, James Cathcart, in Tripoli, asking for his help. The situation in Tripoli had become untenable, Cathcart declared, and perhaps Eaton, who enjoyed far greater success, could pay him a visit and assist him in dealing with the most obstinately recalcitrant, pugnacious ruler on the Barbary Coast.

William immediately agreed and set sail for Tripoli on December 28 on board the *Anna Maria*. It seemed to be his misfortune to travel by sea when the weather was bad. A series of the Mediterranean's most vicious midwinter squalls attacked the brig. As usual, he spent most of his time in his bunk. At least he could console himself with the thought that, thanks to his reading, he knew as much about the political background of Tripoli as any man alive.

The poorest and most primitive of the Barbary Coast states, Tripoli consisted of vast expanses of desert and rock, on which were scattered several large, inhabited oases, of which the capital, which bore the same name as the country, was the largest. Once an important outpost of the Roman empire, it had long been a part of the Ottoman domain; its modern history had begun when the great-grandfather of the present ruler had been appointed its governor by the Sultan of Turkey.

Hamet Karamanli had been an ambitious, ruthless man who had seized power in his own right, although continuing to pay token obeisance to Constantinople, by murdering more than three hundred Turkish officials and army officers in a single bloody night. He quickly established his position as an absolute tyrant and for thirty-two years ruled the land alone. No man, including the highest-ranking nobles in Constantinople, dared to dispute him in anything.

He was succeeded by his son, Muhammed, who tried in all things to emulate him but succeeded in arousing unrest in his subjects, who were weary of terror. Muhammed's rule was short and he in turn was succeeded by his eldest son, Bey Ali Karamanli Pasha, a weak, indecisive man who took the throne in 1754 and held it for forty-one years, until his death in 1795. The country soon paid a high price for his vacillation.

Ali had three sons, the eldest of whom, the competent Hassan, became the ruler of Tripoli. The youngest of the brothers, Yusef, was as coldly ambitious as the founder of the line and at his instigation Hassan was murdered. This brought the somewhat befuddled, weak Hamet to the throne, but it was obvious to all Islam that his position was untenable. Yusef at first tried to work through him, but Hamet's supporters, afraid of the new tyranny that would be established if they gave his younger brother his wishes, managed to stiffen the will of the Bey, and he resisted.

Yusef replied by fomenting a revolution, driving Hamet from the throne and sending him, fleeing for his life, into exile. Yusef took complete control of Tripoli and although his official title was Bey, or governor, he called himself Bashaw, which meant a sultan. No one in Constantinople or elsewhere disputed him. Meanwhile Hamet had become a refugee and drifted around the Mediterranean, finding a temporary home in Malta, another in Tunis and still another in Sicily. From time to time he also visited Gibraltar, and twice made short stays in Algiers and Morocco. Nowhere in Barbary was he really welcome. The other rulers had no desire to become embroiled in a dispute with the ferocious Yusef, and Hamet was a living reminder to their own ambitious relatives that a monarch could be deprived of his throne.

Yusef was so severe in his treatment of his subjects that many began to long for the return of the ineffectual Hamet. But the

Bashaw's grip on the country was secure. His principal supporters were unscrupulous and as willing as their monarch to soil their own hands with blood. One of the most vicious, and certainly the most colorful, was the commander in chief of the cutthroat Tripolitanian navy, Murad Reis, who was really a renegade Scotsman named Lisle. There was a price on his head in Edinburgh and London and it was believed he had also committed murders in Hamburg and Naples. He and Yusef, working together, were an ugly pair.

Tripoli, being the most remote, backward and presumably the weakest of the Barbary states, received smaller blackmail payments from the European nations and the United States than the others. Yusef and Murad Reis used force in an effort to rectify this situation, but their efforts backfired. His Britannic Majesty's Navy informed them that, although preoccupied by the war with France, enough ships of the line would be sent to Tripoli to bombard and destroy the city if British ships and sailors were molested. Napoleon Bonaparte conveyed a similar message, and the three French men-of-war delivering it engaged in target practice that Yusef could see from the windows of his palace.

The smaller European nations followed the example of the great powers, and threatened immediate naval retaliation if the galleys of Murad Reis caused any harm to their property or citizens. That left the weak, distant United States as the only potential source of increased revenue.

The Bashaw, seconded by the omnipresent Murad Reis, made constant demands on John Cathcart from the time he first landed at Tripoli. An experienced hand at extortion, Yusef had managed to force the United States to give him eighty thousand dollars in cash and grain worth another twenty thousand in the period of three and one-half years. But he insisted he was as important as the Dey of Algiers and the Bey of Tunis and demanded sums equal to the amounts paid to them.

Cathcart explained that he was not authorized to make payments on his own initiative, so in May, 1800, Yusef himself wrote a letter to President Adams. The communication is notable because it was one of the most violently insulting documents ever sent by one chief of state to another. It was difficult for Adams, or for Thomas Jefferson, who succeeded him on March 4, 1801, to reply politely without degrading himself and the United States.

By the time William Eaton arrived in Tripoli in January, 1801, American-Tripolitanian relations were strained almost to the breaking point. Within a four-month period the galleys of Murad Reis had captured three American merchantmen, and although their crews had not been molested or enslaved their cargo had been stolen. Both Yusef and his commodore blithely denied any knowledge of the disappearance of the goods, even though the indignant Cathcart saw goods from one of the brigs piled high in the courtyard of the Bashaw's own palace.

From the deck of the *Anna Maria* William Eaton saw a sight he would remember for the rest of his days. Tripoli, with which his name would henceforth be associated, was a city that jutted out into the Mediterranean, its small but perfectly formed crescent-shaped harbor providing excellent shelter for shipping. The community of mosques and flat-roofed buildings, most of them painted a dazzling white, was surrounded by a high wall, part of which dated from ancient Roman times. Aside from the huge palace that the first Bey Hamet Karamanli Pasha had built for himself, the only edifices of consequence were mosques, the largest and most impressive of which had been a church constructed by the Spaniards when they had occupied the place during the sixteenth century.

The walls on the western side of the city were rooted in the desert, which stretched endlessly toward the horizon, but off to the east lay the Oasis of Meshia, one of the most beautiful and verdant in all of North Africa. William noted in his Journal-Diary that it contained more than one hundred thousand palm trees, and he did not exaggerate. Meshia was Tripoli's loveliest asset.

It was difficult to find anything else in Tripoli worth praising, however. Forty-eight hours after William's arrival he met Yusef at the new Swedish Consulate, which had just been established. In his *Life*, William describes the Bashaw vividly: "He was a large, vulgar beast, with filthy fingernails and a robe so spotted with spilt food and coffee that it was difficult to distinguish the original color of the garment. His beard was trimmed, which was a surprise, but he rarely bathed, if ever, and the stench of his body, which mingled with the powerful scent he used to disguise the odors, made Eaton want to retch.

"Had Yusef lived in the United States, he would have been recognized by everyone in his true guise; he was a bully; even in his own realm, surrounded by the sycophants who fawned on him, he was not at ease. His heavy-lidded, dark eyes were constantly in motion, and he searched the faces of those to whom he spoke, seeking always some sign of malevolence. He was an evil man, but evil in a petty, mean way. There was no grandeur in his bearing, his manner or his speech. There are tyrants who clothe themselves with regality, but Yusef Karamanli was not of their number. In Philadelphia he would have been a worker at the docks unable to find employment; in New York he would have been a cutpurse hanged at the gallows; but such are ways of Barbary that in Tripoli he was the master of the world."

William gave another, far more succinct impression of Yusef in a letter he wrote O'Brien, saying, "He is a cur who can be disciplined only with the whip."

Yusef was the third ruler of Barbary William had met, and by this time he certainly had become accustomed to the imperiousness of these princelings. There is more lurking behind his judgment than his disgust for the Dey of Algiers and his reluctant admiration for the Bey of Tunis. There was something intensely personal about his loathing for the Bashaw.

Apparently Yusef felt a similar sense of antagonism. He made it a point to snub the American Consular Agent to Tunis. When William was presented to him he failed to acknowledge the introduction by as much as a nod of his head, much to the embarrassment of Nicholas C. Nissen, the courtly Danish Consul who was to prove himself America's true friend in Tripoli. Thinking that the Bashaw had been preoccupied and had not heard Cathcart's presentation of his colleague, Nissen repeated William's name. Yusef remained stonefaced, immobile and silent.

An incident at the reception caused William to despise the Bashaw even more intensely. Someone jokingly said that there was no lumber in Tripoli to provide the new Swedish Consulate with a flagpole, and that the only way to obtain one would be to take a spar from one of the ships anchored in the harbor.

Yusef replied that there was another way. The flagstaff at the American Consulate might not be needed much longer. Chuckling at his own wit, he added, "It is a difficult endeavor to raise up a flagstaff again, once it has come down. When the American flagstaff comes down, it will be very expensive to raise it again."

The members of the diplomatic corps were horrified by the bald threat, which made all of them feel insecure. Nowhere else in Barbary did rulers spell out their demands so bluntly, and it was evident that if the United States failed to pay a large sum of money in the immediate future, there would be serious trouble.

William and Cathcart discussed the problem far into the night. Was Yusef bluffing? Both thought he had originally intended his stand as a bluff, but they had agreed he had gone too far, in public, to back down without losing face. His "royal dignity," such as it was, had become a major issue in the situation, and as one who had seized power by force and kept himself in power in a reign of terror, Yusef could not keep his throne if he vacillated. Once his own subjects believed his threats were empty, they would rebel against him.

Hoping to learn whether their analysis was accurate, the Americans tried to make an appointment with Yusef. Cathcart went to the palace each day for ten days, and each day was turned away by a major domo who went out of his way to be insulting.

One morning Murad Reis paid an unexpected visit to the

American Consulate, and speaking in Arabic, said, "The door of the palace is closed to you until you pay the Bashaw his due."

Cathcart wanted to know what he considered his due.

Fifty thousand dollars in cash, Murad Reis replied, and another fifty thousand in naval stores. The payments had to be made within the next four months, he added, or the American flagpole would be chopped down. He also made the gratuitous comment that, although Cathcart was too weak to become a galley slave, there were other menial tasks he might be made to perform.

The bullying was more than William could tolerate. "Lisle," he said, addressing the renegade Scotsman in English, "if any harm comes to Mr. Cathcart, I give you my solemn, personal word of honor that I shall hunt you down, put a noose around your neck and hang you from the nearest palm tree. If I can, I shall do it with the aid of the United States Army and Navy. If possible, I shall also enlist the services of the Royal Navy, which has grown tired of the blustering of a traitor. But, if necessary, I shall do it alone!"

No one had dared to speak so frankly to Murad Reis since he had come to Tripoli, and he was too stunned to reply.

William emphasized his words by opening the front door and literally kicking the astonished commander in chief of the Tripolitanian navy into the street.

It was impossible to meet the new demands and both Americans knew it. Months might pass before a ship bound for the United States could carry a message to the State Department. More months would pass while the Secretary of State, the President and Congress considered the impudent new request. And it would take a long time for another ship to bring the American reply to Tripoli. Under literally no circumstances would it be feasible to expect either cash or naval stores in time to meet Yusef's deadline.

William was also deeply concerned about his colleague's personal safety. He and Cathcart expected the entire diplomatic community would hear of the way Murad Reis had been treated, but to their surprise the Scotsman kept the story of his humiliation to himself. Cathcart considered this a good sign and insisted he would be neither injured nor taken into captivity if Yusef should close the Consulate.

Less certain of the outcome than his friend, William went to Nissen, the Danish Consul, and told him the whole story of the incident. Nissen promised to keep a close watch on Cathcart and, should it become necessary, give him refuge in his own Consulate. All of the European powers would be forced to band together and send a punitive expedition to Tripoli if the diplomatic immunity of one European headquarters was violated, so it seemed unlikely that Yusef would allow the violent Murad Reis to make good his threat to enslave Cathcart.

Two more attempts were made to arrange an audience with the Bashaw, but both failed, and William returned to Tunis, sailing on the *Anna Maria*. He left Tripoli on February 20, and wrote to O'Brien that he was uncertain whether either of them would see Cathcart alive again. "It appears certain," he said, "that Yusef is intent upon venting spite on himself. I enclose a communication, to be forwarded by you to the State Department at your pleasure, in which I am compelled to express the unqualified belief that Tripoli will declare war upon the United States at the end of the four-month grace period that Yusef had so graciously granted us.

"Obviously, this state of war will make all the more difficult the relations of the United States with the other nations of Barbary. I anticipate troubles with the Bey of Tunis, and feel certain that, although he may not join actively in the war, he will give the Bashaw his sympathy and support."

In his report to the State Department, William urgently requested that American troops be dispatched at once to the Mediterranean in transports protected by the most powerful fleet of the new United States Navy that could be assembled.

O'Brien also sent a report to Washington City, requesting that a squadron of warships be sent to the Mediterranean at the earliest convenience of the Navy Department.

Cathcart's report was more detailed, but he, like his colleagues, concluded with an appeal for a show of American armed strength. "Karamanli no longer hears the voice of reason," he wrote. "Our cannon must speak for us."

By a stroke of good fortune, the three messages were carried westward in the *George Washington*, a small American frigate that had put into Algiers. The first American warship of consequence to appear in Barbary, in spite of its diminutive size, it made an impression on the Dey. Subsequently, when it arrived at Tunis, the Bey Ahmed Pasha realized that perhaps the United States was not as impotent as he had believed. Certainly a brief visit of the frigate to Tripoli caused Murad Reis to reconsider his threat to Cathcart, and the American Consular Agent there was spared a harrowing personal experience.

Aided by unexpectedly favorable winds blowing from east to west, instead of in the opposite direction, which was more frequently the case in the Atlantic, the *George Washington* reached Baltimore in mid-April. President Thomas Jefferson and his Secretary of State, James Madison, immediately faced one of the new Administration's first international crises. Both men were dedicated to the principle of maintaining peaceful relations with all nations, as they were convinced that the United States could achieve her potential of prosperity and greatness only if wars with other powers were avoided.

But the insulting letter which Yusef had sent to President Adams had been delayed en route to Washington, and had not arrived until the new Administration had taken office. This communication, combined with the reports of Eaton, O'Brien and Cathcart made it necessary for the new President and his Secretary of State to review the country's situation in Barbary.

Jefferson and Madison reached the inescapable conclusion that no matter how deep their commitment to peace the United States would be stripped of all respect in the community of nations if she allowed herself to be bullied, threatened and blackmailed by international brigands. The time had come to take a firm stand.

Therefore the most powerful squadron of warships America could muster was dispatched to the Mediterranean under the command of Commodore Richard Dale, who traveled under specific instructions. He was directed to avoid acts of violence if they could be avoided, but to take any and all steps he deemed necessary against the Barbary Coast states to protect the honor and interests of the United States.

The squadron was followed by a letter, written by Jefferson and countersigned by Madison. Dated May 21, 1801, it assured the Bashaw Yusef Karamanli Pasha of the desire of the United States to keep the peace with Tripoli. Sane nations led by just and sane men, they declared, could and should settle their dispute amicably.

At the same time, the letter continued in an uncompromisingly frigid tone, the President had deemed it essential to the safety and honor of the United States to dispatch "a naval squadron of observation to the Mediterranean Sea." Its purpose there, Jefferson said, would be to "exercise the American seamanship in nautical duties, and to superintend the safety of American commerce."

The communication ended on a bland, diplomatic note. The President commended the ships and their crews to "the hospitality and good offices" of the Bashaw Yusef Karamanli Pasha in the event that they should put into the harbors of Tripoli or Derna, or both.

It is of considerable significance to note that neither Jefferson nor Madison gave serious consideration to Consular Agent William Eaton's proposal that a land force of American troops also be sent to the Mediterranean. The President and Secretary of State were thinking exclusively in terms of making a show of American sea strength off the Barbary Coast, and in this they were supported by the new Navy Department.

Only the War Department found William's suggestion good, but the voices of the high-ranking civilians and military officers of the Department were ignored. At no time, either in 1801 or in the years that followed, did the United States seriously contemplate the dispatch of a powerful army corps to the Mediterranean. William lobbied furiously in favor of this scheme and, as will be seen, eventually persuaded the President to grant him the authority to raise an independent force of his own, although it is possible that Jefferson never quite realized what it was that he approved. It was the execution of William's plan that eventually created lasting peace between the United States and the pirate nations of Barbary.

The new American Navy performed erratically, at times acting too cautiously, at times making the mistakes of an organization that was just beginning to understand teamwork, yet at other times achieving brilliant successes that have become a part of the Navy's treasured heritage. But the hard fact remains that the Navy did not and could not have won the war with Tripoli single-handed. It was not the Navy's striking power, intrepidity or accurate gunnery that brought the troublesome North African states to their knees, but the overwhelming success of William Eaton's march to Derna. Every Barbary Coast ruler was alarmed by his achievement and hastened to change his attitude toward the United States.

A man of strong, stubborn convictions, William believed with all his heart that only a military campaign could compel the Barbary brigands to behave reasonably. That attitude explains, in part, his many disputes with the Navy and his lack of rapport with the commodores. But there is an even deeper reason that he and the Navy officers so frequently failed to understand, like and respect each other.

It must be remembered that William was an alumnus of the Army's officer corps, and felt a strong sense of loyalty to the senior service. Like other Army men, he resented the emergence of the new force into the limelight and, above all, the sums of money being spent on ships and Navy recruiting, cannon and naval stores, while the Army was being forced to live on a starvation diet. The unpleasantness that so often manifested itself in his relations with the Navy was, literally, the first case of interservice rivalry on record.

Let it be noted, however, that when it counted most William and the commodores learned to live with each other and to work together for their common good and that of the United States. All were patriots living in an age when men loved their country unquestioningly and selflessly.

In any event, President Jefferson's letter to the Bashaw was sent from the United States precisely one week after Tripoli broke diplomatic relations and declared war on the United States. Members of Yusef's guards regiment appeared at the American Consulate at noon on May 14, 1801, and chopped down the flagpole in the courtyard. Yusef, remembering his previous words on the subject, thought it amusing to send the pole to the Swedish Consulate as a gift.

Danish Consul Nissen immediately extended his protection to James Cathcart and gave him quarters in his own home, at the same time finding a ship that would take him to Leghorn as rapidly as possible. Lightning had struck at last. America was embroiled in her first formal war since her struggle for independence.

CHAPTER SEVEN

THE END OF DIPLOMACY

Tripoli's declaration of war against the United States immediately complicated America's relations with Tunis, precisely as William had anticipated. The Bey Ahmed Pasha made no secret of his sympathy with his brother ruler and, as was to have been expected, seized the opportunity to increase his own preposterous financial demands.

There were American products that Tunis wanted and needed, and William, since his success in renegotiating the treaty with the Bey, had been cautiously exploring the possibilities of making a new, mutually profitable commercial arrangement. The idea of mutual profit was alien to Ahmed's way of thinking, however, and he considered it fair, proper and financially just for the United States to provide him with whatever he wanted, at America's expense.

Instead of trading, he demanded $50,000 worth of grain annually, as well as $100,000 in prime American timber, already cut into planking. At least half of the wood supply had to be oak, he specified, and under no circumstances was he interested in pine, which was too soft.

William remonstrated with him, saying that American farmers and lumbermen expected to be paid for their products.

"Let your Government pay for them," the Bey replied. "How your President obtains what I need is not my concern, but his."

What would Tunis give in return?

"Peace," Ahmed said. "Rather than join Tripoli in a holy war against you, I will continue to give you my hand in eternal friendship."

William's reply became a classic in the annals of American diplomacy. "I am not certain," he said, "whether we can afford your friendship, be it eternal or merely temporary. I fail to see the difference between what you define as friendship and what civilized nations call enmity."

The Bey bristled angrily, and wanted to know whether William was insulting him.

"Since you think of yourself as the most intelligent of men," the American declared, "I must leave you to puzzle out the conundrum for yourself. Meanwhile, I beg to remind you that our treaty remains in effect."

That same day he sent a formal letter to the *Kasba*, cancelling the negotiations for a commercial agreement.

And before going to bed that night he sent a detailed report of the incident to Secretary of State Madison. He ended the communication with a strong statement. "During our talk of today, the Bey hinted that our present state of hostilities with Tripoli, which require him to increase his own defense strength, will make it necessary for him to obtain ten thousand of the best American-made rifles. I fully expect him to translate this hint into a formal demand for arms within a day or two. His demands on us are endless, and will become even greater as his price of remaining at peace with us. That peace cannot long be kept.

"The Barbary pirates are indulged in the habit of dictating their own terms of negotiations. They are under no restraint of honor, decency or reason. They are unbridled savages whose conduct is at best intolerable and at worst an insufferable offense against the very principles of civilization which we, as Americans, pledge ourselves to uphold.

"We are the only nation on earth against which Barbary can safely cruise.

"I submit, in all earnestness, the following for the consideration of the President. If the Government, in lieu of ships filled with naval stores intended as gifts for the brigands, will give me transports with five thousand infantrymen and cavalrymen of the United States Army, I will offer in return my absolute pledge that within six months all of Barbary will sue for peace on reasonable terms.

"If this force be too large for the Government to send me at this time, I beg that I be given a corps of one thousand Marines, between eighteen and thirty-eight years of age, native Americans all, properly officered. Let them be sent to me under cover of a single forty-four gun frigate. I will pledge myself to surprise Porto Farina, the principal defense bastion of Tunis, and destroy the Bey's arsenal. This will compel him to seek the honorable peace that is the only, ultimate goal of all Americans.

"Take away the club of a bully, and he becomes meek. I earnestly pray that the President will keep this thought in mind when he gives consideration to my proposal. I beg, too, that no time be lost in reaching a decision. The estate of Americans in Barbary is low, and will sink still lower with each passing month. In order that our ships remain afloat and our citizens be spared the whips of Barbary slave-masters, I ask that I be given the men I need at the earliest convenience of our Republic."

The plea would be repeated endlessly in the next few years.

One of William's fascinations, both to his contemporaries and to the modern student, is that he was, simultaneously, a hardheaded realist and a wild-eyed dreamer incapable of separating fact and fantasy. At the same time he was asking the United States Government for troops, in the spring of 1801, Hamet Karamanli, Yusef's older brother who was the deposed Bey of Tripoli, came to Tunis as a refugee. His appearance was the opening act in a drama that would change the history of the Barbary Coast.

94

Hamet and his entourage embarrassed the Bey Ahmed Pasha, but there was little the Tunisian ruler could do to discourage the visit of his unwelcome guest. He pointedly refrained from inviting Hamet to the *Kasba,* but Moslem etiquette made it impossible for him to reject Hamet's shrewd request that he come to the house rented by the wanderer from Tripoli. Hamet's mere presence placed a strain on Ahmed's relations with the bloodthirsty Yusef, yet all of aristocratic Islam would be shocked if the Bey told the uninvited guest to go elsewhere.

William had little to make him happy that spring, but he enjoyed Ahmed's dilemma. It was inevitable that the American Consular Agent and the former Bey would strike up a friendship when they met; the bond that brought and held them together was a mutual hatred for the crafty Yusef. In the course of their conversation Hamet expressed sympathy for the American position in the dispute with Tripoli, and one balmy day, over a kettle of lamb and vegetables, William concocted an idea that was his masterpiece—and almost became the cause of his undoing.

He sent off an immediate letter to Cathcart, who was recovering his health in Leghorn after suffering what men of a later era would call a nervous collapse. In brief, William wanted the reaction of his friend and colleague to a bold scheme: he suggested that the United States initiate, support and direct a campaign to put Hamet back on the throne of his ancestors.

The arguments in favor of the plan were impressive. The worst tyrant on the Barbary Coast would be deposed by American military might, and the chastened, frightened rulers of the other pirate states would be certain to mend their manners, revise their treaties and treat the infant New World nation with the respect she deserved. The grateful Hamet, although not reduced to the impotent and humiliating role of an American puppet, a position that would be sure to create more harm than good in the attitudes of his subjects, nevertheless would be willing to make a new treaty with the United States based on considerations of mutual national honor. Hamet's example would compel the other Barbary sovereigns to conclude similar agreements, and the dangers to American lives and shipping in the Mediterranean would be eliminated almost overnight.

In spite of his enthusiasm for the project he had conceived, William remained cautious, and bluntly told Cathcart he very much doubted that his present instructions from the State Department gave him the authority to pursue the idea. On the surface, at least, he liked to maintain the thought that he was merely a Government servant executing policies conceived by his superiors.

Cathcart thought so highly of the plan that he wrote to friends in the State Department about it, which gave some people the mistaken impression that he was the author of the scheme. William's letter outlining the project, together with Cathcart's approving reply, dispelled any such fancies.

William's own feelings on the subject were so intense that he did not wait to hear from Cathcart. Instead he sent a long letter to President Jefferson, through Secretary Madison, officially giving the details of the idea and requesting permission to put it into effect.

In the summer of 1801 Cathcart, lacking instructions to the contrary from Washington, decided to join William in Tunis. Not only would he be in the closest of all possible observation posts to Tripoli, but in the event that the scheme became operative he would be in a position to help. While crossing the Mediterranean, the American brig on which he was traveling was halted on the high seas by a fleet of Tunisian pirate vessels. Cathcart was subjected to the indignity of being stripped naked on the open deck, and was robbed of nearly all his personal belongings.

When he arrived in Tunis with the story of what had happened to him, William immediately lodged a strong protest with the Bey. Ahmed ignored the communication, Sahibtappa openly laughed at the Americans, and it was said that Joseph Famin, who had been sulking for a long time, was rejoicing.

In the meantime, Commodore Dale had arrived at Gibraltar

on board his flagship, the frigate *President*, with a squadron that also consisted of the *Philadelphia*, the *Essex* and the *Enterprise*. The *George Washington*, currently being refitted in the United States, was scheduled to join the squadron as soon as she was seaworthy and could cross the Atlantic. The display of naval strength was by far the greatest ever made by Americans in the Mediterranean.

But Dale immediately erred. A schooner flying the ensign of Tripoli had arrived a day earlier, and her commander cleverly paid a courtesy call on the Commodore and assured him that rumors of a declaration of war by Yusef against the United States were false. Dale believed him and lingered at Gibraltar for a month, thereby giving Murad Reis time to prepare the Tripolitanian navy for a showdown with the Americans.

Dale, although personally courageous and patriotic, had not been the best of choices for the post of commander in chief of the Mediterranean fleet. Perhaps the most experienced of American officers, he had served in the original United States Navy during the Revolution. He had been the First Lieutenant of the legendary Captain John Paul Jones on board the *Bon Homme Richard*, and had distinguished himself during the battle with the Royal Navy's *Serapis*. He had spent time as a prisoner of war and later became the master of a merchant ship engaged in West Indian trade.

One of the first Captains appointed in the new Navy, he had taken umbrage because three other officers had been ranked above him and, at his request, had retired from active duty and returned to his merchantman. Now, recalled to duty by the Navy, he had been given a post of the greatest responsibility. A moody, shy man who had become increasingly cautious in advancing middle age, Dale was not spoiling for a fight.

Eventually he had to leave Gibraltar in order to visit the State Department representatives in the Barbary States, and on July 8, 1801, the squadron arrived at Algiers. The Dey was impressed by the size and efficiency of the American squadron, and as a consequence was very polite when Dale was received in an audience, accompanied by Consul O'Brien. The ruler of Algiers complained about America's alleged failure to meet her treaty obligations, but he was unfailingly courteous and soft-spoken. The meeting was the first with him that O'Brien had ever enjoyed.

It was from O'Brien that the Commodore finally discovered the truth about the state of war that existed between the United States and Tripoli. Dale was surprised, chagrined and somewhat amused when he realized how badly he had been fooled. O'Brien did not share his amusement.

Dale gave the Consul his first letter of instructions from Secretary Madison, and, before leaving, handed him $30,000 from an emergency fund for the purpose of keeping the Dey tamped down. The squadron then sailed eastward to Tunis.

On the night of July 17, William Eaton, James Cathcart and Eli Danielson were dining at the American Consulate when Aletti burst into the room with the rumor that a fleet of United States warships had arrived off Porto Farina and had anchored there for the night rather than risk moving into the rock-strewn roads of Tunis after dark. There was no way to confirm the story.

But, a short time later, William and Cathcart were summoned to the *Kasba*. There the Bey took the unique step of publicly apologizing to Cathcart for the humiliation he had suffered on his voyage from Leghorn, and gave him a handsome purse that more than recompensed him for the losses he had suffered at the hands of Tunisian brigands. As William and his colleague made their way back to the Consulate, they knew that, beyond all doubt, an American squadron had indeed arrived. Nothing other than the demonstration of great American force could have persuaded the Bey Ahmed Pasha to reverse himself so completely.

On the morning of July 18 the ships sailed into the roads and anchored, a maneuver that was observed by thousands of the Bey's subjects. Joseph Famin quietly disappeared from the city and went off to a desert oasis, where he remained until he was certain the squadron had departed.

For reasons that have never been clarified, William and Dale disliked each other on sight. There is no reason given in William's *Life*, Journal-Diary or correspondence. His first references to the Commodore are scathingly contemptuous, but he gives no explanation for his feelings. Eli, who almost always echoed his stepfather's views, also looked down his nose at Dale, but is equally silent regarding the cause of any possible dispute they may have had.

Dale's first mention of William appeared in his official dispatches to the Navy Department, and were patronizing and cold. He further compounded the mystery by offering no evidence to substantiate his feelings. Unfortunately, he made his views known to a number of his immediate subordinates, with the result that most of the high-ranking Navy officers with whom William subsequently dealt were influenced by his opinion.

Other than the abrasions previously mentioned, chief among them being the rivalry between a former Army officer and the commodores and captains of the younger, more glamorous and currently more favored service, posterity is totally in the dark regarding the sparking of the feud. Perhaps it is an oversimplification to say that there was a personality clash, based on the chemistry of William and Dale, but many men through the centuries have become antagonistic to one another for just this reason. Whatever the origins of their dislike, a legitimate argument developed before the end of the summer that widened the breach and made it permanent.

Dale, accompanied by William, paid a courtesy call on the Bey, and Ahmed went to great pains to charm the Commodore. William, like O'Brien in Algiers, laughed to himself throughout the interview. If Dale had accomplished nothing else, he had temporarily eased the burdens of the State Department representatives in Barbary.

William was given a letter of instructions from his new superior, and Secretary Madison, who was completely out of touch with the situation on the Barbary Coast, was necessarily vague. This suited William perfectly, because it enabled him to take matters into his own hands.

After spending three days at Tunis, Dale sailed off to see for himself what the precise situation might be in Tripoli. The *Essex* remained behind for minor repairs that delayed her for a day or two and was ordered to rejoin the rest of the squadron as quickly as possible.

William had spent a great deal of time during the squadron's visit pondering, and by the time Dale departed had elected to interpret Secretary Madison's orders liberally, so liberally that he proceeded to put his cherished scheme into operation. Before the American warships had disappeared from the American roads, he paid a visit to Hamet Karamanli.

Over coffee the two men reached a provisional agreement. The United States would use force, as demonstrated by the powerful squadron, to restore Hamet to the throne from which he had been deposed. He in turn would make an equitable, lasting treaty with the United States. Hamet gratuitously offered something else. Since he wanted no part of his brother, but wouldn't know what to do with him after regaining his title and position, he told William that he would give Yusef and his family into the keeping of the United States as "hostages" guaranteeing the good faith of Tripoli.

William dutifully reported every detail of the conversation in a report to Secretary Madison. Recognizing its historical significance, he made a careful copy of the report and included it verbatim in his *Life*. Obviously he knew the project would be his greatest achievement, if he brought it off. He must have known, too, that he had as yet been given literally no authority to commit the United States to an enterprise of such magnitude. But his conscience remained untroubled because he felt certain he would obtain the full support of his Government.

He also made another momentous decision, in concert with James Cathcart. Both men felt they had been negligent in allowing Commodore Dale to depart on such a vague mission, and they corrected their oversight by preparing a proclamation, signed by William and countersigned by Cathcart, declaring that Tripoli was under a state of blockade. They gave the document to the Captain of the *Essex*, telling him to give it to Dale as soon as he rejoined the squadron.

A squall delayed the American ships in the Mediterranean, and the *Essex* caught up the squadron at the approaches to Tripoli. Dale responded to the signal from the *Essex* telling him she carried a message from the Consular Agents with word that its delivery would have to wait, as he was preoccupied.

The appearance of the squadron threw Yusef into a panic. Although he had been expecting the arrival of American warships, he was not prepared for the sight of their size and armaments, and a discouraged Murad Reis confirmed his opinion that the Tripolitanian navy was not strong enough to beat off the enemy.

So, using Danish Consul Nissen as an intermediary, Yusef sent out word to the approaching Americans that he was prepared to negotiate with them.

Nissen was acting in an informal capacity, of course, and Commodore Dale replied in kind. He agreed with President Jefferson that peace was preferable to war and negotiation to bloodshed. But the facts of the situation were very simple. A state of war existed because of Yusef's declaration of it. If the Bashaw wanted peace, he could cancel his declaration. If he did not, however, the Commodore's hands were tied because the United States Government had given him no authority to negotiate on her behalf.

Nissen carried his message to Yusef, and while Dale waited for the Bashaw's response, the proclamation signed by William and Cathcart was delivered to him. Dale read it and lost his temper, claiming that any such proclamation should be signed by him, as the Navy's senior representative in the Mediterranean. He could not deny the legal right of the State Department's representatives to issue such a proclamation, but felt they should have deferred to him and that by issuing the document under their signatures rather than his they were deliberately slighting him.

It must be remembered that Dale had reverted to an inactive

101

status several years earlier rather than accept a status junior to several other officers. No man was more conscious of rank and dignity. Perhaps his reasons were trifling, but he now had a grievance against William Eaton that he considered legitimate.

Nissen remained ashore a very short time, returning to the *President* with word that Yusef felt a retraction of his declaration of war would be regarded everywhere as a surrender. If the American Commodore refused to negotiate, the war would continue.

Dale could have taken the time to copy the proclamation declaring Tripoli under blockade and sign it himself. He was not that petty, however, and instead handed Nissen the document bearing the signatures of William and Cathcart. The Danish Consul went ashore and the American ships moved out to sea to establish their blockade, the Commodore feeling he had been cheated out of a place in history that was rightfully his.

Whatever his personal sensitivities, Dale knew how to conduct a tight naval blockade. No ships succeeded in entering or leaving the harbor and only one tried. The sloop *Tripoli*, the pride of Murad Reis' fleet, made an attempt to put out to sea, but was intercepted by the American schooner-of-war *Enterprise*, commanded by Lieutenant Andrew Sterrett. The *Enterprise* attacked at once, and Sterrett signalled the Commodore that he needed no help. Dale took him at his word, and in three hours the *Tripoli* was reduced to a shattered hulk, while the *Enterprise* was unscathed.

Of the *Tripoli's* crew numbering eighty men, twenty had been killed and thirty-one wounded. Because the United States had not declared war and was officially at peace, the *Tripoli* was stripped of all her equipment, armaments and gear except for an old sail and single spar. Sterrett then allowed her to limp back into the harbor with her dead and wounded. The object lesson was not lost on either Yusef or Murad Reis.

Only once did Dale make direct contact with the enemy. Several officers of Yusef's guard and a number of merchants from Tripoli were intercepted off the coast on board a Greek merchantman and, acting through the ever-obliging Nissen, the Commodore offered to trade his prisoners for any Americans who might be in Tripoli. There were three, the exchange was made, and on September 3 the Commodore gave up his blockade because he needed supplies in Gibraltar and his men, after so long at sea, were clamoring for shore leaves.

The squadron put into Tunis en route to Gibraltar, and there William and Dale had a furious argument. William accused the Commodore of having been derelict in his duty because of his failure to bombard Tripoli and capture as many prisoners as he could take. Dale replied he had no orders from the United States Government to do either, and would not commit himself beyond expressing the hope that he might find fresh orders waiting for him at Gibraltar. William, compromised by his understanding with Hamet, was wildly indignant.

The months that followed were frustrating for everyone except Yusef and Murad Reis. There were no orders for Dale at Gibraltar. After waiting in vain until December for instructions from Washington, he sailed for home, leaving two ships to patrol the Mediterranean, the *Philadelphia* and the *Essex*, with Captain John Barron in overall command. Barron's hands were tied even more effectively than Dale's had been, and although he was a competent officer, the Commodore had left him with no instructions authorizing him to take any action, overt or indirect, against Tripoli.

The distressed William Eaton, waiting in vain at Tunis for his countrymen to attack Yusef or, at the very least, resume the unofficial blockade of Tripoli, cursed the Navy. His own problems were multiplying rapidly. Once the American squadron had sailed away and given no evidence of returning, the Tunisians took heart and the Bey Ahmed Pasha renewed his unceasing demands for cash and naval stores and grain, rifles and gunpowder. Sahibtappa, although afraid to attack American merchant shipping for fear of reprisals from the warships which he knew to be at Gibraltar, nevertheless halted several Yankee brigs in the Mediterranean to emphasize his point that

Tunis could, if she wished, turn the screws tighter at any time.

Commodore Dale had given William no funds and the Consular Agent, forced to make repeated token payments to the Bey, found his treasury rapidly vanishing. The bulk of his private fortune was in the United States and, although he made strenuous efforts to obtain loans from Tunisian bankers and moneylenders, they were not interested in advancing cash when the security for the loans was so far away.

At this unhappy juncture Hamet Karamanli became a pauper. It was expensive for a former Bey to live in the style to which his birth and the murder of his elder brother had entitled him, and the nest egg he had taken with him from Tripoli in both cash and jewels was exhausted. It was small wonder; his household consisted of his three wives and their eleven children, approximately thirty nobles and their women, and servants—most of them slaves, who nevertheless had to be fed and clad—whom no one bothered to count.

Hamet's situation was even more perilous than that of his benefactor, and he sat down with William to discuss the economic facts of life. He badly wanted to regain his throne and, if possible, would rely on the Americans to help him. But he had rent to pay, many mouths to feed, bills for clothing and medical treatment to pay, and even found it necessary to provide discreet entertainment on occasion for his bored but still loyal nobles.

If no funds were forthcoming from the United States, he would have to make his peace with the detested Yusef. In fact, Yusef had sent an intermediary to him in recent weeks, and had offered him the governorship of the province of Cyrenaica, where Tripoli's second and third cities, Derna and Benghazi, were located, if he would sign a document giving up all claims to the throne for himself and his heirs. Hamet hated to accept, to admit defeat, but a man, his family and his followers had to eat.

William first took steps to determine that Hamet was not merely subjecting him to a subtle form of the usual Barbary

104

Coast pressure. Cathcart conducted a quiet investigation, and all that Hamet had said proved to be true. The ex-Bey was at the end of his financial rope. If the Americans did not come to his rescue, he would be forced to make a permanent, humiliating peace with the brother who had driven him from his throne and homeland.

William's situation was desperate and he resorted to desperate measures in order to deal with it. He saw no choice for himself and decided to gamble. A brig recently captured by Tunisian pirates, the *Gloria*, believed to have been of Danish ownership, was put up for auction sale. No other potential owners appeared, and William was able to purchase the vessel for the surprisingly small sum of one thousand dollars. But he quickly discovered, now that he was the owner of a merchantman, that he had just started to pay out money.

The hiring of a competent master, an Italian, and an experienced crew of seamen from many nations cost him a considerable sum, as officers and sailors alike demanded wages in advance for their first voyage. A cargo of Tunisian olive oil and almonds, tanned hides and pottery used up the last of his personal reserves. Then, when the ship was about to sail off to the European shores of the Mediterranean to sell the cargo, Sahibtappa stepped in. The Keeper of the Seals refused to supply the American with a navigation passport that would insure the *Gloria* of immunity from pirate attack for less than $15,000 in cash.

William neither had such a large sum available nor could he acquire it. He stormed and begged in vain; Sahibtappa refused to budge.

The American found himself trapped in an impossible situation of his own making. Even if he abandoned the one plan that, in his unalterable opinion, would create a permanent, just peace between the United States and the nations of the Barbary Coast, he had already invested so much money in his venture that he would suffer crushing financial losses if he gave up the *Gloria* now. Apparently it did not matter to him that,

105

as a high-ranking official of the State Department, he was engaging in activities contrary to every ethical principle of diplomatic service. He was doing what he believed essential, had no desire to make a profit for his own sake, and stubbornly refused to change his course.

Using the *Gloria* and her cargo as security, he borrowed money to arm the brig with a number of 14-, 12- and 6-pounder cannon. Then, because of the increased risks, he had to give the ship's officers and men a substantial bonus before they would undertake a voyage. He was almost completely without funds when the brig finally sailed away.

The next weeks were among the most anxious of his life, but he finally received word from the master of the *Gloria* that the vessel, after several narrow escapes from brigands, had reached Leghorn and had disposed of her cargo for a fat profit. Most of the crew had walked out, however, and refused to return because the hazards were too great.

The profits of a single transaction would be helpful, but the *Gloria* had to remain active if she was to serve William's purpose. So he improvised, brilliantly. Sweden and Tripoli had just broken diplomatic relations, and for all practical purposes were at war, which gave the always resourceful William an idea. He borrowed more money, and went off to Leghorn, where he had a long, earnest meeting with Karl Andersen, the Swedish Consul there. Since the units of the United States Navy berthed at Gibraltar were doing nothing to protect Mediterranean shipping flying the American flag, William offered Andersen a one-third interest in the *Gloria*. In return the brig would fly the Swedish ensign and would be guaranteed the protection of the strong, aggressive Swedish squadron stationed in the Mediterranean. Andersen was interested, but his own code of ethics made it impossible for him to agree.

So William pocketed his profits and, accompanied by a skeleton crew, sailed off to Gibraltar. There he laid his problem before Captain Barron, who proved sympathetic to him and his grand scheme. Never at a loss for ideas, William presented

106

a new one to Barron. If the Captain would issue a certificate temporarily incorporating the *Gloria* into the United States Navy, he would make the brig available for purposes of assisting in the blockade of Tripoli—at no cost to the American Government—whenever the Navy wished. She would continue to operate as a merchantman until her services were required, but several Navy officers could travel on board as passengers, ready to take command instantly in the event of need. What William would gain in return for his generosity was the valuable protection of the United States Navy flag. By flying it the *Gloria* would be safe from all Barbary pirates except units of the now relatively inactive fleet of Murad Reis. The Moroccans, Tunisians and Algerians would not want certain war with the United States, which would inevitably follow an attack on a unit of the American Navy.

The idea was ingenious, unethical and without question illegal. Never had the government of a self-respecting nation indulged in such a flamboyantly transparent ruse. But William was a convincing talker and before the naive Barron quite realized what was happening, he agreed. William promptly hired a new crew at Gibraltar and, with two lieutenants of the United States Navy on board, himself took on a cargo and set sail for Algiers with it.

From December, 1801, until May, 1802, the American Consular Agent assigned to Tunis cruised the Mediterranean engaging in lucrative, illicit trade, his brig protected by the Navy's flag. Not once was the *Gloria* called on to assist in a blockade of Tripoli or participate in any other act of war. Finally, in early May, after the apprehensive Barron had learned that a new squadron of American warships was on the high seas sailing for the Mediterranean, the agreement was cancelled.

William returned to Tunis with his pockets bulging. Whether the *Gloria* flew the Navy's pennant on this voyage is a question that has never been settled. William's enemies in the United States, a group that multiplied rapidly as he enjoyed continuing, increased successes, claimed that even though the privilege had been withdrawn he flew the Navy's banner on this final voyage in order to protect his cash profits locked in his cabin, his ship and his person from brigands of the sea. William, in his *Life*, hotly denies the charge.

In any event, he reached Tunis without incident.

It is of interest to note that Captain Barron never suffered because of the part he played in the curious, unorthodox affair. Although William incurred the increased hostility of several senior officers who came to the Mediterranean, Barron escaped censure. In Washington he was actually regarded as something of a joint hero with the remarkably resourceful Consular Agent Eaton and won the praise of senators, congressmen and his civilian superiors in the Navy, including the Secretary of the Department.

A new crisis confronted William when he reached Tunis. The Bey Ahmed Pasha had learned of Hamet's agreement with the American Consular Agent, had notified Yusef of it and had been working closely with the Bashaw, trying to persuade Hamet to make his peace with his brother. The easily influenced Hamet, whose dependents were now living on the charity of the Bey of Tunis, had agreed to return to Tripoli. Forty burly guards, all members of Yusef's household regiment, had arrived to escort the wanderer home.

William intervened swiftly and delicately. At a private meeting with Hamet he gave the former Bey of Tripoli enough money to satisfy the demands of even the most insatiable Barbary Coast aristocrat. Then, working out a clever escape plan, he allowed Hamet and his entourage to sail for Tripoli by way of Malta. Meanwhile the *Gloria* vanished from Tunis, manned by sailors given a bonus for particularly hazardous duty.

At Malta, which was protected by the Royal Navy, Hamet dismissed his brother's broad-shouldered guards and, in spite of their angry protests, took his party on board the *Gloria*, which quickly put out to sea. The Tripolitanian warship on which Hamet and his entourage had been traveling had disappeared, and after conducting a fruitless search, Yusef's men returned home empty-handed.

Meanwhile, the *Gloria*, which had been hiding in a cove, reappeared. Hamet and his followers went ashore to live in comfort on Malta until William could put his plan into effect.

As for William himself, he repaid his debts with his remaining profits from the brig's trading voyages and was able to afford the luxury of an association with a young, very attractive Italian mistress whom Aletti found for him. His daring venture had been completely successful and although he did not yet know it, events in the Mediterranean were about to take a new, totally unexpected turn.

CHAPTER EIGHT

ANCHORS AWEIGH

President Jefferson, always a cautious optimist in his approach
to international relations, took a moderately hopeful attitude
toward the Barbary Coast problem after he received Commodore Dale's report on the situation there. Secretary Madison's
reaction was similar, and both saw grounds for the possibility
of reaching a peaceful solution. Certainly the Bashaw Yusef
Karamanli Pasha's expressed desire to talk rather than fight
hinted that some reasonable compromise might be found.

Both Houses of Congress exploded, however. Tripoli's insults to the American flag, James Cathcart's humiliation and
the constant harassment of American shipping in the Mediterranean were more than senators and representatives could bear.
The walls of both chambers in the new, raw capital, Washington, rang with denunciations of the evil Yusef and his corrupt
followers. In its burst of patriotic enthusiasm Congress voted
a medal to Lieutenant Sterrett, who had smashed the warship *Tripoli* in battle, and unanimously agreed to commend
Consular Agent William Eaton. A select committee prepared
the commendation, which was one of the most flowery documents ever written by members of a body noted for their
ornate language.

110

Then Congress buckled down to consider the realities of the situation. The United States, through ignorance of Tripoli's declaration of war, had not replied in kind. It seemed rather absurd, the better part of a year later, for America to retaliate with a declaration of her own.

Secretary Madison's testimony before the Senate Committee on Foreign Relations was illuminating. By issuing a formal declaration of war, he said, the United States would limit the elasticity of her response to future developments. In the event that Yusef could be maneuvered into making an agreement that would guarantee a just and lasting peace, the technical machinery leading to that agreement would be ponderously heavy. The Secretary much preferred, he said, to let American representatives on the spot handle the situation as they saw fit. The Barbary rulers, Yusef in particular, were so flighty and unstable that American civilian leaders and military-naval commanders in the area should have the right to seize any opportunities beneficial to the United States that might present themselves at unexpected moments.

Congress agreed that Madison made good sense, yet at the same time had no desire to let Yusef go unpunished for the acts of aggression he had committed. Therefore an ingenious formula was devised and adopted. Both Houses of Congress passed a resolution specifically stating that the nation was not at war with Tripoli, but that, in view of Yusef's unilateral declaration of the previous year, a situation similar to a state of war had been created. Under such circumstances, it was necessary for Americans to defend themselves by all available means.

A large sum was voted for an additional expansion of the Navy. A request was made to the President, in his capacity as Commander in Chief, to dispatch a strong squadron of warships to the Mediterranean at the earliest possible moment, under instructions to take any steps her senior officer deemed necessary to protect American honor, lives and property. In brief, Congress was authorizing the United States to participate in armed

111

combat, but without actually identifying that activity as war.

The reactions to William Eaton's plan to drive Yusef from the throne of Tripoli and replace him with his brother was complicated. Jefferson and Madison, as leaders of a country too young to have developed her own strength as yet, were ultra-sensitive to the interference of any nation in the internal affairs of another. All too frequently Great Britain still treated the United States as though she were still a colonial possession, the attitude of France in the recent undeclared naval war had been unbearable, and it was common knowledge that Spain was trying to woo the territories of the American West with gifts of money and land as well as promises of influence to men who held political power in the area.

It was the view of most congressmen that the two situations were dissimilar. The treatment that Britain, France and Spain accorded the United States was, in the main, "civilized." But the Barbary states seemed unaware of the etiquette essential to international intercourse. It would be a shame to let scruples that applied to one circumstance color America's feelings in another. It might well be that the opportunity to get rid of Yusef and replace him with the more amenable Hamet would be lost if the Executive branch of the Government took too rigid a stand.

Some congressmen were in favor of a public declaration that would spell out America's intention of dethroning Yusef and replacing him with the brother who was actually Tripoli's rightful ruler. The alarmed Secretary Madison pointed out that any such public statement would tend to force the other rulers of Barbary to make a common stand with Yusef. So far, a tenuous peace had been maintained with Algiers, Morocco and Tunis, and it was far better for a country still recovering from an eight-year war for independence waged only two decades earlier to fight as few enemies at any one time as she could.

Giving this point of view additional weight, Madison cited passages from reports submitted by O'Brien, Eaton and Cath-cart which expressed the unanimous opinion that the defeat of one Barbary state in armed conflict would cause the others to behave more circumspectly. Eaton had been even more vigorous than his colleagues in stressing this belief.

The matter was debated at some length, and President Jefferson finally solved the issue by side-stepping it. The United States Government neither endorsed and accepted the Eaton proposal nor rejected it. The high-principled Jefferson, who never approved of chicanery, may or may not have understood the full import of what he was doing by doing nothing, but the move—or lack of a move—was very clever.

The full burden was being left on William Eaton's shoulders. If he succeeded, the United States would reap the benefits of his plan. If it failed, however, the Government could claim that his idea had never won the approval of his superiors.

There was only one possible hitch in the way Secretary Madison carried out the Administration's policy. It would be impossible to drive Yusef off the throne and replace him with Hamet unless violent action was utilized. Such action cost money. Madison, following in the President's footsteps, managed a neat evasion. Eaton was being sent new funds and, presumably, would use them as he saw fit. He was not specifically directed to give every penny to the Bey of Tunis and other Tunisian officials. If he chose to spend some of the money elsewhere, the State Department was prepared to close its eyes.

Also, the Navy squadron being dispatched to the Mediterranean was not being sent on a pleasure cruise. Never before had so many American warships with such great fire power been gathered together as a unit. The Secretary assumed that Commodore Richard Morris, the squadron's commander, would get together with Consular Agent Eaton to work out the details of coping with the Barbary pirates.

Madison was assuming a great deal.

The squadron consisted of the Commodore's flagship, the *Chesapeake*, a new frigate of thirty-six guns, the *Constellation*, also with thirty-six guns, the *New York*, another thirty-six-gun frigate, and the new *John Adams*, with twenty-eight guns, just

113

commissioned. The schooner-of-war *Enterprise*, with twelve guns, and three still smaller ships made up the rest of the squadron. Their combined force was sufficient to destroy the navies of all the Barbary states and, if necessary, reduce Tripoli, Algiers and Tunis to ruins. The hopes of Congress and the country soared high when the squadron sailed for the Mediterranean, with only the new *John Adams*, which was completing her sea trials, scheduled to follow a little later in the year.

Although no one yet knew it, the squadron was suffering from a debilitating weakness, her commanding officer. Commodore Morris was a good sailor and an excellent gunnery officer who should not have risen higher in the service than the rank of captain. When he served under someone else, he executed orders reliably and punctually. But when he himself held the post of ultimate responsibility he was so confused and uncertain that he became incapable of rendering positive decisions. He was further handicapped by a complete lack of political experience that made him the most naive of officers ever to have risen to what was, at that time, the highest rank in the Navy.

Unfortunately for Morris, for the United States, and for William Eaton, the orders given to the Commodore prior to his departure left unsaid far more than they said. He was directed to "make the most handsome and most military display of force, and so conduct maneuvers as to excite an impression that, in the event of negotiations failing, you intend a close and vigorous blockade."

These orders were in keeping with the country's formal posture of being a nation at peace. What Morris failed to take into account, or perhaps to understand, was the sense of the resolution passed by Congress. The wording of that document had made it specific that the armed forces of the United States were to "conduct themselves as though this nation were at war with Tripoli, such a state having been declared publicly by the ruler thereof, albeit not recognized by these United States."

The captains of the squadron knew what was meant. It was their understanding that Morris was to make an attempt to negotiate with the Bashaw Yusef and if the effort failed to establish a blockade of Tripoli, capture prisoners and, should it be necessary, shell the city. Since Congress had not declared war, the Commodore's orders had necessarily left unsaid that which was obvious. But none of the subtleties were obvious to the literal-minded Richard Morris.

The squadron reached Gibraltar in mid-June, 1802, and Morris remained there for ten weeks, to the despair of William, O'Brien and Cathcart. The ships, regardless of their strength, were useless when anchored in a British port. William sent the Commodore a full report on the state of his negotiations with Hamet, who was still living at Malta on the funds earned by the *Gloria's* commercial cruises. Morris, who found nothing in his orders authorizing the scheme to put Hamet back on the throne, sent a brief, curt reply in which he flatly refused to have any part in carrying out the plan.

While William was reeling from the shock, all Americans in the Barbary states were humiliated by what came to be known as "the *Franklin* tragedy." The *Franklin,* a brig out of Philadelphia, was captured in international waters by three ships belonging to Murad Reis' navy. They put into Algiers with their prize, but O'Brien went at once to the Dey and his anger peeled paint from the walls of the *Kasba.* Using the presence of the American squadron at Gibraltar as a threat, he told the Dey at length what would happen to Algiers if the Tripolitanians were given refuge.

The Dey promptly told his allies to leave and they sailed on to Bizerta, the second city of Tunisia. William, without realizing it, reacted precisely as O'Brien had done. He went straight to the Bey Ahmed Pasha, and his threats, delivered in a voice loud enough to raise the minarets of the *Kasba* into the air above the walls, were very explicit. Again the corsairs of Murad Reis were invited to leave, and they did, abandoning the *Franklin* at Bizerta, but taking the seventeen officers and seamen of her crew with them to Tripoli as prisoners.

There two of the officers and one seaman were identified by

115

the British Consul as English, and were released. A number of others, who also were not American nationals, were set free, too. But the *Franklin's* master remained a captive, and four of his American-born sailors were sold into slavery.

Commodore Morris, when the news was related to him, found it impossible to believe that any nation could deal in such a crude manner with prisoners. The story was exaggerated, he declared, and although he sent several of his ships out to cruise the Mediterranean and prevent future raids on American merchantmen, he continued to do nothing at Gibraltar.

His supine inactivity was embarrassing to both William and O'Brien. Not only was the United States taking no retaliatory measures, but Yusef's agents spread the word that the American Navy was afraid of him. The danger that all of the nations of the Barbary Coast might band together became distinctly greater.

William's personal position in Tunis was rapidly becoming untenable. Morris' failure to act on behalf of Hamet, or at the least to send a ship for the claimant to the throne of Tripoli and escort him to the American headquarters at Gibraltar, made it evident to the Bey and Sahibtappa that William was receiving no support from his own country's Navy. The Keeper of the Seals, never one to forgive or forget, started a rumor to the effect that Consular Agent Eaton no longer enjoyed the confidence of his own Government.

"In God's name," William wrote to O'Brien, "what ails Commodore Morris? Unless he unlimbers his cannon soon, we will be driven from the Mediterranean!"

Both men thought of resigning, reconsidered and tightened their belts. William's contracted far more than O'Brien's. He was still supporting Hamet and the large ménage of refugees from Tripoli, and his funds were not unlimited. He parted with his expensive young Italian mistress and as he had not yet received the money from the State Department that Morris was supposedly bringing him, he took the desperate step of making a gift of the *Gloria* to the Bey, claiming he was presenting it on behalf of the United States. For the moment Ahmed stopped clamoring for blackmail, but William's resources once again were exhausted.

Suddenly, in October, the entire Barbary Coast was electrified by the news that Hamet Karamanli had landed at Derna. Tired of waiting for American support, the usually lethargic Hamet had taken matters into his own hands. According to Aletti, who assiduously gathered gossip and news for William, the people of Derna received Hamet with greater enthusiasm than the originator of the plan had dared to hope. The still-trusting Hamet was spreading the word that the American squadron, which had just moved most of its units from Gibraltar to Malta, would sail to his support in the immediate future. Men from every part of Tripoli began to rally to his banner. The move to depose Yusef had become a reality and it appeared that, with luck and American help, it would succeed.

Although it was difficult to confirm the rumors, the Tunisian authorities were so concerned that William was convinced the news was fairly accurate. Within a few days the Danish Consul received a hastily-prepared communication from the faithful Nicholas Nissen; the reports were true.

Here was the opportunity William had so long awaited. The mere appearance of the American squadron off Tripoli would multiply the pressures on Yusef, and a bombardment of the capital without question would cause the frightened Bashaw to sue for peace. The stronger the American display and use of armed might, William believed, the greater became the possibility that Yusef could be persuaded to give up his throne "voluntarily" and go into exile.

"At last," William wrote to Commodore Morris, "our long-awaited chance to attain peace for America and Americans on the Barbary Coast is at hand. If we are bold and act with vigor, every pirate nation will beg for a treaty similar to those on which civilized nations make their peace with one another. If we press our cause with dispatch, it will never again become necessary for American Governments to pay tribute to the petty tyrants of this savage corsair world.

"I urge you, with every fiber of my being, to muster your full

117

strength and sail at once for Tripoli. Victory is within grasp of the United States!"

Richard Morris, before sailing with the better part of his squadron to Malta, had performed one act that he considered within the range of his instructions. Just before he had left Gibraltar, one of Murad Reis' warships, the cruiser *Meshouda*, had put into port there. So he had left the *John Adams* on patrol duty to prevent her from leaving the harbor.

The rest of the American ships took part in the elaborate ceremonies celebrating the birthday of King George III, and the roar of their cannon firing 21-gun salutes sent seagulls and other alarmed birds flying high into the air. This was literally the first time the American guns had been fired since the squadron had come to the Mediterranean.

A few days before the Commodore received William's letter, a small schooner-of-war arrived at Malta with a message for Morris from the Navy Department. If he no longer had urgent use for the *Constellation*, the communication said, she was needed elsewhere, and should be sent home. The Commodore promptly released one of his most powerful, efficient ships, and she sailed for the United States.

When Morris read William's communication, he obviously realized it was no longer possible for him to evade taking a firm stand. He had been ordered to parade his ships before Tripoli if he could not negotiate with Yusef, and it evidently occurred to him that he could do neither from the sanctuary of Malta. So, detaching the *Enterprise* for independent patrol duty in the Mediterranean, he sailed for Tripoli.

When he arrived off the city, the gunboats of Murad Reis at anchor in the harbor fired, ineffectually, at the American warships. Yusef assumed that the Americans had come to do battle with him, and, in an attempt to force them to keep their distance, also had his shore batteries open fire. The gunnery of the Arabs was frightful and not one shot hit the targets.

A more aggressive officer would have returned the fire. But Morris contented himself with writing a long report to the

118

Navy Department explaining that the hostile acts of Yusef's subjects were making it impossible for him to initiate the negotiations that President Jefferson and Secretary of State Madison wanted. Having justified his passivity, he paraded his ships back and forth across the harbor entrance. For all practical purposes this became a blockade, since no Tripolitanian ship dared to enter or leave the harbor.

The blockade—or simulated blockade—was maintained for approximately three weeks. The weather was very bad, so Morris thought it wise to return to Malta until spring, when the cessation of storms would make the task of maintaining a patrol much easier.

When William learned the blockade had been abandoned, he virtually lost all hope. Knowing Arabs, he realized that Hamet's supporters would desert him and return their allegiance to Yusef. The grand scheme was collapsing.

In addition, William was at the end of his diplomatic and financial rope. The Bey Ahmed Pasha was making new demands on him, and he had no funds left with which to pay tribute. The abandonment of the new blockade made the Bey and Sahibtappa so contemptuous that it appeared Tunis would in time—probably a very short time—break diplomatic relations with the United States.

The status quo was further complicated by the one positive act taken by a ship of the Commodore's squadron. The *Enterprise* had captured a Tripolitanian sloop-of-war, and had taken her to Malta. The Bey claimed that he was part owner of the vessel, and although he was undoubtedly lying, he could use the incident to declare war on the United States.

When Commodore Morris reached Malta he discovered that the claim made by the Bey of Tunis was holding up the award of the Tripolitanian sloop, the *Paulina*, to the United States Navy. This, more than anything else, is probably what impelled him to pay an immediate visit to Tunis. He arrived there with his whole squadron on February 19, 1803, nine months after his arrival in the Mediterranean.

119

The sight of powerful American warships and cannon had their usual effect on the Bey and Sahibtappa, who suddenly became meek. William found it difficult to be civil to the Commodore who had made a shambles of his plans, but instead of sulking he wisely seized this last, unexpected opportunity to persuade Morris to see reason.

"When he chose to exercise it," Eli Danielson wrote of his stepfather after his death, "General Eaton had a charm so great and a logic so persuasive that he could have talked Satan into abandoning hell and applying for a new post as a minor angel."

William used all his powers of reason and all his charm on Commodore Morris, who was soon agreeing that his campaign to put Hamet back on the throne of Tripoli made great sense. He also agreed that William's need for more money was urgent, and promised—according to William's account, at least—to support the request in his own reports to Washington.

After the two Americans had talked amicably for the better part of a day, William took Morris to the *Kasba* for an audience with the Bey. Rarely had any interview been so excruciatingly embarrassing. Ahmed brought up the subject of the *Paulina*, and the Commodore bluntly expressed his disbelief that the ruler of Tunis was her part owner. Ahmed complained that William was behind schedule in his tribute payments, and Morris expressed his opinion of such extortion in language so plain that the official interpreter did not dare to translate his remarks until Ahmed insisted.

William tried repeatedly but in vain to halt the increasingly heated exchange and "was dismayed and dejected beyond all previous experiences of such feelings," as he wrote in his *Life*, when the Commodore suddenly stood, turned his back to the princeling and stalked out of the audience chamber. Never had a ruler of a Barbary Coast state been treated with such impudence by a Christian foreigner.

While William remained behind in an unsuccessful attempt to repair the damage, Morris collected James Cathcart and Captain John Rodgers of the *John Adams*, who were waiting

120

in an anteroom. Refusing to listen to Cathcart, the two Navy officers picked up their gear at the American Consulate and, with Cathcart still accompanying them, stalked to the water-front, where they had left a gig that would take them to the squadron anchored in the outer harbor.

Three hundred Tunisian soldiers armed with scimitars and rifles blocked their path. Sahibtappa was waiting, and told them they would not be allowed to leave until the question of the *Paulina's* ownership was settled and William Eaton's tribute was paid. Morris, instead of threatening to level Tunis to the ground unless he was permitted to pass, became embroiled in a long argument with Sahibtappa, each man haranguing the other at length.

The humiliated Navy officers were forced to return to the Consulate. The enraged Morris insisted that William was to blame for his degradation, and Rodgers, who had not been present in the Bey's audience chamber, naturally believed his own superior. This, unfortunately, thereafter clouded the relations of William and the future Commodore Rodgers, one of the finest officers in the Navy.

The stalemate remained unbroken for days. Troops stayed on duty at the docks, making it impossible for the Navy officers to leave. Morris stormily rejected all suggestions made by William and Cathcart that he return to the *Kasba* and observe the amenities so vital to the pride of the petty rulers of Barbary. Instead he ranted at both Consular Agents, and the longer he was forced to remain in Tunis, the angrier he became.

William made several trips each day to the *Kasba*, where he used both diplomatic language and threats in an effort to persuade the Bey that he was doing irreparable damage to Tunisian-American relations. But Ahmed, whose pride was still outraged by the refusal of the Commodore to make even a token apology for his rudeness, no longer cared what happened. He made scenes, swore that he would join Tripoli in her war against the United States, and berated William incessantly.

After five days the hurricane winds began to subside, if for no other reason than because both sides were exhausted. At last William was able to persuade the Commodore to become more reasonable, but the obdurate Bey raised his price. A determined, spirited William finally forced Morris to admit that he had funds in his possession that had been given him for the use of the State Department's representatives, but, as a matter of principle, that he hated to pay blackmail.

William finally convinced him that neither of them were in a position to change a policy established by a treaty to which the United States was still a party. So Morris grudgingly agreed to pay the Bey twenty-three thousand dollars. Ahmed, aware that he was winning, also insisted that the Americans relinquish their claims on the *Paulina* to him. The bewildered Morris agreed, capping his degradation.

Wiliam had won the release of the Navy officers, but had to pay the highest personal price. His own sessions with the Bey had been so violent that it was no longer possible for him to do diplomatic business with Ahmed. After all, the entire court had heard the American Consular Agent shouting at him.

The Bey announced that he required a new American representative "whose disposition is more congenial to the Barbary interests." In the language of international diplomacy, William became *persona non grata* in Tunis, and had to leave.

Rodgers was to remain behind to work with Cathcart in handling the details of the negotiations, and Dr. George Davis, a Navy physician, temporarily replaced William. A final hitch developed when the disgusted William finally showed his own feelings in the matter by refusing to sail with Morris. Instead he waited for Rodgers, and then he and Eli Danielson sailed with the future Commodore on board the *John Adams* to Algiers. William's departure from Tunis was not only sudden but permanent. He never returned.

His policy was destroyed, he believed himself in permanent disgrace and believed he would have to leave the employ of the State Department. Never had his feelings been so low, never had he considered himself such an abject failure.

CHAPTER NINE

YANKEE DOODLE CAME TO TOWN

A scant two hours before the departure of the *John Adams* from Tunis, the Bey Ahmed Pasha suddenly decided that James Cathcart was no longer welcome in his realm, presumably because he had been William Eaton's close associate and friend, and Cathcart joined the other State Department representatives on board the frigate. William was gloomily silent on the voyage, and a brief notation in his Journal-Diary indicates his state of mind during this trying period.

"I fear," he wrote, "that all the United States has tried to accomplish in Barbary has been in vain. Unless something drastic is done to reverse the decline in our fortunes, and I know not what it might be, the United States soon will be forced to abandon the entire Mediterranean Sea."

When the *John Adams* reached Algiers, he discovered that the situation was even worse than he had imagined. It had deteriorated so badly, in fact, that although the American squadron was anchored in the harbor, Commodore Morris had carefully refrained from going ashore. The Dey, in emulating his colleague in Tunis, was actually going him one better.

Consul O'Brien had recently paid the Dey thirty thousand dollars in cash out of his last remaining reserves, in lieu of the naval stores that, according to treaty, he was supposed to receive. Now the American warships had brought him the stores, and he demanded these supplies in addition to the cash. The patience of O'Brien was exhausted, and he said the Dey could have one or the other, but not both. The burly Algerian monarch insisted that the stores be landed and cited the treaty, but would not give back the cash. O'Brien refused to land the stores. The Dey retaliated by expelling him from the country.

The Emperor of Morocco decided the time had come for him to stand beside his brother rulers of Barbary in the growing crisis, and sent a note to Commodore Barron, declaring that the Tripolitanian cruiser *Meshouda*, which was being blockaded at Gibraltar, was actually his property. Commodore Morris unwisely recognized the claim and allowed the blockade to be lifted.

The diplomats held a conference of their own. O'Brien decided to accompany the squadron to Malta and do what he could from there to prevent the complete collapse of America's diplomatic relations with Algiers, Tunis and Morocco. It was agreed that Cathcart would remain with him.

Of primary importance was the need for someone who knew the entire situation to return home and explain matters candidly to President Jefferson. O'Brien felt that the outspoken, persuasive William was best suited for the task and Cathcart concurred. Although William was reluctant to leave the Mediterranean, he also recognized the need for prompt corrective action by the Executive branch of the Government, and said he would go.

Commodore Morris was glad to be rid of the man he considered responsible for the "disgrace our flag has suffered," as he put it in a report to the Navy, and sent William back to the United States on board the *Chesapeake*, which was commanded by Captain John Barron. The voyage was thoroughly unpleasant for both the Captain and his guest. On the first night of the voyage, when they dined together, the discouraged and exasperated William was less diplomatic than he should have been, and

124

forcibly expressed the opinion that the Navy had bungled. Captain Barron, loyal to his service, repeated Morris' charge that it was William who had been at fault. The conversation became heated, then icy, and the two men did not speak to each other again for the rest of the voyage. Captain Barron thereafter dined alone, while William and Eli Danielson, who was accompanying him, ate with the ship's officers. These patriotic young gentlemen had heard of the dispute between their Captain and the civilian, and of course took Barron's part. The atmosphere at the dinner table was reserved throughout the entire crossing.

The *Chesapeake* landed at Philadelphia, and William, wasting no time, hired horses for himself and Eli and departed the same day for Washington. He went straight to the State Department on his arrival, leaving Eli to find them sleeping quarters in a lodging house.

Secretary Madison, who had been given no warning of what had happened in Tunis, was astonished by the unexpected appearance of his subordinate. The aroused William, who had been waiting a long time for this occasion, informed Madison that he wanted to see the President as soon as possible, and would explain to them jointly what had happened in the Mediterranean.

They rode together to the newly built Executive Mansion, and there William was closeted for more than four hours with Jefferson and Madison. "Eaton," William wrote in his *Life*, "gave the President a candid account of events that had led the United States to her present, sorry state in Barbary. Mr. Jefferson," he added in an understatement, "was much chagrined."

The United States was, at this time, on the threshold of becoming a major world power much more rapidly than even the most ardently patriotic American had dreamed possible. Jefferson and Madison were in the process of closing a deal with France for the purchase of the Louisiana Territory, a vast expanse of more than 828,000 square miles stretching to the Rocky Mountains, which would increase the area of the United

States by approximately 140 percent. Napoleon and his Foreign Minister, Talleyrand, had agreed to sell the huge tract for the absurdly small sum of $15,000,000. The reasons France was willing to make the sale were complicated, and were predicated principally on her desire to be rid of her New World holdings so she could concentrate on European expansion and her war with Great Britain.

The importance of the transaction to the United States was overwhelming. As Robert R. Livingston, the American Minister to France said, "This is the noblest work of our lives!"

The treaty was signed at Washington on April 30, and both the President and his Secretary of State were preoccupied in the days immediately prior to the day that would transform the United States from a minor international power into one with the potential for becoming one of the strongest and greatest on earth. It was on April 25, unfortunately, that William Eaton held his long meeting with Jefferson and Madison, and it was even more unfortunate that both had matters on their minds that made it difficult for them to concentrate on their country's problems in the Mediterranean.

William's difficulties were compounded by events of which he knew nothing. Secretary of the Treasury Albert Gallatin was a cautious man intent on saving money when he could. It was his theory that any project that failed to produce tangible results should be cut back or eliminated, and the failure of the Navy to bring peace on the Barbary Coast had caused him to recommend that the squadron in the Mediterranean be reduced. The President had agreed, and Robert Smith, Secretary of the Navy, was forced to comply.

William argued long and vociferously that a strong expedition be sent to the Barbary Coast. Only if the masters of the pirate states were severely chastised, he explained, would they behave. He had been preparing his speech for a long time, and was cogent, persuasive, even brilliant. As Madison later remarked, "Eaton is a devil's advocate whom I would not like to see opposed to any plan of mine. There are few men in the

126

Congress with his ability to present a case for that in which he believes."

But the results of his meeting were disappointing. As he observed in his Journal-Diary, "The President became reserved, and referred the Barbary question to his Cabinet, seeking advice. Mr. Madison, who believes as the President does in all things, says nothing, and leaves everything to the Navy Department. The Secretary of War believes it would be too great an effort and expense to send troops to Barbary, and thinks it both easier and cheaper to pay tribute to the savages, even if it should become necessary to double or treble our tribute payments. Only Secretary Smith of the Navy supports me. He, by the way, is as much a gentleman and a soldier as his relations with the Administration will suffer. Gallatin, like a cowardly shopkeeper, shrinks behind the counter and tries to make himself invisible in the presence of the robbers.

"On May 11th, whilst the whole of the United States was celebrating the purchase of the Louisiana country, truly a great event in our history, I appeared before the Cabinet to explain the Barbary conundrum and offer my solution. It was disheartening to find only Smith supporting me. The President remained silent, saying nothing, and the Secretary of State also resembled a tomb.

"I am discouraged, but will not surrender."

Secretary Smith was William's ally and together they began a campaign to win the President's support. Smith, like William, was aggressive, and both realized that it was only the approval of Jefferson they needed. There was still so much resentment of the Barbary Coast treatment of Americans being manifested in Congress that it was simple to gain the backing of articulate members of both Houses, and a steady stream of callers at the Executive Mansion pressed Jefferson to adopt a more belligerent pose.

Spurred by William and encouraged by Smith, the senators and representatives argued that the shrunken squadron now operating in the Mediterranean was too small and too weak to

127

perform the task assigned to it. No matter how much territory the nation had acquired through the Louisiana Purchase, the lack of respect engendered in other countries would sooner or later cause even more serious problems. The British, finding it more difficult to man the ships of their expanding Navy, were impressing American merchant seamen. France, now that the Louisiana deal was completed, was treating America with such open contempt that James Monroe, the special envoy sent to Paris to complete the negotiations for the purchase of Louisiana, commented bitterly in his dispatches on the attitude shown by the French government. Spain was becoming increasingly bold in her efforts to woo men who might be persuaded to create new nations carved out of American territory in the West. Something had to be done, the congressmen insisted.

It was inevitable, in the course of William's many discussions with Secretary Smith, that Commodore Morris' name should come into the talks. William pulled no punches in making his own views of Morris clear. Captain Barron of the *Chesapeake* was called to the Navy Department and although he tried to defend his superior, Smith realized that all of William's charges were true.

Armed with the evidence of Morris' incompetence, Smith went to see the President, and spoke bluntly. Jefferson wanted no scandal and was reluctant to replace a senior officer, but finally agreed there was no choice. Once his thinking had gone this far, he was ripe for the next step, and Smith brought William to another conference at the Executive Mansion held a few days later. All of the arguments in favor of a firm Mediterranean policy were presented once again to the President and Secretary of State.

Jefferson, still hoping to avoid war with all of the Barbary Coast states, wanted to hold a final discussion of the matter with his Cabinet, and a meeting was scheduled for the next day. The session was held behind the closed doors of the President's office, and in spite of Gallatin's opposition, Smith's will prevailed.

The Navy Department immediately took action. Two of the nation's largest and strongest frigates, the *Constitution* and the *Philadelphia*, were ordered to proceed to the Mediterranean as soon as they could be made ready for extended sea duty. In the meantime, two new sloops-of-war, the *Argus* and the *Vixen*, currently making sea trials, were directed to join the squadron, too, when they were ready for action.

In the meantime orders were issued recalling Commodore Morris and giving command of the squadron to John Rodgers. Smith wrote a candid personal letter to Rodgers, that said, in part, "We have been for some time much disappointed with the conduct of Commodore Morris. He has not done anything that he ought to have done, and we despair of his doing anything. As a mark of our disapprobation, it has been determined to suspend him."

In a postscript the Secretary declared, "We can obtain from Morris no information on what he is proposing to do. We have to rely on others to give us some general information with respect to his movements. Be good enough not to emulate him in any thing."

A Navy schooner, the *Nautilus*, carried the Secretary's orders and letter to the Mediterranean, and Morris returned home on the same ship. Because of his long and faithful service to his country it was deemed preferable to avoid a court-martial, if possible, and Morris was given the chance to retire quietly from the Navy. He indicated, at first, that he wanted to fight, but friends managed to persuade him he would be disgraced, so he chose to retire.

Morris knew, of course, that William Eaton was responsible for the abrupt termination of his Navy career, and became the enemy of his tormentor. There was nothing overt he could do to hurt William, but he wrote innumerable letters to friends in the Navy, and many accepted his judgment. It is small wonder that there were Navy officers who felt antagonistic to William until the end of his days.

The immediate problem facing William was his own part in

the new schemes being concocted to bring the Barbary pirates to heel. The policy of taking a firm, aggressive stand against the corsair states was his more than that of any other man. His plan to put Hamet Karamanli on the throne of Tripoli had collapsed, to the best of his belief, because Morris had not supported it. He had literally no idea what might have become of Hamet who, if captured by Yusef, in all probability had been put to death. He still entertained hopes, however, that Hamet was alive and free, in which event he might be able to revive his idea. Stubbornly persistent, he had no intention of giving up.

Smith, his admirer and new friend, was also determined that the man responsible for the new, firm American policy in the Mediterranean would not be left out. The Secretary of the Navy promised William he would participate in the new campaign. "It was promised Eaton by Secretary Smith," William wrote in his *Life*, "that he would return to Islam with the new fleet units, but he had no idea of the role he might play. Since he was in the employ of the State Department, the Navy could give him no instructions to regulate his conduct."

The air was being cleared, however, and William understood the limitations under which he would be operating. The War Department had recommended so strongly to the President that no Army corps be dispatched to Barbary that Jefferson refused to consider such a plan, the War Department's stand coinciding with his own desires to keep hostilities to a minimum. And only a few marines were assigned to the warships, all of them on board the warships for purposes of repelling enemy boarders and, when necessary, acting as policemen when sailors obtained shore leaves.

Therefore it would be impossible to lead either American soldiers or marines in a land campaign. William recognized the fact that he would have to settle for less. No one knows precisely when he concocted the idea for his great adventure, that of leading a corps of mercenaries and dissident Arabs against Yusef, preferably but not necessarily for the purpose of putting Hamet on the throne of Tripoli. The notion may have come to him at this time; perhaps he had dreamed of it earlier.

In any event, it is certain that the plan was firmly in his mind during the period of his stay in Washington during the spring of 1803. He sent Eli Danielson to Philadelphia and New York on a confidential mission to obtain $20,000 of the fortune he had made in land speculation. Eli also bought tents, saddles and cooking equipment, which were packed away in boxes that would accompany both men on their return to the Barbary Coast.

Eli also went to New York's most prominent swordsmith, Morton Jones Martin, with instructions to make a perfectly balanced scimitar of the finest steel. William drew a sketch of the weapon himself, and in his written orders for the weapon directed that "the blade must be perfectly balanced so that its handle will lie without strain in the palm of a man's hand. It must be light in weight, yet so durable and strong that no other sword could shear it in twain. It must be so sharp that, should a man so desire, he could remove his beard with either the outer or inner edge."

Martin had obtained a quantity of the steel used in Toledo, Spain, for the making of swords, and fashioned the scimitar of it. He followed William's orders, and the blade lived up to all of its owner's expectations. Martin charged $85 for the scimitar, an outrageous price at the beginning of the nineteenth century, but William did not care what he had to pay. He got what he wanted, and the scimitar was packed away, too. It did not reappear until the beginning of his march to Derna.

But William still had a long time to wait. The State Department was reluctant to send him back to the Mediterranean until he had a specific assignment to fill, and the Navy squadron sailed off to the Barbary Coast without him. Smith continued to promise him that he would play an active part in coming events, and for the present he had to be content.

As it happened, William's enforced holiday in the United States furthered his cause. While he went off to Massachusetts for a visit to his wife that no longer could be postponed, a new era for Americans was beginning in the Mediterranean. While he languished in Brimfield, Commodore Rodgers and the man

131

who succeeded him late in the year, Commodore Edward Preble, began to attack Barbary pirate ships molesting American merchant shipping. Most of these engagements took place in the western Mediterranean or the open Atlantic beyond it and, as it happened, three of the pirate vessels were Moroccan. All three were captured, their crews were made prisoner and the Emperor became so alarmed that he asked for a revision of his treaty with the United States on terms far more favorable to America. Rodgers and Preble made him aware of the remarkably accurate gunnery of the Navy and he was intelligent enough to realize that the era of threats and blackmail had come to an end.

The Emperor voluntarily proposed that a new treaty of friendship be executed, in which the payment of tribute by America—in any form—was eliminated. This request reached Washington late in 1803, when Commodore Rodgers arrived home. The firm policy so long advocated by William Eaton was paying spectacular dividends, and although Rodgers could not be considered William's friend, he threw his full support behind the "Eaton arrangements," as they were being called. Like so many other senior Navy officers, Rodgers, as an executor of these policies, was aware of their unqualified success.

The defeatist followers of Commodore Morris had been in the minority for some time, and now vanished, the entire Navy urging that the Barbary pirates be taught a permanent lesson. The increase in Navy morale was sharp, and everywhere in the United States young men began to volunteer for service. It became easier to recruit officers, too, the masters of merchant ships and their mates suddenly finding the prospect of Navy careers more attractive.

William, who had returned to the nation's capital from Massachusetts after another totally unsatisfactory visit with his wife, found himself being hailed as hero in Congress and in some departments of the Executive branch. Secretary of the Navy Smith praised him everywhere, and Secretary of State Madison declared himself highly pleased. The most important reaction was that of President Jefferson, who finally became convinced that a firm, aggressive policy would succeed. Even the penny-pinching Albert Gallatin admitted that in the long run the utilization of strength would save money, although he continued to oppose the sending of an Army corps to the Mediterranean, as did the War Department.

On December 5, 1803, the President sent a special message to Congress on the subject of the Barbary Coast crisis, and by promising to take a firm stand in the future indirectly, at least, apologized for his previous caution.

The time was ripe, almost over-ripe, for William to advance his own cause. On December 8th he was advised by Secretary Smith that he would encounter no difficulty in getting whatever he wanted from the President. Two days later William went to the Executive Mansion, summoned by Thomas Jefferson.

Secretary Madison had been scheduled to attend the conference, too, but was suffering from an attack of indigestion that day, so only William and the President were present. The precise nature of the understanding they achieved was never made clear. William had his own, very specific ideas, which Jefferson neither confirmed nor denied. It may be that the President of the United States was reluctant to admit publicly that he was committing his Government to the overthrow of a reigning monarch. This is the probable reason for his silence. Another theory, that he did not know what William had in mind, is also realistic. It is unlikely that the President or anyone else guessed that William intended to recruit a corps of his own and march across the desert with it.

Only Eli Danielson knew that closely guarded secret. The President unquestionably realized, however, that William intended to depose Yusef by force and replace him with Hamet. After all, Jefferson personally initialed the memorandum authorizing the State Department to advance to William the sum of forty thousand dollars "for use in restoring peaceful relations between the United States and Tripoli."

It must be assumed that James Madison, who secured the funds from the Treasury Department and gave them to William, also had a fairly good idea the money would be spent to remove Yusef from his throne. Madison was also the agent for obtaining one thousand rifles from the War Department and handing them over to William.

The very subject of these rifles is something of a mystery. No record in the War Department files indicated that the President or Secretary of State had requested them. In fact, the first mention of them appears in a memorandum signed by Colonel Ezekiel Gale of the War Department, and states, simply, "One thousand long rifles have been delivered to Mr. W. H. Eaton at the order of the Secretary of State."

The embarrassed State Department preferred to pretend that the weapons did not exist. In fact, Madison and his subordinates decided it was more convenient not to have William on the payroll. Although still technically an official of the Department, he was loaned to the Navy, informally, and his lack of a precise status suited his own purposes. The State Department assumed he was working for the Navy, and the uniformed officers of the Navy considered him a State Department man.

This ambiguity allowed him far greater latitude in making his own preparations and carrying them out. He had so much freedom, in fact, that a suspicion arises: was he himself responsible for this convenient status? Perhaps he and Secretary Smith, his mentor, worked it out together. It was Smith, certainly, who gave him the grand but essentially meaningless title he carried with him to the Mediterranean. He was the "United States Naval Agent on the Barbary Coast."

No one, Smith included, specifically outlined his duties, and he was the only man in the history of his country ever to hold such a title. Smith also made another contribution to William's cause, instructing the Navy to "provide Mr. Eaton with such artillery as he may require for his purposes."

No American ever traveled under such vague authority, with forty thousand Government dollars in cash locked in his cabin, one thousand rifles stacked in the holds of warships and the official demand of the Secretary of the Navy that the Mediterranean squadron supply him with artillery. No one, it seemed, wanted to specify William's "purposes," and no one asked too many questions.

Commodore Rodgers, on his return to the United States, had brought with him information that had galvanized William into action. Hamet Karamanli's unsupported attempt to crush his brother had failed. When it had become obvious to the oppressed people of Tripoli that the United States was not going to help Hamet, the rebellion had collapsed. Even the nobles who had gone into exile with Hamet and wandered around the Mediterranean with him for years left Derna for Tripoli to make their personal peace with the Bashaw.

And Hamet, knowing his fellow countrymen, had fled again before zealous officials who had joined him when he had first landed at Derna cast him into prison in order to win favor with Yusef. Commodore Rodgers did not know what had become of Hamet, but had heard rumors that he had gone to Egypt as a refugee.

Those rumors were all William needed to revitalize his favorite project. He knew Hamet was alive and living somewhere in the Mediterranean, so could be found. The Navy, operating with the largest force it had ever sent to the Mediterranean, was under instructions to take vigorous action against Tripoli —and the ships of any other Barbary state that dared to harm American merchant shipping interests.

The delays had been long and odious, but the effulgent dawn of a glorious new day was breaking.

CHAPTER TEN

SNARLS IN THE ROPE OF FATE

While William Eaton was at work in Washington and dreaming of his return to Barbary, the United States Navy squadron in the Mediterranean was bringing increasingly heavy pressure to bear against the ruler of Tripoli who had declared war on America. Captains were ordered to seek, find and destroy all vessels flying the banner of Yusef Karamanli Pasha, and they did. From September 1 to October 15, 1803, four Tripolitanian warships were captured and two others sunk. Murad Reis was forced to become increasingly cautious and kept most of his navy close to home.

Hoping to bottle up the enemy completely, Preble directed Captain William Bainbridge of the frigate *Philadelphia* to establish a close blockade of Yusef's capital. The American ship arrived off the coast of Tripoli on October 20. There was no more efficient, courageous officer in the Navy than Bainbridge, who later became a Commodore, and his officers comprised an extraordinary group, too. The First Lieutenant, David Porter, became a great hero in the War of 1812 and gained additional fame as an explorer in the Pacific. Five other lieutenants also achieved the rank of captain and served with distinction. Perhaps, as Bainbridge himself suggested some years later, the ordeal they suffered after the *Philadelphia's* ill-fated cruise was a crucible that tempered them.

On October 31, while chasing a small Tripolitanian warship, the frigate suddenly went aground on a reef at the entrance to the city's harbor, and was in acute danger of breaking up. The Tripolitanian cruiser immediately opened fire on the American ship, and Murad Reis' gunboats swarmed out of the harbor to join in the attack. Beset on all sides and in ever greater danger of foundering, Bainbridge fought off the enemy as long as he could, but by four o'clock in the afternoon, after a struggle that lasted the better part of the day, it became obvious to him that the *Philadelphia* could not be hauled off the reef.

A very brief council of war was held on the quarterdeck, and the officers agreed there was no way to save the ship and escape. Bainbridge, with tears streaming down his face, hauled down his flag and surrendered. Tripolitanian gunboat crews claimed possession of the *Philadelphia,* and the officers and men of the frigate were taken ashore. The elated Yusef suddenly found he had more than three hundred Americans to use as pawns. And after several days of labor Murad Reis was able to float the frigate again. After she was repaired, the renegade Scotsman boasted, she would be capable of meeting any American warship on equal terms.

The sudden capitulation of the *Philadelphia,* which shocked so many Americans and was deemed inexplicable until the full story became known almost two years later, requires an additional word. The frigate was in strange waters and appeared to be breaking up on the reefs. Bainbridge, Porter and the junior officers, all of whom later demonstrated their exceptional valor in the War of 1812, were not panicky, neophyte seamen who gave in when the foe appeared to be on the verge of overwhelming them.

In their best judgment, and this cannot be stressed too strongly, they honestly believed their ship was sinking. Therefore, they assumed it would not fall into the hands of the enemy. Events proved them wrong, but their error was an honest one, as an exhaustive inquiry later proved. Nevertheless, their mistake had far-reaching consequences.

The story of the nineteen months of captivity endured by the crew of the *Philadelphia* is a familiar one and has been told many times. The enlisted men were treated as slaves and were forced to work on harbor fortifications and other defense projects. Rebels and malingerers were whipped and starved into submission. The treatment of the sailors was brutal. It was small consolation when they were assured that they were not being handled any more harshly than other Americans who fell into Tripolitanian hands.

Bainbridge and his officers were helpless, unable to intervene, although the Captain repeatedly protested to Yusef, both in person and through Danish Consul Nissen, who did everything in his limited power to help the captives. The officers were confined in an old fortress overlooking the sea, and the more they agitated, the more severe became their own treatment. Those who tried to escape were held in solitary confinement and when the United States Navy began its subsequent bombardment of Tripoli, the *Philadelphia's* officers who signaled their colleagues at sea, helping to direct the American gunnery fire, were put on reduced food rations.

Yusef made certain that none of the prisoners died of hunger or were beaten to death, as they were worth far more to him alive than dead. Totally misunderstanding the temperament of Americans, he sent a new message to the United States Government through Nissen. The price of peace had risen: the Bashaw would sign a treaty and release his captives in return for a down payment of $500,000 and an annual tribute of the same sum, in perpetuity.

News of the *Philadelphia's* tragedy and Yusef's impudently greedy demands created a major sensation in the United States. The Congress immediately increased taxes on all imports in order to raise additional revenues, and authorized the President to recommission several warships that had been put into drydock, and to build others. No one in the United States seriously considered paying Yusef the blackmail he demanded. Even the families of the prisoners urged the Government to use force.

The *Philadelphia's* fate influenced and colored the thinking of every responsible Government official during the long months that William was trying to obtain permission to put his pet project into operation. It is impossible to say whether he would have obtained greater support had the frigate not foundered on the rocks of Tripoli's harbor, but it is certain that many officials were in no mood to think in terms of elaborate schemes. Everywhere in the United States the blunt, direct frontier mentality was overwhelming; when a man was hit, he struck back, twice as hard. "Bash the Bashaw!" some newspapers urged, while others said simply, "Destroy Tripoli!"

William was so thoroughly convinced his own plan would succeed far better than the exclusive use of sea power that, in his final meeting with President Jefferson, he flatly declared that he would refuse all compensation for his services "except for a sufficiency to cover my actual expenses," as he wrote in his Journal-Diary.

He also declared, in the same statement, "I can therefore say, as a Spartan Ambassador to the King of Persia's Lieutenant, when asked whether he came with a public commission or on his own account: 'If successful, for the public; if unsuccessful, for myself.' "

Unquestionably the capture of the *Philadelphia* and her crew caused the pacific Jefferson to adopt a more stringent policy toward the states of the Barbary Coast, but in the furor most officials forgot the long-range goal of obtaining just treaties with the pirate nations. Members of Congress and the Executive branch alike sought the release of the prisoners in Tripoli, and the attainment of this end was the primary objective of the Navy.

Before leaving the United States, however, William was finally given a specific task. He was directed to secure a lasting, equitable treaty with Tripoli.

Having been given an assignment, he was immediately handcuffed. Colonel Tobias Lear, a veteran soldier and diplomat, was appointed United States Consul General at Algiers, and also was given a special Presidential directive to act in a new post, Political Commissioner with the Mediterranean Fleet. William was told nothing of the precise nature of the work that Lear was to do, and Lear himself, like a good soldier, was closemouthed.

William and Lear were unable to define their relationship and areas of responsibility. The latter now held the State Department's highest-ranking post in Barbary, and his title of Consul General, the first granted to an American representative in North Africa, was an indication that he had the full confidence of Jefferson and Madison. His assignment as Political Commissioner with the Mediterranean Fleet signified that he, above all others, would work with the squadron's commander in chief, and would be responsible for the solution of non-military problems.

On the other hand, William had been loaned to the Navy by the State Department, and therefore appeared to be the "Navy's diplomat." At the same time, he had been given a specific State Department assignment, that of concluding a new treaty with Tripoli, presumably after Yusef was compelled by force of arms to become reasonable. Further complicating the situation was William's off-the-record order—or perhaps it was no more than an informal agreement with the President—to foment an armed revolt in Tripoli and if possible put Hamet on the throne as Bey.

It is small wonder that Lear and William were confused. There were areas of overlapping authority that were not clarified by President Jefferson, Secretary Madison or other members of the Cabinet. Lear assumed that William was required to report to and through him; William took it for granted, deliberately or otherwise, that he was operating independently.

Fortunately, the two men established a personal rapport that eased the embarrassments of their relationship. They had been acquaintances for some years, and occasionally had dined together. Now, as two former Army officers required to live and work closely with the Navy, they were drawn closer. Lear, like William, was a moderate consumer of alcoholic beverages in an age when most men drank heavily, and rarely touched any spirits stronger than wine and ale. Both enjoyed reading the ancient Greek classics in the original and discussing them, and both were frontiersmen ready to improvise and seek unorthodox solutions of problems that could not be approached in conventional ways.

Their differences were equally great. Lear was a moderate in all things, William an extremist; Lear was self-effacing, a perfect diplomat, while William still hungered for renown, applause and a permanent place in history. Lear was a traditionalist to the extent that he always followed orders and under no circumstances would have exceeded them. William was an innovator who found it convenient to forget or "misunderstand" orders when he felt he could attain his goals in his own way.

Five powerful frigates were made ready to join the Mediterranean squadron. It was evident that the United States intended to use all of its power to obtain the release of the *Philadelphia's* crew. The vessels were the *President,* of forty-four guns, the *Congress,* of thirty-six, the *Essex,* of thirty-two, and the *Constellation* and *John Adams,* which had just recently returned from the Mediterranean. The unit's commander, Commodore Samuel Barron, was the older brother of Captain Barron, with whom William had been at odds on his return voyage home.

With Captain Barron transferred to the command of the *President,* the Commodore elected to use another vessel as his flagship, and although the forty-four gun *Constellation* would have been a natural choice, he decided to cross the Atlantic on board the *John Adams,* the smallest ship in the subsquadron. He invited Lear, William and Eli Danielson, who once again was accompanying his stepfather as an assistant, to accompany him. They had no choice, of course, although the *John Adams* would be crowded and all three would have to share a single, small cabin.

There were innumerable, frustrating delays that made Wil-

141

liam wonder if he would ever return to Barbary. A number of gunnery crews were still in training, and the Commodore refused to leave until they became expert marksmen. Some of his ships needed minor repairs that nevertheless took a long time to perform, and while a less meticulous commander might have waived this work, he insisted it be done. He planned to sail in April, 1804, then in May, but it was June before the squadron was ready.

Before weighing anchor, the Commodore and his civilian passengers heard news that soon had Americans everywhere lighting bonfires. Commodore Preble, the Mediterranean commander, had been afraid that Murad Reis planned to send the captured *Philadelphia* to sea, and took steps to prevent the incorporation of the frigate into the Tripolitanian navy. He sent an exceptionally able and daring young officer, Lieutenant Stephen Decatur, sailing into the harbor of Tripoli on the night of February 16, on board a bomb ketch, the *Intrepid*, with a crew of seventy-five men and armaments of twelve cannon.

Decatur succeeded in boarding the *Philadelphia*, driving her Tripolitanian crew into the sea, setting fire to the *Philadelphia* and then withdrawing on the *Intrepid* without the loss of a single man. The *Philadelphia* burned to the water line, became a charred wreck and soon sank. Congress voted Lieutenant Decatur a sword of honor for his exploit, and the Navy promoted him to the rank of captain.

Preble was handicapped that winter and spring by the small size of his squadron; he was operating with only one frigate, the 44-gun *Constitution,* his flagship. He had two sloops, the *Argus* and *Syren,* each of sixteen guns, the schooners *Vixen* and *Nautilus,* of fourteen and twelve guns respectively, and two converted prize ships, the *Intrepid* and *Scourge.* Unwilling to wait for the powerful reinforcements being sent him from home, he sailed to Tripoli, and sent Consul O'Brien ashore to negotiate.

Yusef held the upper hand and knew it. "War is my life,"

the Bashaw said, and threatened to torture, then behead all of the prisoners from the *Philadelphia* if the Americans dared to bombard the city. Preble was forced to sail away, but began to collect reinforcements on his own initiative.

He bought six gunboats and two bomb ketches from the Kingdom of the Two Sicilies, and by early summer took his entire squadron to Tripoli, where he established a tight blockade of the city. Now it was his turn to threaten, and he sent word ashore to Danish Consul Nissen that if any of the prisoners died or were executed, he would begin an immediate bombardment.

The haughty Yusef did not deign to reply and instead strengthened his shore batteries. The Americans could see men at work on them, and through their glasses the officers recognized the tattered American uniforms of laborers being driven by overseers armed with whips. Preble found it increasingly difficult to wait until the frigates arrived, but forced himself to remain patient. Meanwhile Nissen sent word to him that Yusef had mobilized a garrison of twenty-three thousand men to protect his capital. The Americans on blockade duty numbered only one thousand, so the odds were one-sided.

The subsquadron sailed from the United States in mid-June, when the weather should have been good, but the frigates were delayed by squalls and did not reach Gibraltar until late July. On a voyage of this length it was almost inevitable that William, Commodore Barron and Colonel Lear should become well acquainted. Before the subsquadron left the United States, relations between William and the two men who, in a sense, were his immediate superiors, were eased considerably when Secretary of the Navy Smith, William's staunch supporter, dined with the other two men and praised his friend at length.

Commodore Barron was a man of unusual, judicious temperament. Although he had heard William roundly condemned by his brother, he preferred to form his own judgments. He was well aware of the errors that Commodore Morris had made on his tour of duty in the Mediterranean, and felt that William's complaints to the President had been just. According to letters Eli Danielson wrote to Smith's attractive daughter, Ann, in whom he had become interested during his Washington sojourn, Commodore Barron indicated on a number of occasions at the dinner table that he, had he been Morris' superior, would not have hesitated in suspending him.

The subsquadron needed supplies at Gibraltar, and several of the frigates required minor repairs. Barron was anxious to let Commodore Preble know that he had arrived in the area, and therefore sent his smallest ship, the *John Adams*, to carry the word to the squadron on patrol in the waters off Tripoli. William was so anxious to reach Tripoli himself that he sailed on the little frigate, even though his rifles and the boxes containing his personal gear were stored in the holds of the *Congress* and the *Constellation*. He carefully carried his money with him, however, forty thousand of it in Government funds and twenty thousand of his own.

Eli was particularly pleased, as he was able to move from the hammock in the very crowded quarters he had been sharing with the ship's junior Lieutenants into the cabin with his stepfather. There, he wrote Ann, he enjoyed the luxury of sleeping in a real bunk instead of a swaying hammock. Members of the Eaton family were never good sailors.

On August 9 the *John Adams* reached *Tripoli*, and her Captain informed Commodore Preble that Commodore Barron would be arriving in the immediate future. That night the always courtly Preble invited William to dine with him on board the *Constitution*. Like his colleagues, Edward Preble had heard William damned by many Navy officers, but nothing in his manner indicated that he might share their opinion.

He brought William up to date on the operations he had been conducting, and was filled with optimism. A number of Tripolitanian cruisers and smaller vessels trying to run his blockade had been either sunk or captured, and he had also taken possession of several merchantmen flying Yusef's banner. His own losses had been light throughout the campaign—fewer than fifty officers and men killed or wounded.

144

Now, with the strong frigates joining him, he felt certain he could force the Bashaw to capitulate within a short time. William did not agree, but believed it his duty to communicate with Yusef, even though successful negotiations would bring peace before he could put his own scheme into effect and win the glory he sought.

On the morning of August 11 Commodore Preble sent him ashore under a flag of truce in the *Constitution's* gig, escorted by two gunboats. Several small Tripolitanian warships hovered nearby, but made no attempt to dishonor the white flag. A number of prisoners from the *Philadelphia* were at work on fortifications near the wharf where William was landed, and cheered him as he stepped ashore.

"Their overseers," William wrote in his *Life*, "cracked their whips menacingly to force the poor, ragged wretches to resume their cruel labors, but the stout fellows ignored the threatened punishment and sent cheer after cheer echoing across the harbor."

Consul Nissen was on hand, having hurried down to the wharf when informed that an American party was coming ashore, and greeted his old acquaintance warmly. William, pretending to address him, actually spoke to the American sailors. He told them the strongest unit of warships ever sent by the United States to the Mediterranean was arriving shortly, and assured them that their fellow countrymen were determined to obtain their freedom. "Be of good faith," he told them. "All America stands with you!"

Nissen escorted William to his house, and sent word to the Bashaw, who undoubtedly knew of the envoy's arrival, that an American diplomat wanted an audience with him. While they waited, a messenger went to the fortress where the *Philadelphia's* officers were imprisoned, carrying a letter from Nissen requesting that Captain Bainbridge be allowed to come at once to his house. Under the terms of incarceration that the Danish Consul had arranged, it had been agreed that Bainbridge could visit him at any time he chose.

The Captain soon arrived, and William devoted a long sec-

tion of his *Life*, to a description of their meeting. Bainbridge
was in fairly good health and had no complaints about his personal treatment, but was deeply worried about his men. William brought him up to date on the fleet strength in the
Mediterranean, on the support for the prisoners in the United
States, and was tempted to tell the Captain of his own scheme
in order to give him greater courage, but refrained. He promised Bainbridge he would exert every effort on behalf of the
captives when he saw Yusef.

The Bashaw kept the visitor waiting until early afternoon,
when Nissen accompanied William to the palace. Murad Reis
was on hand as an interpreter, and exchanged icy greetings
with the American.

William informed Yusef that he needed no interpreter, and
Murad Reis left the room. The Bashaw could have insisted that
his naval chief remain, but allowed himself to be outmaneu-
vered, which gave his visitor something of a psychological
advantage.

Well aware of the American's identity, Yusef taunted William for having failed to achieve his goal of putting Hamet on
the throne. Instead of rising to the bait and becoming angry,
William managed to draw out the Bashaw, and eventually
found out what he was so anxious to learn, that Hamet was
now living obscurely in Egyptian exile.

Only when he began to press, inquiring whether Hamet was
in Cairo, Alexandria or some small community did Yusef
realize that he had said too much, and that perhaps the plan
to depose him was not as dead as he had apparently assumed.
He became silent.

William knew he would learn no more and turned to the
immediate business at hand. He was authorized by the President of the United States to negotiate a new treaty, he declared.

Yusef side-stepped repeatedly, but finally began his hard bar-
gaining, and his tune was far less strident than it had been
the last time he had made demands. Instead of requesting
$500,000 at once and $500,000 per year, he said that "for the

sake of humanity" he would release the *Philadelphia's* officers and men for $150,000, and would be satisfied with an annual payment of $250,000.

It was evident that the blockade was hurting him, but it was equally clear that he still failed to recognize the extent of his vulnerability.

William was not surprised. A man of Yusef's mentality had no understanding of justice, and the American's reply was subsequently printed by virtually every newspaper in the United States. "The national honor of my country will be redeemed by steel, not gold!"

Yusef lost his temper and, shouting so loudly that members of his court raced into the throne room with drawn scimitars, threatened to execute all of the American prisoners he held.

William was thoroughly familiar with the etiquette of a Barbary Coast court: under no circumstances was a ruler denigrated, ridiculed or insulted in the presence of his subjects. But the safety of more than three hundred Americans depended on a stern rebuff, so William disregarded Barbary protocol. If one prisoner died, no matter what the cause of his death, the Naval Agent declared in a calm but firm tone, Commodore Preble would hang the Bashaw from the yardarm of his flagship. That was a promise, and William called on every man present to witness the sincerity of his declaration, and would remind the group of it when the Bashaw swung from a gibbet.

Yusef was so angry he became inarticulate. Finally, when he recovered, he swore he would have William beheaded before sundown that same day.

Several officers of the royal household guard caught hold of William, who made no attempt to resist. Now, he decided, was the strategic moment to reveal that four of the most powerful frigates in the United States Navy would arrive off Tripoli at any time to join the blockading squadron. Speaking slowly, with emphasis, he named the ships, their armaments and their commanding officers.

The Bashaw may have thought he was bluffing, but preferred

to take no unnecessary chances. He ordered his men to release the American.

The unruffled William reminded him that manhandling was a violation of a flag of truce.

"The Bashaw," William writes in his *Life*, "became so flustered that he ordered Eaton from his presence. Greatly fearful that the American fleet, which had not yet used its full striking power out of regard for the prisoners at the mercy of Tripoli, might vent its terrible wrath upon him if anything amiss should happen to Commodore Preble's Ambassador, the Bashaw charged his men to see Eaton safely back to his gig."

So many men hastened to obey that Nissen, who was waiting for the American, found it difficult to reach his side. Their conversation was restrained because Murad Reis made himself a member of the bodyguard, so William experimented, and addressed Nissen in French. "The perturbation of Murad Reis was so great," continues the *Life*, "that Eaton and Nissen knew at once that he could not understand the language, even though he recovered quickly, and for the sake of the Arabs clustering about him pretended to know the tongue. Therefore Eaton and Nissen conducted their business in the alien tongue of the Emperor Napoleon I."

When William returned to the *Constitution* and reported on his fruitless meeting with the Bashaw, Preble realized the blockade had to be intensified. Some of his ships had been on duty for five months and were running short of supplies, so the *Enterprise* was sent to Malta under orders to return with all the provisions she could carry.

William, in a private conversation with Preble, told the Commodore he thought it unlikely that a blockade, even if accompanied by a heavy, prolonged bombardment of Tripoli, could induce Yusef to surrender.

"Preble listened politely and said little," William writes in his *Life*, "but his very manner of listening indicated he thought otherwise."

The *Enterprise* rejoined the squadron on August 27, her

mission accomplished, and brought word that the frigates, which had been delayed by minor but vexing problems, were due to arrive within a few days. Equinoctial gales that might drive all of the American ships out to sea would threaten within a short time, so Preble decided not to wait for Commodore Barron before opening the next phase of his operation.

On the morning of August 28, with William an observer on the *Constitution's* quarterdeck, the squadron sailed into Tripoli's harbor. Ignoring the inaccurate gunnery of the land batteries, the American warships pounded the vessels at anchor in the harbor, sinking five Barbary merchantmen and seven gunboats. The following day the Yankee sloops, schooners and ketches returned, and concentrated on the Bashaw's castle. William comments in his *Life* that he later learned Yusef prudently found urgent business elsewhere until the Americans sailed out of the harbor at sundown.

On September 4, after daily shelling, the *Intrepid* was boarded by Tripolitanian seamen and soldiers while carrying out her assigned task in the operation. Rather than lose his ship and allow his men to become prisoners of the enemy, Captain Richard Somers blew up the *Intrepid*, with all hands on board. Since she was loaded with bombs, the explosion rocked the entire harbor, and considerable damage was done to the closest shore installations.

Both sides were stunned, and the Americans, grieving for the courageous Somers and his men, withdrew to the waters outside the harbor. That night the frigates under Commodore Barron's command finally arrived. The two senior officers conferred in private on board the *Constitution*, and then William, Colonel Lear and the Captains were called in for a council of war.

Everyone present—with the exception of William—agreed that the Bashaw must be ready to sue for peace. From the windows of his shell-scarred palace Yusef could look out on the installations leveled by the explosion of the *Intrepid*, at the hulks jutting up from the bottom of the harbor, and, beyond the reefs, at the newly arrived frigates. Commodore Preble said it was obvious that Tripoli would lose the war. Commodore Barron added that any sensible ruler would sue for peace. The Captains concurred, and so did Lear.

William quietly insisted that none of his colleagues understood the mind and character of the Barbary Moslem. Yusef might be cornered, but that would only impel him to fight all the harder. A man who had killed one of his brothers and sent another into penurious exile in order to gain the throne of his country would not yield to any force unless he had literally no choice.

But Yusef undoubtedly believed he had many choices. The coming bad weather might mean the siege would be abandoned for a time. He might persuade the other Barbary states to join in the war for the sake of their own survival. Allah, who was all-powerful, might perform miracles on his behalf. Yusef, William argued, was not only stubborn, but one who neither thought nor acted as Americans and Europeans did.

The Commodores, Lear and the Captains literally failed to understand what William was talking about. Preble called for a vote, and, with William abstaining, it was unanimously agreed that Yusef should be given another opportunity to surrender.

So, the following morning, William was rowed into Tripoli again in the gig, accompanied by a curious and confident Tobias Lear. William's subsequent written report tells the story of what transpired: "Though the Bashaw is heartily sick of the war, he swears he will not give up the prisoners without ransom. His honor forbids it! He swears that in a dernier extremity he will retreat with them to the mountains."

Lear's eyes were opening by the time the audience ended. The two diplomats returned to the squadron and the truce ended.

That afternoon the frigates went into action for the first time and laid down what American newspapers called the heaviest artillery bombardment in history. The fire was so fierce that two small Tripolitanian warships tried to escape out to sea and were captured.

The prisoners, both officers and enlisted men, were taken aboard the *Constitution,* where the Commodores questioned them, Lear sitting in as an observer, with William acting as interpreter. The interrogation helped to dispel some American illusions. The Arabs said they had been told that Americans were wealthy merchants, not warriors, that they were—according to William's *Life*—"infidels, cannibals and monsters of cruelty who had unprovokedly made war upon the Bashaw with the intention of taking the country away from its people and subverting their religion."

The Arab prisoners were learning that what they had been told was untrue, at least insofar as the American ability to fight was concerned. But they repeatedly expressed the conviction that Yusef would neither surrender nor release the American prisoners in his hands. Even if the city was totally destroyed, they swore, he and his subjects would retire to the interior and continue to wage war until Allah saw fit to grant them victory.

William launched on a tack of his own and questioned the prisoners closely about the attitude of the tribes of the interior. Were they loyal to Yusef? Would they continue to support him if he suffered a severe defeat?

The Arabs stumbled and stuttered. It became clear, at least to William, that in the interior of Tripolitania itself and in the important province of Cyrenaica, Yusef stood on ground as treacherous as the shifting desert sands that made up the better part of his kingdom. It was obvious—to William—that the time had come at last to put his own pet scheme into operation and topple the Bashaw from his throne.

Lear couldn't see matters in the same light, and William quarreled with him. The Commodores, and Commodore John Rodgers, who joined the squadron a few months later, remained obdurate in their conviction that the Navy alone could conquer Yusef.

William had waited long enough, and his patience was exhausted. He made up his mind early in the autumn of 1804 to take charge of the situation himself, in his own way, regardless of the consequences. Commodores and diplomats, he confided to Eli, were fools, and he did not intend to let the United States lose her great, golden opportunity to win a resounding victory and create a lasting peace on the Barbary Coast.

CHAPTER ELEVEN

THE WHEELS TURN

In the autumn of 1804 William Eaton began to wonder whether he was one of those men whose ambitions and dreams would be forever unrealized. He knew the time was ripe for the inauguration of his grand scheme to replace the belligerent Yusef on the throne of Tripoli with the more amenable Hamet, but everything went wrong. Commodore Preble was relieved by Commodore Barron, and went home. Commodore Barron fell ill, and in turn was succeeded as commander in chief of the Mediterranean squadron by Commodore John Rodgers.

Barron sailed to Malta on the *President*, inviting William to accompany him, a request that could not be refused. His illness growing worse, he sailed on to Syracuse, the base of American operations in the area, and William found himself increasingly cut off from activities on the Barbary Coast. Not only was he physically removed from the scene of the war, but even the most optimistic review of his situation was disheartening.

If there was one officer in the United States Navy who had a low opinion of him, that man was Commodore Rodgers, who had been forced to share the humiliation of Commodore Morris in Tunis and who still believed William was responsible for that degradation. Rodgers was a brilliant commander, a gentleman and a splendid prototype for future generations of Naval Academy graduates, but his horizons were limited by the boundaries of his profession.

In his opinion William was responsible for his personal embarrassment and, far worse, that of the proud young Navy he represented. It happened that he was a close friend of Colonel Tobias Lear, William's immediate superior, and that, just prior to William's departure from the seas off Tripoli with Commodore Barron, Lear and his subordinate quarreled.

It was unimportant that the cause of their dispute was trivial, so insignificant that neither could recall what had upset them. "Papa and Lear," Eli wrote to his betrothed, "had hot words at supper last night, and both were sorry for their displays of bad temper, but they are men who cannot find it within their own natures to apologize with ease, so there is bad blood between them."

While William was sailing across the Mediterranean to Malta, and thence to Syracuse, Lear aired his grievances to his old friend, and Rodgers, already prejudiced against someone he considered hotheaded and incompetent, quickly sympathized. Members of the new commander's staff wondered, with good cause, whether Naval Agent Eaton might be ordered to return to the United States with the ailing Commodore Barron.

Rodgers raised his flag on the *Constitution* and took charge of the blockade of Tripoli. William, meanwhile, had nothing better to do than visit some ancient mineral springs and examine some early Roman ruins in Syracuse. The few scribbled entries in William's Journal-Diary from mid-September to mid-November indicate that he had become gloomily lethargic. He thought of buying himself a plantation in Georgia with the fortune he had won in land speculation. Afraid that such a life might be too quiet, he wondered whether he might be happier investing in a Philadelphia or Boston inn. He knew Rodgers disliked him and was convinced that Lear would oppose any venture with which he was connected. He spoke at length with his step-

son about retiring from Government service, and he tried to
find solace with a redhaired young woman identified only as
Maria.

She was incapable of making him happy, of course, a task
too great for any temporary mistress. But, in spite of his waning
hopes, William continued to keep his finger on the Tripolitanian pulse. He sent two espionage agents to Derna at his own
expense, an operation about which he says nothing in his *Life*
and mentions in a single laconic line on his Journal-Diary.

The spies returned to Syracuse with news he believed to be
of the utmost significance. Derna, they said, was ripe for revolt.
All of Tripoli was eager to be rid of a tyrant whose excesses
were becoming worse with each passing month, and a spark
ignited in Derna would cause the whole country to explode in
flames.

Commodore Rodgers had just arrived in Syracuse after temporarily abandoning the blockade for the winter months, Commodore Preble had not yet gone home and Commodore Barron was at yet undecided whether his health would force him
to resign his command. So William took advantage of an
unusual opportunity and presented the evidence of the espionage agents to all three senior officers.

Preble, who liked William and recognized his talents, was
very much in favor of initiating a campaign to take Derna by
land. Barron was too ill to contribute much to the discussions,
but Rodgers was strongly opposed to the idea, pointing out
that no troops were available for the purpose. Colonel Lear,
still quietly feuding with William, supported Rodgers.

The crucial moment was at hand, and William delivered
the most important oration of his life, not one word of which
has ever been recorded. Preble, after returning to Washington,
told Secretary of the Navy Smith that "Eaton argued most
persuasively for more than two hours, often invoking the name
and majesty of the President and Secretary of State." The results of his impassioned speech were worth the effort.

The Commodores agreed to support a campaign carried out

by a military corps, and William was ordered to find Hamet Karamanli, who was living somewhere in Egypt, and persuade him to take command of this force. It was assumed by all of the Navy officers that the soldiers—or irregulars—would be directed in their operations by Hamet and his followers. It was clear to everyone concerned that President Jefferson and Secretary of State Madison had approved of a Tripolitanian campaign, conducted by Tripolitanians. The United States would supply funds, which William had been given for the purpose, as well as the arms carried in the holds of warships from the United States.

Even the dubious Rodgers, who thought exclusively in terms of sea power, could not object to a plan which his own commander in chief had deemed appropriate. In fact, it was Rodgers who took the active lead in working out the details of the cooperation the United States Navy would give in order to insure the success of the operation. The Mediterranean squadron, he promised, would intensify its blockade of Tripoli and would step up its bombardment of the city in order to prevent Yusef from sending reinforcements eastward.

William kept only one aspect of his plan to himself, knowing that neither the Commodores nor Lear would grant him their permission to lead an Arab army himself. It was easy for him to keep his secret, as none of the others thought of him as a military man. He was a State Department representative attached to the Navy on temporary duty, and although the Commodores and Lear knew he had been an Army officer, it could not have crossed their minds that a retired Captain intended to promote himself, in a single, dizzying leap, to the exalted rank of General.

All at once everything seemed to favor the scheme. Captain Bainbridge of the *Philadelphia* smuggled a message out of Tripoli, assuring his colleagues that they need not harbor unnecessary fears for the safety of his officers and crew. Yusef, he wrote, was showing increasing signs of uneasiness, and apparently realized that, if he harmed his prisoners, he and the members of his family would be held personally responsible for criminal acts. "Every shot you fire into this city," Bainbridge wrote, "brings closer the hour of our liberation. Let our gunners exert their utmost for the honor of the American flag!"

Perhaps Lear was skeptical of the evidence presented by William's espionage agents. In any event, he sent his own secret representatives to test the climate in Derna, and they returned with word that corroborated everything William's spies had said. There was no reason to delay the expedition any longer.

In later years Lear claimed that he had enjoyed William's complete confidence during the planning stage of the campaign, and both Preble and Barron hinted that they, too, knew what was in the wind. Only the austere Rodgers bluntly admitted that he had been told nothing of William's personal plans. It is difficult to believe that, if he was in ignorance, the other Commodores and Lear would have kept something of such importance from the man who would lead the Navy's assault on Tripoli.

Rodgers was the most energetic officer the Navy had ever sent to the Mediterranean, and proved his efficiency in the winter of 1804-5. Two or three American warships maintained a close blockade of Tripoli, no matter how bad the weather, the ships operating on a rotating schedule. Meanwhile he used all of the funds allocated to him for the purpose by Secretary Smith to purchase gunboats from every Mediterranean power willing to sell them to him. Men from each of the warships were assigned to the crews of the boats, and went through a rigorously exhausting period of specialized training that included practice in the ramming and boarding of larger vessels, mining shore installation facilities and storming the streets of an enemy city.

Rodgers was preparing for any eventuality. He had, as yet, set no specific date for his major thrust against Yusef, but was planning to launch his operation in late April or early May. He had no way of guessing that a determined William Eaton was going to do everything in his power to beat the Navy to the punch.

The place of Tobias Lear in this period of methodically

frenzied preparations is obscure. Lear carried private instructions from President Jefferson, signed by Secretary Madison, ordering him to negotiate a satisfactory peace with Yusef Karamanli. Apparently neither William nor the Commodores knew that any such instructions existed. If they had, their own efforts might have been less intense. It can be argued, of course, that no representative of the United States was in a position to negotiate reasonably with the Bashaw at this time, and as a consequence Lear left matters in the hands of those who planned to force the despot to behave in a more civilized manner. In any event, there are no known documents indicating that the Commodores or William were aware of Lear's instructions.

Late in November, 1804, William was at last ready to embark on his great adventure. The rifles carried from the United States were transferred to the hold of the little *Argus*, as were his personal effects, which included his tent, scimitar and field equipment. Certainly the soft-spoken Lieutenant Isaac Hull, commander of the *Argus* and subsequently one of America's great heroes in the War of 1812, had no idea what was packed away in the boxes containing William's personal gear.

Hull's orders from Rodgers were simple and plain. He was directed to conduct Naval Agent Eaton to Egypt, escorted by a British warship that would insure the American vessel safe anchorage at Alexandria, which Great Britain had occupied after Lord Nelson virtually demolished a powerful French fleet in Egyptian waters.

William's own orders were equally direct and simple, or so the Commodores thought. Accompanied by his stepson, he would find Hamet Karamanli somewhere in Egypt, give him guns and money, and persuade him to gather together an army that would coordinate an attack on Tripoli with Rodgers's planned April or May assault.

William reached Alexandria early in December, and almost immediately after going ashore learned that Hamet was somewhere in the vicinity of Cairo. He unhesitatingly decided to proceed at once to that city.

The decision was not made lightly. Egypt was in a state of near-anarchy, thanks at least in part to the war between Great Britain and France. Turkish control of the country was nominal, and at least three major factions, as well as several smaller groups, were struggling with each other in an attempt to gain command. Egypt's Christian residents, a tiny minority, were pawns in the fight, and each faction was trying to gain the support of fanatical Moslems by threatening to exterminate them. Travel through the Egyptian countryside was dangerous.

But William entertained no fears for his personal safety, and the British Consul at Alexandria, Samuel Briggs, granted him a travel permit after reading a warm letter of introduction written by Sir Alexander Ball, the British Governor of Malta. William promptly hired barges and oarsmen for himself, Eli, their baggage, the cases of rifles and bags of silver for Hamet.

Lieutenant Hull was jittery, knowing that he would be held responsible for the safety of Naval Agent Eaton, and insisted on assigning William an escort from the crew of the *Argus,* commanded by a Lieutenant named Blake. A fifteen-year-old midshipman and twenty-three sailors made up the rest of the party. Before the group departed via the Rosetta branch of the Nile River, a man of somewhat questionable esteem also joined them. He was an old acquaintance of William's, a physician named Mendrici, who had been expelled from Tunis a year or two earlier after arguing with the Bey. Mendrici, who claimed that the Turkish Viceroy of Egypt and other distinguished personages were among his patients, said he was anxious to reach Cairo, too, and since he supposedly knew the countryside, William welcomed him.

The barges flew the American and British flags, the American sailors stood sentry duty day and night, armed with small cannon and rifles, and the peace of the 130-mile journey was marred by relatively few incidents. Only once, about twenty miles from Cairo, was it necessary for Lieutenant Blake to order the cannon fired for the purpose of dispersing a mob. Violence was commonplace in Egypt, and apparently no one attached any significance to the incident. William did not refer

159

to it in any of his correspondence or other writing, Blake's report on the subject was brief, and Eli gave no details in a rather breezy letter to his betrothed.

The ancient city of Cairo was a maze of walls, winding streets so narrow that it was sometimes difficult for two men to walk abreast, vast seas of minarets and palaces, tiny shops and some of the most shockingly unsanitary living conditions to be found anywhere in the Near East. Most of the Americans were stunned, but William, who changed into Arab attire, seemed completely at home. He had read so much about Cairo that he was able to make his way through the labyrinth of streets like a lifelong resident, much to the chagrin of Mendrici, who often became lost.

The arms having arrived safely, Lieutenant Blake returned to the *Argus* at Alexandria, but Hull, still worried about William's safety, sent a small party of marines, commanded by Lieutenant O'Bannon, to act as Naval Agent Eaton's escort.

William was already enjoying the time of his life, and entertained himself one evening by debating the relative merits of Christianity and Mohammedanism with the Turkish Viceroy. Members of the Viceroy's court were astonished, and William, ever conscious of what he was doing, proudly notes in his *Life* that "Eaton's presentation of the tenets of the Christian faith were the first ever heard at the court of a Muslim ruler." He exaggerated, but not much.

Meanwhile his party was growing larger. Two "Englishmen" joined him, one a Captain Farquhar, the other a Captain Vincenzio, who spoke with a decided Neapolitan accent. Neither William nor Eli explains how these two men "happened" to attach themselves to an American Naval Agent in Egypt on official business, but it is obvious that William had started recruiting his corps of adventurers.

He was having far more difficulty finding Hamet. Several of the deposed Tripolitanian ruler's former courtiers were new hangers-on at the court of the Viceroy, and each of them claimed to know Hamet's present location. Each promised to reveal it in return for money, but William, knowing men of their caliber in the Arab world, agreed to pay only when he received a reply. He wrote five identical letters, which messengers carried off in five different directions. William was inclined to believe that Hamet was living at a small oasis called Minyeh, about one hundred and twenty miles from Cairo.

Although he was tempted to go to Minyeh himself, his common sense caused him to hesitate. For one thing, he had no positive proof that Hamet was there. For another, conditions were chaotic in the city of Cairo, and were said to be even worse in the desert. The citizens of Cairo rioted daily, men were murdered in the streets by their personal enemies, and anyone who looked prosperous ran the risk of being shot or stabbed.

The Americans ventured out together and stayed close together when they left the lodgings William had rented for them only a short distance from the Viceroy's palace. He himself showed no concern for his own safety, however, and, ignoring the remonstrances of Lieutenant O'Bannon, went out every day in flowing Arab robes, a pair of pistols and his superbly fashioned scimitar in his belt. On one of his sight-seeing jaunts in the city he saw a number of Arabs attacking a man in Western attire, and promptly went to the assistance of the victim, wielding his scimitar so effectively that the crowd dispersed and vanished.

The man he rescued claimed to be an American, called himself Leitensdorfer and said he was a military engineer. He was enrolled on the spot as a member of William's brigade of adventurers, and as he had no money, received advance wages of fifty dollars in silver.

A messenger returned from Minyeh with word that Hamet was indeed living there, and William went to the Viceroy, who himself wrote to Hamet, promising to provide him with an escort of Turkish troops if he would come to Cairo.

Funds disappeared rapidly in Egypt, where every hand was extended, palm upward, and William decided it would be wise

161

to increase his capital. His experiences in dealing with the nations of the Barbary Coast had taught him that cash was far more potent than principle, and he was discovering, too, that soldiers of fortune charged high prices for their services.

So he wrote to Lieutenant Hull, who was still waiting for him at Alexandria, and for the first time hinted that he did not intend to confine himself to diplomatic activities. "We shall need at least four or five thousand additional dollars," he declared. "If the Government should reprove our arrangement, we shall reimburse them from the spoils of Benghazi, which I already calculate upon as ours."

Isaac Hull, who would acquire a reputation for taciturn candor when he became a commodore, sent a succinct reply: "You inform us that most likely you will need four or five thousand more; if so, God knows where we shall get it, unless you have means at Cairo or Rosetta, for I know of none here." Suspicious of the Naval Agent's activities, he also asked why so many persons of dubious background were being attached to William's suite. He was sent no reply to his question.

Early in January, 1805, William received his long-awaited reply from Hamet, who promised to come to Cairo two days later. The Tripolitanian did not appear, however, and a few days later, in another letter, suggested a meeting at a small oasis near Minyeh. The Turkish Viceroy was the formal ally of Yusef, and the cautious Hamet had no desire to be cast into an Egyptian prison or, even worse, sent off to his brother as a prisoner.

Ignoring the advice of everyone from the Viceroy to his newly hired mercenaries, William set out across the desert, accompanied by his entire party. Catastrophe overtook him at the oasis town of Damanhur, where a Turkish garrison was located, and the foreigners were hauled off to the local jail. They were charged with fomenting treason, and each was held in a separate cell.

"It is impossible," Eli Danielson wrote to the prim and proper Miss Smith, "to describe the interior of a Turkish prison to you, or to convey some idea of the existence one is forced to endure there. The stench is beyond imagination, there are vermin and rodents everywhere, the slops one is fed are unpalatable, and the brutality of one's guards is but further proof that, in this part of the world, human life is regarded as cheap. I can only pray that the brave lads from the *Philadelphia* are not being made to suffer such severe conditions of incarceration. We are more determined than ever before to effect their release at the earliest possible moment."

William spent no more than a few hours in his cell. He astonished the sentries assigned to stand watch over him by speaking fluent Arabic, and was hauled before the commandant for questioning. Taking full advantage of his opportunity, he charmed the Turk, who enjoyed little relief from the monotony of garrison life, and who invited him to dinner.

At some point during the long evening's discussion a sum of money discreetly changed hands, and William half-convinced the officer that he was bound for Minyeh and a meeting with Hamet Karamanli. The Turk had no desire to give strangers the freedom to wander where they pleased in his district, and suggested that, instead, Hamet be brought to Damanhur. This would not only prevent the foreigners from stirring up trouble, but would keep them close at hand, where he could watch them. In all probability it would save their lives, too, since no Westerner was safe in the desert.

William had no choice, and graciously consented to remain at Damanhur provided he and his companions were given comfortable quarters. The others were released from the jail, and William was given a suite of rooms in the commandant's own house. For the next ten days he discussed Turkish military tactics with the officer and watched the troops of the garrison drill. He soon proved to them that he was superior to them in handling a scimitar, either on horseback or dismounted, and won their respect.

At last, in mid-January—the exact date is unknown—the lugubrious Hamet arrived at Damanhur with the few personal followers who had remained with him in poverty. The Turkish commandant, who sat in on William's meetings with him, was satisfied that the American had told him the truth and wrote a relieved letter to the Viceroy. But Hamet was unhappy.

The time for real action had come, and the deposed Bey of Tripoli infinitely preferred a subsidy that would enable him to live in peace and safety. It would be far better to think, talk and plan for an invasion that might or might not take place in the dim future. Perhaps, having been disappointed so frequently in the past, Hamet wondered whether the Americans really meant business this time. If so, no one could have blamed him for his reluctance to make another attempt to regain his throne.

But William was not to be denied. "General Eaton," he says in his *Life*, "waxed rhetorical, and at last succeeded in persuading Hamet that he would need to join at once with his deliverers or forever abandon all hope of regaining his heritage, in which event he could look forward only to the life of a refugee in an inhospitable and alien land."

After spending several days pondering his problem, Hamet, constantly prodded by the volubly persuasive William, decided to accompany an expedition to Tripoli and act as its nominal leader. A major obstacle had been overcome.

But William's troubles were not yet ended. A false rumor reached Alexandria, and was duly reported by Lieutenant Hull, to the effect that Naval Agent Eaton had raised the American flag at Damanhur. The Governor demanded an apology, and petulantly refused to grant permission for Hamet and his followers to enter the city gates. William immediately sent the Turk a long letter, but could not persuade him to change his stand.

So it became necessary for Hamet and his party to go to Burj el Arab, forty miles west of Alexandria, and wait there for the rest of the party. William had good reason to doubt that Hamet would go to the place, or, if persuaded to make an appearance there, that he would wait for the corps William intended to recruit in Alexandria and its vicinity. Hamet's

164

enthusiasm for the project was so feeble that he needed constant bolstering, and there was a strong possibility that, if William left him for even a very limited period, he would become discouraged and return to Minyeh.

Although he himself was only a halfhearted figurehead, his presence was vital to the success of the long-planned expedition. For one thing, his presence would give the invasion a legality that would otherwise be lacking, and the position of the United States, in the eyes of the world, would be even more dubious when men elsewhere began to question the legitimacy of an invasion. Equally important, William was relying on support from Tripolitanians who had fled into exile by the hundreds during Yusef's years of rule. Without Hamet's presence, these men would disappear, too, and the American would have no one but his small band of adventurers to follow him in his projected invasion of Derna.

But there was no choice. The Governor of Alexandria remained adamant, so Hamet departed for Burj el Arab, with misgivings. William sent out a call to Cairo, Alexandria and several smaller Egyptian communities, asking for Tripolitanian volunteers to proceed at once to the Arab's Tower for a march into their homeland. Meanwhile he and his own party went back to Alexandria.

There he wrote an urgent letter to Commodore Barron, whose health had improved somewhat, and who had remained at Syracuse, where he exercised overall command, if not sea command, of the Mediterranean squadron. Now that the time for action was at hand, William dropped all pretense of diplomacy and worded his request in blunt military terms. In addition to the *Argus*, he said, he wanted two sloops-of-war and a bomb ketch, all of which he expected to await him at Derna, where the Navy could coordinate its attack with the invasion "that will be made in overwhelming force by the army of the Bey Hamet Karamanli Pasha." The fact that this army would be led by William H. Eaton of Connecticut and Massachusetts was not mentioned.

William also asked for two cannon the army could use, a

force of one hundred United States Marines to accompany the corps and act "in a disciplinary and advisory capacity," and the sum of $10,000 in cash. Lieutenant Hull sailed off in the *Argus* with the letter.

Barron was not surprised and, having been ordered by his own superiors at home to work with William on the project, honored the better part of the request. The schooner *Nautilus*, twelve guns, commanded by Captain John H. Dent, and the sloop *Hornet*, ten guns, commanded by Captain Samuel Evans, were sent off with the *Argus*.

As William himself wrote in his *Life*, "Although the instructions of the Secretary of the Navy left entire discretion in the Commodore concerning the cooperation of the Navy in this enterprise, the Government had, nevertheless, calculated that such cooperation would be given."

Barron sent William a cordial letter, congratulating him on having overcome so many grave difficulties in bringing the expedition alive. He also promised to do what he could to fulfill the other requests. The money would be forthcoming soon, he said, and so would the cannon. On the subject of the marines, however, he remained discreetly silent, apparently having decided it would be inappropirate for a full company of uniformed Americans to march with the Arabs.

On the other hand, in a voluntary gesture that did much to ease William's immediate burden, Commodore Barron sent a letter to Hamet, in which he promised the Tripolitanian that he enjoyed the full support of the United States Government. That communication, more than anything else, kept Hamet at Burj el Arab and prevented him from bolting for the remote sanctuary of Minyeh.

The British authorities at Alexandria were impressed by William's energy and plans and worked with him, offering him their enthusiastic assistance as he began to purchase supplies for the army and recruit more adventurer volunteers. Only Isaac Hull remained uneasy. The unfortunate reference to Benghazi that William had written to him lingered in his mind, and he entertained a strong suspicion that Naval Agent Eaton intended to accompany the expedition, if not lead it. William was so evasive whenever Hull mentioned the subject to him that the Lieutenant wrote letters to Commodores Barron and Rodgers, expressing to both the fervent hope that Eaton would not cause embarrassment and trouble for the Navy. Neither of the senior officers could quite believe, however, that William seriously intended to become the commander in chief of a corps of Arabs and soldiers of fortune.

No sane American, they agreed, would march hundreds of miles across the desert wastes of North Africa at the head of an undisciplined body of men whose talents as fighting men were at best questionable. All that Barron and Rodgers hoped was that Hamet and his followers would create a diversion. Derna, they felt, could actually be taken by the Navy, and they expected that Naval Agent Eaton would rejoin the squadron, now that his work was done.

Never had men in high places so badly underestimated William's intent or burning ambition.

CHAPTER TWELVE

A BAND OF ROGUES

A great deal of unpleasantness could have been avoided had William Eaton observed the amenities of the Ottoman Empire and crossed the palpitating palm of the Governor of Alexandria with silver. But he had no funds to spare for greedy officials, and the Governor retaliated by making it difficult for him to buy provisions, ammunition and gunpowder. Finally, after an impressive quantity of stores had been purchased, the Governor sent a company of troops to confiscate the goods.

Lieutenant O'Bannon, standing guard with his little squad of marines, told the Turkish officer in command of the company to take his men elsewhere. A full battalion of Turks returned within an hour, and O'Bannon conveyed the impression that it would be healthier not to try taking the stores by force. Later that same day an entire regiment of Turkish infantry came to take possession of the disputed property. O'Bannon remained firm. One officer and seven men were establishing a tradition for the Marine Corps.

An angry William went to the Governor and swore that, if the harassment did not stop, the American warships in the harbor would shell Alexandria. He had no right to make such a threat, which would have been an act of aggression on the part of the United States against the Ottoman Empire, and would have horrified Jefferson and Madison, had they known of it. But the saber rattling was effective, staying the hand of the Governor long enough for William and the British Consul to send urgent letters to the Turkish Viceroy in Cairo.

For reasons totally unconnected with the American Naval Agent and his purchases, the Viceroy directed his subordinate to permit William to go where he pleased, buy what he pleased and take his property anywhere he wanted to take it. The Governor, it seemed, was an ambitious man, and was trying, through his friends in Constantinople, to win an appointment for himself as Viceroy. The present Viceroy was aware of the efforts, and was opposed to anything the Governor favored. William had learned of this feud, and was able to utilize it to his own advantage.

The American spent most of his time in Alexandria recruiting officers for his expedition, yet keeping news of his activities from Hull and O'Bannon. It is quite possible that the young Marine officer knew what was happening but chose to close his eyes and ears. He had his own yearning for adventure, and the prospect of a march across hundreds of miles of trackless desert wasteland appealed to him almost as much as it did to the man whom Mendrici, Leitensdorfer and Farquhar were now calling "General."

One of the first of the new mercenaries hired in Alexandria was a former officer of the elite corps of the Turkish army, the Janissaries. Not until later was it discovered that the retirement of Selim the Janissary, as his colleagues knew him, had been forced by his insatiable thirst for alcoholic beverages, which no Mohammedans were allowed to drink, and which were strictly forbidden in the ranks of the Janissaries.

Soon the staff posts were filled, and William's officer roster glittered with the names of some of the most illustrious members of the Near Eastern underworld. Among them were:

Captain Luca Ulovic, a Macedonian.

Lieutenant Constantine, a Greek who claimed to have been

born near Delphi, but later was discovered to have been a life-long resident of Athens. No one asked him about the discrepancy, as it was considered bad manners to pry into the past of anyone living in Egypt.

The "Chevalier" Davies, who spoke and read French fluently and was therefore believed to be a Frenchman. In moments of great stress he reverted to Spanish, but his peers politely pretended to be unaware of these lapses. He was a superb horseman, an excellent pistol shot and could handle both cavalry sabers and scimitars with great dexterity. He was a personable young man in his late twenties, drank moderately and made it his business to entertain William with an endless supply of stories. He was rewarded for his proficiency and charm, and was appointed aide-de-camp to the commander in chief, which made Eli Danielson jealous.

Lieutenant Connant, who sometimes claimed to be English, sometimes American, occasionally West Indian by birth, was utterly ruthless, and made no secret of his hatred for all Arabs. On one notable occasion, soon after the start of the expedition, he put down a mutiny singlehanded by cutting off the head of a Tripolitanian tribesman who was threatening to desert.

Mendrici, whose qualifications were very dubious, was made Medical Officer.

Percival Farquhar, an Englishman who had joined William in Cairo. He appeared to know much about food and proved adept at buying bargains, so he won the post of Quartermaster.

Richard Farquhar, his younger brother. His familiarity with military life and the British infantry's manual of arms made it likely that he had served in one of King George III's regiments, but it was far less probable that he had been a Captain, as he claimed. William's manservant, Aletti, disliked the younger Farquhar, and swore he had never held a rank higher than that of sergeant.

Leitensdorfer was made the corps' Adjutant, and, as it happened, William eventually learned the entire story of his life, recounting it in full detail, first in his Journal-Diary, then in his unsigned biography. He swore the details were true, and seems to have believed them himself.

Leitsendorfer had been born near Trent, in 1772, and had been baptized under the name of Gervasio Santuari. A farmer when he reached manhood, he married, but soon grew tired of his wife and, to escape her, joined the Austrian army. He served at Belgrade in 1789 and 1790, and seven years later had risen to the rank of sergeant major. When Mantua surrendered to Napoleon Bonaparte in 1797, the Austrians collapsed, and Napoleon had no organized enemies anywhere.

Leitensdorfer therefore found it expedient to desert, and the same day enlisted in the French army under the name of Carlo Hossondo. He knew so much about the Austrian army and its life, however, that the French suspected him of being a spy. Learning he was about to be placed under arrest, he fled to Switzerland, where he adopted the name of Eugene Leitensdorfer. Necessity forced him into the jewelry business, and that business eventually took him to Egypt.

There he made a precarious living by serving both the French and the English as an informer, marrying a girl in Cairo, where he operated a profitable coffee house, and acting as a procurer of women, among them his wife, for high-ranking Turkish officials. After the Battle of the Nile, he thought it might be wise to leave Egypt for a time, as he was too well-known to both the British and the French. So, abandoning his second wife, he made his way to Messina in the disguise of a priest.

At Messina he entered a Capuchin monastery under the name of Father Anselmo, but found the life insufferably dull. It is easy to understand why one accustomed to activity and excitement found a monstery too tame, and left, but his reasons for returning to Islam are less clear. In any event, Leitensdorfer made his way to Constantinople via Smyrna and arrived during one of the many serious insurrections that upset the stability and destroyed what was left of the Ottoman Empire's serenity.

Officers were desperately needed, so he was granted a com-

171

mission in the Turkish army, and fought the rebels for the better part of a year. The army was trounced, suffering many casualties, but Leitensdorfer, displaying his highly developed instinct for self-preservation, managed to return unscathed to Constantinople. Street rioting against the army made it dangerous to wear an officer's uniform, so he adopted the role of a holy man, and again changed his name, this time calling himself Murad Aga.

In this capacity, he alleged, he helped cure the Pasha of Trebizond of a serious ailment. Since he knew virtually nothing about medicine, it is difficult to accept his claim seriously, although he did have the grace to admit to William that the rites he performed at the Pasha's bedside were as meaningless as the unguents and other medication he prescribed for his patient. The Pasha, he confessed, would have recovered even had he done nothing.

But he did win the official's gratitude, became a prominent member of his suite and traveled with him to Mecca, Suez and Jeddah. There a wealthy Englishman hired him as an interpreter, and he spent several years traveling through Africa, particularly along the east coast. During this time he perfected his ability to speak, read and write English, and was so accomplished that he was able to pass as either an Englishman or an American.

He had returned to Alexandria only a few months earlier, and had been delighted by a rumor to the effect that his wife —whom he had made no attempt to support during his long absence—had died. It was enough for his purposes that she had disappeared, so he made no attempt to find her, counted his blessings and went off to Cairo, where he set himself up as a "military engineer." His new career was a failure, and the arrival of William in Egypt saved him from starvation. He appeared to know a great deal about army life and was painstakingly thorough in his work, which was enough to satisfy the American. Leitensdorfer proved to be an efficient Adjutant.

The background of Davies, the self-styled French "Chevalier" with an English name, was less flamboyantly dramatic, but was typical of the soldiers of fortune who joined Eaton's corps. According to one of Davies' stories, he was a staunch supporter of the house of Bourbon, had been a member of the staff of the decapitated Louis XVI, and had fled from France during that country's tumultuous Revolution. Another of his tales, however, presented him as a former personal aide to the Emperor Napoleon, with whom, he said, he had quarreled over a woman. Although dismissed from Napoleon's personal service, he had remained in France until friends had told him it would be wise to leave the country.

One of Davies' failings was a faulty memory, and although he told each of his stories with sincerity, apparently he could not remember what he had last said about himself. The jealous Eli Danielson, who had hoped to act as his stepfather's aide-de-camp, enlisted the help of the ever-useful Aletti in conducting an investigation of Davies' background.

According to the British Consul at Alexandria and two members of his staff, Davies was probably an Englishman, and was believed to be a sergeant of Royal Household Cavalry named Henry Roberts, who had spent several years as the personal servant of a brigadier, the military attaché at the British Legation in Paris prior to the break in diplomatic relations between Great Britain and France.

Eli went to his stepfather in triumph with the news, explaining that the British Consul in Alexandria found it too much of a chore to arrest deserters and send them back to England. There were too many of them in Egypt, and it was not easy to verify their real identity.

But William had no intention of dismissing Davies. His real nationality was his own business, and, as he behaved like a gentleman, it didn't matter whether he was a French aristocrat or an English commoner. What was important was his ability to ride, shoot and use a sword, as well as his obvious familiarity with military life.

The commander of a band of adventurer-rogues knew better

173

than to inquire too deeply into the past of his subordinates. Perhaps the most impressive aspect of William's recruiting campaign was his good judgment. The men he hired to work closely with him were scoundrels, yet all of them—with a single notable exception—remained loyal to him throughout his campaign, endured hardships without serious complaint and exposed themselves to constant hazards. In return, they received small wages, won little glory and entertained small hopes of obtaining more than a minimum of booty. All were familiar with the Arab world, and knew there were no more than a small handful of wealthy men in Derna from whom they could steal loot of consequence. Since none of them wrote memoirs or other documents explaining their philosophy, it must be assumed that they enjoyed danger for its own sake.

William also worked to recruit a hard core of European horsemen in Alexandria, and this task proved as simple as he had anticipated. There had been Greeks in the city ever since it had been founded more than 2,200 years earlier by Alexander the Great. Ever since the times of Roman occupation it had been in decline as a center of Western culture, and the Greeks living there were now in the minority, despised by the Turkish overlords and cordially hated by the poverty-stricken Egyptians. In order to earn food for themselves and their families, many had been mercenaries as early as the fourteenth and fifteenth centuries, and the tradition was still strong.

Consequently it was no problem for William to devise riding and shooting tests, interview volunteers and then hire as many as he could afford on his limited budget. He was tempted to go into debt in order to build up his squadrons of Greek cavalry, but wisely refrained, afraid that the conservative Commodores of the United States Navy might refuse to honor his obligations. Hard-bitten Greek mercenaries would turn on him, he knew, if they did not receive their wages, and he had no desire to be slaughtered immediately after winning the glorious triumph he knew awaited him.

In the last days of February a number of additional rogue

174

adventurers became members of the expedition, but literally nothing is known of them. William refers to them in his *Life* and Journal-Diary, and they are mentioned in the correspondence of Eli, O'Bannon and Hull, but details are lacking. All sources appear to agree that the group included Englishmen, Frenchmen, "other Europeans a scattering of Americans." These men served as junior officers in the corps, and if they are heroes, their exploits must remain unsung. They provided the little army with its backbone of discipline, and they, more than their superiors, prevented the mercurial Tripolitanian Arabs from deserting at discouraging moments, some of which occurred daily. Like the senior officers, these foreigners in North Africa served for pleasure, received tiny wages and endured countless hardships.

The precise number of men William led on his march to Derna has never been satisfactorily determined. His own figures vary from time to time, the account books of Adjutant Leitensdorfer are hopelessly muddled, and even Eli Danielson, who took pride in his ability to keep accurate records, often changed his mind. There were approximately five hundred to seven hundred Tripolitanian Arabs in the corps, and there may have been as many as fifty to one hundred Egyptians. The confusion arises in part from the imprecise boundary separating Tripoli and Egypt. No one knew where the exact border was located in the desert, and no one except William really cared. The rulers of the Ottoman Empire had given up trying to separate their subjects in the desert by nationality, and lumped them together.

William, trying to present his expedition to the world as a corps of Tripolitanian patriots seeking vengeance against a tyrant, made no mention of Egyptians. Leitensdorfer, who had no ax to grind, may have been more honest. If so, it was the first time in his life he had ever told the truth.

The exact number of Christians who marched to Derna is also open to some question. The senior officers, including the Quartermaster and the Adjutant, were able to line their own pockets more easily if they had fewer men to feed and clothe, so they minimized the size of the Greek cavalry units. William, on the other hand, spent so much out of his own pocket that, according to Eli's hints after the campaign ended, he enlarged the number in order to regain funds he had lost.

Therefore the lowest figure given for the Greek cavalry was that of a single squadron consisting of fifty men. The largest figure, advanced by William after his return to the United States, was that of four squadrons, each made up of approximately fifty men.

In the last days of February, 1805, the courtly and honorable Lieutenant Isaac Hull had good cause to feel apprehensive. Naval Agent Eaton no longer dressed in Western attire, but was seen everywhere in Alexandria wearing flowing Arab robes. The rogues who always accompanied him, and who also dressed as Arabs, invariably called him "General."

Hull bluntly inquired what he had in mind.

William, uncertain whether the forthright young Navy officer would try to halt his bid for glory, was too honorable to lie. Instead he merely laughed off any suggestion that he intended to command the corps of rabble.

Hull, who believed him sane and sensible, wanted to believe him, and assumed until the very last moment that William would sail with him on the *Argus* to Derna.

By this time Lieutenant O'Bannon, his midshipman and six enlisted men knew better, but all kept their mouths shut. The marines were thirsting for adventure, too.

On March 1 Hull discovered that William planned to accompany the expedition, but was assured—by Dr. Mendrici, as William himself was so busy he could not be found—that the Naval Agent intended to act as an observer, and did not expect to take an active role in the campaign. Undoubtedly Hull entertained serious doubts, but could not prove that William was going to command the corps. His own authority being limited, the Navy officer was forced to content himself with keeping an accurate account of developments, as he heard and learned them, in his log. His principal concern was still his fear that William might embarrass and cause trouble for the Navy.

At last all was in readiness. Troops and their officers had been mobilized and given a very brief period of training which, if it accomplished nothing else, taught them the rudiments of working together. Meanwhile the Tripolitanian hordes had been flocking to Hamet's banner at the Arab's Tower, and glowing reports indicated that thousands were assembling there. William and his staff officers, knowing the people with whom they were dealing, quietly reduced the estimate.

Finally, on March 1, the adventurers and their Greek mercenaries left Alexandria, much to the relief of the Governor and, when he heard the news in Cairo, of the Viceroy. Although the Ottoman Empire had been decaying, growing increasingly impotent, the Turks were masters of the art of maintaining at least a semblance of cordiality between the various segments of the domain under their nominal rule. It had occurred to the officials in Egypt, belatedly, to be sure, that if Hamet's enterprise failed, the Bashaw Yusef Karamanli Pasha would be sure to seek revenge against the men who had permitted the expedition to be mounted on the soil of neighboring Egypt.

William said his farewells to Lieutenant Isaac Hull in writing rather than run the risk of being asked too many embarrassing questions at a personal meeting. He would see Hull at Derna, he said, and expressed confidence that the Navy's subsquadron would be waiting off the shore of the port to coordinate its attack with that "which the Bey Hamet will launch." In the event that the cannon and cash which Commodore Barron was expected to send arrived in time, perhaps a party of seamen could bring the weapons and money ashore to a rendezvous near Derna.

No one was on hand to watch the departure of the rogues and paid soldiers. William had spent freely to assure every man a mount, arms and a brass helmet from a supply of old equipment that the British Consul had been delighted to sell him at a bargain price. Perhaps some of the old, veiled women and small, naked boys of Alexandria peered at the adventurers as they rode their mounts through the quiet streets of Alexandria soon after daybreak. But no fife and drum corps played spirited tunes and no crowd was on hand to cheer William as he began his long-planned march to glory.

The first leg of his journey was brief. He halted at the supply depot he had established and maintained under guard just outside Alexandria, and there found a man referred to in his *Life* as Sheikh el Tayeb waiting for him. The Sheikh owned a large number of camels, and William was anxious to rent several hundred from him. Since negotiations in the Arab world always took time, both parties settled down to haggle at length and leisure.

The Sheikh demanded a fortune for his camels. William offered a pittance. One cut his request, the other offered a little more, and the talks continued until March 4, when a settlement satisfactory to both sides was finally reached. The Sheikh paid William the highest compliment in his repertoire of usually flowery and verbose language by saying, simply, "Eaton Pasha, you are an Arab."

On March 5 William, now accompanied by a large camel train, proceeded to the Arab's Tower, where Hamet and the Tripolitanian refugees awaited him. Having had his fill of promises made by Barbary Coast rulers, William insisted on drawing up a formal agreement with Hamet, a convention containing fourteen articles which provided for every contingency he could foresee. It read, in part, that "under the terms signed this day, this covenant shall insure

"I. Perpetual peace and free, reciprocal intercourse between the United States of America and the Pashalik of Tripoli.

"II. The restoration of the Bey Hamet Karamanli Pasha, as the rightful and legitimate ruler thereof and Viceroy of the Grand Sultan of the Ottoman Empire therefor, to the throne of Tripoli.

"III. The provision by the United States of America of the requisite means and material for the accomplishment of this end.

178

"IV. The immediate, unconditional release of all citizens of the United States of America and persons in the employ of the United States of America now being held captive as prisoners in the Pashalik of Tripoli.

"V. The tributes paid, in this year, by Denmark, Sweden and Bavaria to Tripoli shall be paid, in turn, to the United States of America to defray the expenses outlined in Article III.

"VI. The fulfillment, in order to obtain and secure the payment of these tributes, and thereby to implement the said pledge contained in Article V, by the Bey Hamet Karamanli Pasha, of all conditions contained in the currently existing treaties between the Pashalik of Tripoli and Denmark, Sweden and Bavaria.

"VII. The consideration, by the Bey Hamet Karamanli Pasha, of the renewal of diplomatic relations between his Pashalik and the Kingdom of the Two Sicilies.

"VIII. The irrevocable guarantee that General William H. Eaton shall serve as Commander-in-Chief of the expedition that shall restore the Bey Hamet Karamanli Pasha to his throne, said guarantee to place all final decisions concerning all phases of the said expedition in the hands of General Eaton.

"IX. A general amnesty to be extended to the supporters of the pretender to the throne of Tripoli, Yusef Karamanli, with the exception of Yusef himself, Murad Rais, and such of their associates as shall be determined jointly by the Bey Hamet and General Eaton.

"X. In the event that the United States of America and the Pashalik of Tripoli should go to war against each other at some future time, a catastrophe both nations are anxious to avoid, persons captured by either side to be treated honorably as prisoners of war and exchanged; under no conditions to be enslaved.

"XI. The Flag of the United States of America to provide asylum for suppliants, who shall be immune from arrest and apprehension whilst under its protection.

"XII. The Bey Hamet Karamanli Pasha to be left in full and exclusive possession of Tripoli, the defenses of which shall be left intact and neither damaged nor dismantled following any damage inflicted during military and naval operations designed to bring about the final deposition of the Pretender, Yusef Karamanli.

"XIII. The Convention to be expanded beyond its present limits on the application of either signatory nation, the other nation promising its full cooperation in the extension to include new clauses favorable to both.

"XIV. The Convention to become operative at once, no further ratification by the Bey Hamet Karamanli Pasha being required, but the ratification by the President and Senate of the United States of America being required under the Constitution thereof."

William and Hamet signed the agreement, with P. N. O'Bannon, Lieutenant of Marines, Pascoe P. Peck, Midshipman, Marine Corps, and Dr. Francisco Mendrici witnessing their signatures.

Although the language of the treaty reflected the haste of its composition, William won everything that the President and Senate could ask. The gesture on behalf of the Kingdom of the Two Sicilies was a gracious bow to the nation that had provided the Mediterranean squadron with most of its badly needed gunboats. The principle of granting asylum was unique to the countries of the Barbary Coast. And the influence of the United States would be great in Tripoli.

While William and Hamet were working out the details of the agreement, a detail of sailors from the *Argus* and *Hornet* arrived with two small cannon and their ordnance, which had just arrived at Alexandria on the latter ship. Even more welcome were the strongboxes of metal and leather containing the sum of $20,000 in cash. Commodore Barron had delivered handsomely.

The days of planning and preparation were at an end. Now William would march across the desert, coordinate his army's attack on Derna with the Navy's assault on the city by sea while, simultaneously, Commodore Rodgers began his investment of the city of Tripoli. At last William Eaton's great adventure was about to begin.

CHAPTER THIRTEEN

THE GREAT ADVENTURE

The Tripolitanians, Greeks and motley assortment of officers gathered at Burj el Arab packed their gear in a final step before setting out across the desert, and the Arabs were in such a jovial mood that the European senior officers had to restrain them from wasting gunpowder. Every Tripolitanian, it seemed, was seized by the urge to fire his rifle into the air.

General William H. Eaton had no cause for celebration, however. Eli, Davies and Leitensdorfer came to him less than an hour before the column began its actual march to inform him that one of the Farquhar brothers had disappeared, taking with him approximately fourteen hundred dollars worth of supplies which could be diverted into silver in the markets of Alexandria. There was no sign of the culprit anywhere, and his brother professed to know nothing of the theft.

Which of the Farquhar brothers was the thief is a question that has never been solved. William says in his *Life* that it was Richard. O'Bannon and Eli Danielson claim that it was Percival. Perhaps the point is academic; the supplies and a trusted officer were gone.

The most significant aspect of the incident is that the remaining Farquhar was not dismissed and sent packing. William ignored the advice of his subordinates and refused to blame

181

one brother for the criminal act of the other. He was a sufficiently good judge of character to reap the benefits of his decision. The remaining Farquhar served with distinction throughout the campaign, demonstrated unswerving loyalty to the commander in chief and was loud in his condemnation of his brother. Even soldiers of fortune, it seemed, observed a strict code, and a man's sense of personal honor was more important than his blood ties.

Hamet created some last-minute problems, too. A chance remark that William overheard caused him to make a swift investigation into the deal for camels he had concluded with the Sheikh el Tayeb, and he learned that Hamet and the Sheikh had made a private arrangement behind his back. In brief, Hamet was receiving a generous percentage of the funds William was paying for the renting of his camels. O'Bannon, Eli and Peck were outraged, and some of the English and European officers indicated that they, too, were disgusted, but William calmly took the revelation in his stride.

Hamet, he explains in his *Life*, had been forced to live by his wits for years. He had been a beggar at the courts of Barbary, the recipient of American, British and Turkish charity. The opportunity to make money on the rental of camels to the army that intended to restore him to his throne was too great a temptation to resist. "The Arab," William declares, "does not live according to the moral precepts of the Christian. We of the West cannot judge him as we judge ourselves.

"His philosophy is alien to us, as is ours to him. General Eaton was convinced that Hamet was afraid for his future. So often in the past he had reached for his crown, only to find it eluding his grasp. General Eaton believed he was fearful that the grand campaign would fail, and that he would become, once again, penniless. With the money he obtained from the Sheikh el Tayeb, Hamet, his wives and his children could return to Minyeh and fill their stewing pot with lamb for many months."

William immediately showed Hamet and his Tripolitanians

182

that he, too, could adopt the attitudes and approach of the Arab when it suited his purposes. He summoned the Sheikh, took him to Hamet's tent and quietly announced that he was changing the agreement. He was willing to pay a fair price for the camels, but had no intention of lining Hamet's purse with more American silver. Therefore he was cutting the rental price accordingly, deducting the percentage Hamet was receiving.

The abashed Hamet was in no position to object, but the Sheikh bellowed his protests. He would take his camels and depart at once, he said. William summoned his marines, whose numbers had been augmented earlier in the day by the arrival of a sergeant. The uniformed Americans stood stiffly at attention, their polished rifles gleaming. O'Bannon and Peck drew their swords. The squad was very careful not to threaten or intimidate the Sheikh, who would have lost face had too direct a confrontation been forced on him.

But it was impossible for him to miss the point William was making. He subsided meekly, agreed to accept the lower terms when it was emphasized that he himself would lose nothing, and the incident ended on a conciliatory note.

Mules were used to haul the cannon, and twenty-eight men were assigned to the little artillery battery, with Selim the Janissary in command and Rocco and Connant acting as his lieutenants. William was uncertain whether the cannoneers had really fired such weapons, and ordered Selim to put in an hour of target practice for at least thirty minutes every night, after the day's march ended.

By midafternoon all was in readiness, and a Marine trumpeter sounded a fanfare. Arab rams' horns replied, and the long column straggled out of Burj el Arab into the desert, as Eli wrote to Miss Smith, like a band of "untidy robbers about to raid a bazaar." What little sense of discipline had been instilled in the corps immediately vanished. Arabs staged impromptu horse and camel races, and the army spread out across the desert. Rifles were fired into the air, and a company of

Bedouin tribesmen tried to bring down several buzzards circling overhead.

William called a halt, then ordered the entire corps back to Burj el Arab. He realized the corps would not reach far-distant Derna unless some sense of disciplined unity was established, and, far more than on any previous occasion, he showed his deep insight into the character of the North African.

He made a long, impassioned speech in Arabic, playing heavily on the pride and sentimentality of his listeners. For the better part of an hour he derided them, cursed them, called them old women and heaped scorn on them. Then he changed his tune, little by little, and gave them the opportunity to rehabilitate themselves. If they behaved like true soldiers, they would win immortal names for themselves. Their fame would resound throughout Islam. They would be honored, even revered, until the end of their days.

After speaking for almost two hours, he added a final, chilling note. All of his senior officers were ordered to shoot any man who strayed from his assigned place in the ranks, and the commander in chief made it plain he expected them to shoot to kill. Then he dismissed the corps for the night with the announcement that the march would begin again before dawn the next morning.

An hour before daybreak on March 6, 1805, the lines were on the move. This time the riders held their ranks, there were no camel or horse races, and not a single weapon was fired into the air. The Arabs had learned they were being commanded by a man who understood them, who would tolerate no nonsense, and they behaved accordingly.

Had William marched by the shortest possible route from Burj el Arab to Derna, he would have covered five hundred and twenty miles of desert wilderness. The actual march was much longer, and it is impossible to estimate how far out of its way the corps traveled. William, Leitensdorfer, O'Bannon and Eli each guessed the mileage of every day's march, but only rarely did any two figures agree. Certainly the corps traversed at least six hundred and fifty miles of desert, and the overall total may have been closer to eight hundred miles.

One of the greatest difficulties William faced was the maddeningly frustrating lack of knowledge of the area. The few maps he had so painstakingly acquired through the years soon proved to be fanciful works of imagination that bore little resemblance to reality. Officers who had boasted that they knew every inch of the country were revealed as liars. Bedouin and other tribesmen who acted as guides and, presumably, were familiar with the area, soon showed their own ignorance; a Bedouin might be thoroughly familiar with a very restricted area, but was lost when he rode more than a few miles beyond terrain he had visited previously.

William had to rely on himself, and it is a tribute to his genius that he was able to lead the column to its destination. His own experiences in the desert had been limited to the brief visits he had made to the interior during his stay in Tunis, but his instincts for desert living were unerring. Frequently his "guides" swore the corps would reach an oasis after a morning's march, or an afternoon's, but no such oasis was found. William then rode off by himself to a high rock, and after studying the layers of sand blown by the winds, set a new course.

Again and again he led the army to oases and water holes. He was so accurate that proud sheikhs who had spent their entire lives in the desert followed him without hesitation, and within ten days of the column's departure from Burj el Arab, virtually every member of the army believed he was endowed with magical powers. Even his adventurer-rogues began to suspect that his ability to find water and grass was supernatural. Lieutenant O'Bannon, a Marine to the core, believed in no nonsense, but said after his return to the United States that "General Eaton's instincts were uncanny."

Only Hamet complained, and he made up for the blind devotion of the rest of the corps. In spite of the many hardships the deposed Bey had suffered during his long years of exile, he already imagined himself restored to the rule of his Pashalik, and acted accordingly. The days were too hot, he was given too little time to rest, neither he nor his gelding liked the unending miles of hard rock underfoot, the sand irritated his eyes, the nights were too cold.

For a short time William tried to humor him, but had too much on his own mind. Dr. Mendrici was given the unenviable task of soothing Hamet, but his own patience was limited, and the past-and-future monarch of Tripoli was forced to vent his grievances to any unfortunate member of the corps who could be persuaded to listen to him for a short time.

The army, its attitudes becoming more crisply military each day, marched steadily across hills and valleys of rock and sand, making its way across ridges and the bone-dry beds of rivers that came to life only briefly each year. Occasionally the barren landscape was relieved by fields of barley planted by the Bedouin immediately following the winter rainy season. Now and again tiny, brilliantly colored flowers were seen growing in crevices exposed only to limited sunlight, and when William jauntily began wearing one in his burnoose each day, his officers started decorating their helmets with them.

The march was the grand climax of a lifetime, for which William had been preparing since childhood. Not only was he as completely at home in the desert as the Bedouin and other tribes, but he appears to have been a natural leader of Arabs. Other troops might not have followed him as readily, nor might he have enjoyed as great a success with them. His accomplishments had been solid in Anthony Wayne's Legion and in Georgia, but his achievements in the American West and South had not been spectacular. It may be significant that, with the single exception of his spirited leadership during an Indian attack, he had done his best work alone.

Something in his nature responded to primitive peoples, and he established his greatest rapport with the desert tribesmen of North Africa and the savages of the North American forests. Perhaps it is unfair to compare his early career with that of his prime, and it can be argued, certainly, that he was not yet ready for mature leadership on a large scale when he served as a captain in the United States Army. Nevertheless, it is true that no American soldiers served him with the ferocious loyalty and dogged devotion of his Arabs.

The mystique of kismet had bemused him for years, and now, at an age when most of his contemporaries were happy to lead less active lives, he met his own fate. Had he felt elated, inspired, it would be somewhat easier for the modern student of his life to comprehend, but his calm throughout the long, 6-week march across the desert was monumental, rarely broken. This was the kismet that had always been in store for him, and his reaction to hardships and difficulties without number would have done credit to a veteran warrior shiekh of the Libyan Desert or the Sahara. He shrugged, improvised and invariably found ways to solve his dilemmas.

The single greatest need of both men and animals on the trek was water. The sun blistered the faces of the hardiest, and William himself was tanned almost beyond recognition. In a land where there was literally almost no rainfall from early March until the following January, the air was so dry that men's throats and noses stung, swallowing was painful and the craving for water was ever-present. Only at the few, scattered oases and water holes could any of the precious liquid be found. Some oases were occupied by nomad tribes whose proprietary claims to these patches of green were traditional, and who were ready to drive off intruders.

A heavily armed corps of hundreds was capable of taking possession of any oasis in the desert, of course, and it would have been a simple matter to scatter the relatively small groups of nomads, whose fighting men rarely numbered more than ten to fifteen adult males and older boys. But William knew that a single hostile act committed against one group of desert wanderers would unite all the nomads of the region against him. Word would spread across the wastelands far faster than he could travel, and his corps would have to fight its way, foot by foot, mile by mile, all the way to Derna.

He preferred to rely on the hospitable kindness that Arabs

showed to those who did not molest or intimidate them. Out of his own pocket he had bought large quantities of knives and other small arms in Cairo and Alexandria; he had purchased inexpensive jewelry at the bazaars of Egypt's two principal cities, and had also acquired stores of cooking utensils and bolts of coarse cloth.

At each occupied oasis he rode ahead of his corps alone and politely inquired whether he and his men might share the water and grass for a few hours. Often the nomads looked askance at the hordes of mounted men waiting to ride toward them. But no member of the corps drew a weapon or shouted an insult. The leader, speaking faultless Arabic, had the manners and air of a great and noble chieftain. Arab courtesy made it mandatory for permission to be granted, and William, no matter how tired or busy, always made it his business to chat with the nomad elders and shiekhs.

Then, before departing again after spending a night with the tribesmen, William distributed largesse. Never condescending, never actually offering payment for the use of the oasis, he gave gifts to every man, woman and child in each nomad band. Not once had any of his men tried to molest the nomads' women and girls, which was fortunate for the troops, as the commander in chief had promised to decapitate with his own scimitar any soldier who caused trouble. Not once was any property of the nomads stolen, which was a tribute to the vigilance of his officers and sentries, particularly Lieutenant O'Bannon and his marines.

The American's reputation preceded him. Eaton Pasha, the protected of Allah, was a good and generous man, fair to all who met his friendship with friendship. Not all the nomads chose the olive branch instead of the sword, however. There were some bands which regarded the corps as intruders on territory that strangers entered only at their peril, and these tribesmen waged guerilla warfare of sorts on the motley army. They fired at the column from the protecting shelter of rocky ridges, then disappeared into boulder-strewn hills or rode away at full tilt across beds of gravel or seas of sand.

During such assaults William encountered his greatest difficulty in maintaining order. His Tripolitanians and other North Africans ached to exterminate their tormentors, and even the European senior officers of the corps wanted to chase their foes. But, for many days, William refused to let any unit in his column break its formations. He was afraid that too much precious time would be lost chasing nomads who, although nuisances, did little harm. Even the dreaded Bedouin, he discovered, were execrable marksmen, particularly when shooting moving targets.

But the army became increasingly restless as the annoyance of these attacks continued. William sensed the temper of his men and, realizing that something had to be done, devised a way to meet the threat and satisfy the yearning of his troops for revenge, yet lose no time on the march. He ordered each company to elect a small number of its best riders and rifle shots to participate in the work of a new, special unit.

This elite company was assigned the task of retaliating against nomad attacks. When such an assault took place, the elected few were directed to drop out of their usual places in the ranks, form new lines on the flank nearest the fire, and then take off in pursuit of the foe. In theory the idea was sound, but in practice the "Janissary Company," as the unit was called, accomplished virtually nothing. By the time the pursuers reached a rocky ledge or row of boulders, the nomads were gone.

After several fruitless attempts had been made to counterattack, the frustration of the corps became more intense and bitter. Afraid that his whole army might take off after a band, William decided to lead a counterattack in person. He did, with results as spectacular as they were devastating. When muskets first began to fire from hidden positions behind the crest of a sand dune on the far side of a gravel-strewn gully, he spurred his own horse in the direction of the fire, ignoring the concentrated efforts of men armed with ancient muskets and pistols to bring him down.

Members of the "Janissary Company" streamed across the gully after him, and when he twirled his scimitar above his head in a dramatic display calculated to impress the primitive Arabs, they rode still faster. The nomads apparently were fascinated by the reckless courage and scimitar-wielding skill of the enemy sheikh, and hesitated a few moments too long before turning to flee.

By then it was too late. William galloped into their midst, killing one man and wounding another with his scimitar, then gravely injuring a third with a pistol shot at close range. By then the troops of his "Janissary Company" had caught up with him, and in a few moments of swift, ruthless terror completely wiped out the nomad band. Rifle and pistol fire disposed of the majority, and the wounded, shown no mercy, were put to the sword. In all, eleven adult males and five boys in their teens were killed.

William's men stripped the bodies of their foes, divided the loot, and took the nomads' horses. But no attempt was made to bury the dead, and their bodies were left for the vultures already circling overhead after appearing from nowhere. Desert justice was inexorable, cruel and, it seemed, necessary. After a similar punishment had been meted out to several such bands in the same manner, the nomad attacks on the column stopped.

Daytime temperatures soared regularly into the nineties, and sometimes exceeded 100°F., if the records of a later period are any criterion. William and the members of his expedition who wrote of the march used the same language to describe their experience. The days, they said, were "intolerably hot." The nights were always cool and sometimes cold; during the early part of the march, the corps was surprised at three or four oases by brief, heavy rainfall. After the rain stopped, William says in his *Life*, "the nights were so cold, so disagreeably raw, that Eaton found it hard to believe he was in the same land wherein the heat of day stifled him and made it difficult for him to breathe."

There were serious problems that beset the corps during every phase of its long march, but the American dreamer who had studied Arabic and the philosophy of Islam in the swamps of Georgia was able to master all of them. Even had everything gone smoothly, the successful march would have been an extraordinary achievement; that it was made under so many handicaps was miraculous, and some of the rogue adventurers, marveling at William's skill, refused to believe that he was new to desert life. "General Eaton," Dr. Mendrici said in a comment frequently quoted in the United States the following year, "is the inheritor of the mantle of Alexander the Great! The sands of the desert part before him, and the mountains melt away. He conquers all that lies in his path!"

The conqueror had his hands full. The last oasis supplied with adequate water was visited on March 8, soon after the march began, and thereafter the men were forced to drink limited quantities, filling their goatskin pouches with even less water for use during the day. Occasionally the Arabs threatened mutiny, always adding that the hazards of the journey were so great they needed higher wages. The first few times William responded to the threat with one of his own: the Arabs could do as they pleased, he said: he would take the Christians back to Alexandria, Hamet could fend for himself, and his supporters would get nothing.

The punishment of ringleaders fomenting trouble was a far easier way to deal with the situation, however. William acted as his own judge, prosecutor, jury—and executioner. One day in late March—the exact date is not recorded—he listened briefly to demands for more money presented to him by two Arab spokesmen, whose comrades clustered in the background behind them, listening. All were armed, and William stood alone.

He tried to silence the spokesmen, telling them they were repeating a familiar story. They, however, thought they had

191

him where they wanted him, since the column was now closer to Derna than to Alexandria, and could not turn back. After warning the men a second time, William drew his pistols and put a bullet through the forehead of one and the heart of the other.

The scores of stunned Arabs who witnessed the execution could have rushed him, but were afraid of his scimitar. There was nothing other than the great force of his personality and the authority he exercised to prevent them from shooting him down with their own firearms, but they did nothing. He ordered them to disperse, and the mutiny collapsed. It was the last attempt made to extort more money from him.

William wrote several pages in his *Life* justifying the incident and explaining that the laws of Western civilization were inapplicable in the desert. "Had General Eaton failed to act with dispatch," he declared, "he and the Americans, as well as the Europeans, in his command, would have been slain that very evening. By putting to death, with his own hands, the leaders of the conspiracy, he saved many lives and made possible the successful completion of the march to the city of Derna."

About three weeks after setting out from the Arab's Tower, the column crossed the ill-defined border into Cyrenaica, and the water shortage became more acute. Presumably the Tripolitanians were familiar with this, their own territory, and William had been assured repeatedly that wells were deep and filled with water. He soon discovered that the wells were deep, but the flow into them was very slow through the hard, rocky soil. Rations of water were reduced, although the Tripolitanians insisted that if the General would wait long enough, more water would appear. The General, however, had no desire to tarry indefinitely in the desert. His "rendezvous with Destiny at Derna," as he called it in his *Life*, could not wait.

Eli Danielson lamented to Miss Smith privately, in the letter to which he added a paragraph or two every few days. "I hope," he told her, "that after this march ends, I will never taste goat meat again. The General thrives on it, and eats it

192

with as much enthusiasm as the most bedraggled, starved nomad of the desert shows for boiled goat stew. I need only smell the odor emanating from the kettle, and want to retch. I am forced to conclude that, unlike the General, I am not at heart an Arab."

At no time on the march did the expedition visit a permanent settlement. Occasionally the corps halted for the night at a large oasis where goats, goat butter and goat milk were for sale, along with melons and dates. At one oasis several cows were purchased, and the Americans and Europeans feasted on beef for two days. As food soon spoiled because of the heat, the beef had to be consumed quickly, and most of the officers made gluttons of themselves. William, however, refused to touch the beef and remained on his stringent diet of goat stew, claiming he would become too ravenous for beef if he tasted a single bite.

Messengers from the west continued to meet the expedition, usually bringing tidings of woe that William, at least, would not believe. According to the most spectacular of these reports, Yusef had sent eight hundred of his best horsemen to reinforce the garrison at Derna, and these men allegedly had already reached Benghazi and were starting on the final lap of their journey. The staff officers were impressed, and wondered whether it would be possible for a combined military and naval force to take Derna under such circumstances. Hamet became panicky, and when he indicated that he was giving serious consideration to the idea of abandoning the campaign and returning to Egypt, his followers showed a sharp decline in their already weakened enthusiasm for the venture.

William's attitude was one of cynical skepticism. He believed that Yusef, menaced by the major units of the American Mediterranean squadron, would hold his strongest forces at Tripoli rather than scatter his troops and increase the risk of his own capture by Commodore Rodgers. The alarm of Hamet gave him new problems, however, and in order to restore order in his ranks he found it necessary to use the threat of fresh punitive measures. Anyone, Hamet included, was free to leave the corps at once, he said, but only those who remained would be fed. Those who left would be regarded as deserters, and could starve in the desert.

The corps was camping at the time on the site of an ancient, abandoned Roman town hundreds of miles from civilization. Men who went off on their own would be certain to starve, and the commander in chief took the wise precaution of setting up a strong guard over the provisions, the marines and half of his senior officers standing sentry duty. Hamet was the first to buckle, preferring the possibility of an encounter with his brother's elite troops at some future date to immediate starvation. And when he changed his mind the other Arabs did the same. Once again William won the battle of wits and wills.

At the end of March, perhaps early in April, the corps reached a large, fertile oasis which William, in his Journal-Diary, calls Eu Korrar-ke-Barre. Its exact location is unknown, since he did not pinpoint it on any chart or map, and the name is unlike that of any oasis known in later times. But the place was no mirage, other members of the expedition also mentioning it, and the benefits reaped from the stay there were substantial.

Barley was ripening, and, according to William's estimate, three to four thousand nomads were gathered at the oasis. His supplies of knives, cooking utensils, cloth and trinkets was running low, but he gladly depleted them in order to trade with the wandering Arabs. He purchased large quantities of barley, many sacks of dates and enough melons to enable his troops to eat their fill.

But he enjoyed far more than the replenishing of his stores. As he put it in his *Life*, "For the first time since General Eaton had contemplated the grand expedition, he encountered men whose love of country was greater than their love of self."

One hundred and twenty of the Bedouin horsemen volunteered their services with the corps, requested no pay and asked only to be given a place of honor in the vanguard when the assault was made on Derna. For years Yusef had treated his Bedouin subjects with contempt, and these tribesmen were anxious to play an active role in removing him from his throne.

William was delighted, and remained at the oasis for an additional day and night, his longest halt on the entire march, in order to recruit openly. At his instigation Hamet made an address to the nomads, but was so pale and colorless that William followed the talk with a fiery speech of his own. In it he appealed to Bedouin sense of freedom and love of wild adventure. He was cheered far more loudly than Hamet. Another ninety horsemen joined him, making more than two hundred newcomers in all.

These men had a motive other than personal gain that was impelling them to fight, they were excellent horsemen and relatively good shots, and were less inclined to panic than most Arabs. As an added bonus, they brought their own food and ammunition with them. The corps was infinitely stronger because they joined it, and even the perennially pessimistic Hamet became a trifle more cheerful.

William felt as he had from the first, that the outcome of the campaign was not in doubt. He spoke only in terms of victory, and his Journal-Diary, which was not written for publication, consistently reflected his conviction that he would take Derna and march on to the city of Tripoli.

Aletti caused trouble a few days later during a stop at a smaller oasis. Two or three small parties of nomads were stopping there, and William's manservant saw a young girl he coveted. There had been no trouble with women on the march, the General having refused to allow his troops to bring mistresses or wives with them, and from the outset he had discouraged camp followers who had wanted to travel in the wake of the corps.

The ever resourceful Aletti felt certain he could handle his master, however, and bargained with the girl's parents. They finally agreed to sell her to him for a bag of figs equal to her weight, and Aletti calmly stole the necessary supplies from the commissary wagons. The girl spent the night with him under the palms behind William's tent, but at dawn the next morning, as the corps was preparing to start out on its day's march, the outraged father of the girl appeared and denounced Aletti loudly. The figs, he claimed, were spoiled.

Aletti denied the charge, and a bitter quarrel ensued. William was forced to intervene, and settled the matter in his own way. A new supply of figs was purchased from the nomads, and the cost was deducted from Aletti's wages. The girl was returned to her parents, who were paid fifty dollars in American silver, that sum also being taken from Aletti's future income. The manservant, William estimated, would work for the next twenty months without receiving a penny. Worst of all, Aletti was in disgrace, chiefly because the dispute delayed the departure of the corps by more than an hour.

"Lust," William writes sententiously in his *Life*, "is the most expensive of vices."

No sooner was one problem settled than another arose. The Arabs began quarreling among themselves. There were at least three major factions—William and Leitensdorfer counted four—and Hamet contributed nothing to the situation by siding first with one, then with another. One night, soon after a halt, a member of one group was stabbed by unknown assailants, and refused to name his killers before he died.

William was afraid that a serious blood feud might erupt and realized his ranks might be decimated before peace could be restored. So he summoned the entire command to a meeting before his own campfire and announced that unless those who had knifed the dead man gave themselves up voluntarily he would execute two soldiers from each company.

By any standards other than those of the Barbary Coast, this threat was cruel, extreme and barbaric. But it seemed fair to the Arabs, who responded to it in their own way. A dozen men identified the two enemies of the dead man who had perpetrated the deed. William ordered the culprits put to death at once.

They were executed by a firing squad made up of the corps' European senior officers. By selecting them to perform the thoroughly unpleasant task, William again demonstrated his foresight. The friends of the executed men almost certainly would have become involved in a new blood feud with other Arabs who shot their comrades, but, the General reasoned, would be less inclined to seek vengeance against foreigners.

Events vindicated William's judgment. There were no repercussions, and although the rogue adventurers slept with their firearms beside them for many nights, no attempts were made on their lives. Lieutenant O'Bannon summed up the sagacity of the corps' leader when, testifying before a House of Representatives Committee after his return to the United States, he said, "General Eaton always was able to read the minds and enter the hearts of the Arabs he commanded. He knew them better than they knew themselves."

The army continued to grow, too. The news that Bedouin warriors had volunteered their services spread through the desert, and other tribesmen with grievances against Yusef appeared at oases or on the march to offer their rifles to the cause. Perhaps some were motivated by a desire for excitement, and some undoubtedly wanted booty, but the majority appeared to be patriots anxious to take part in terminating the rule of a tyrant. William comments in his *Life* that few of the Tripolitanians showed any positive enthusiasm for Hamet; the volunteers appeared interested in getting rid of Yusef, and weren't thinking of anything else.

The expansion continued at a rate that soon became alarming. Scores of tribesmen appeared and soon numbered in the hundreds. William's own estimate is that his force was augmented by approximately seven hundred fighting men. Adjutant Leitensdorfer's figures show that more than one thousand flocked to the colors. O'Bannon admitted bewilderment, and Eli, writing to Miss Smith about ten days before the column reached the walls of Derna, declared, "There are now thousands in our camp."

197

The confusion was caused, at least in part, by the fact that many of the new arrivals brought their wives and children with them. William had been successful up to this point in his efforts to make the campaign a masculine venture, but the tide became too strong and he could no longer swim against it. When two hundred stalwarts appeared, ready to give their lives for him, he was in no position to send away the wives and offspring of these warriors, women and children who literally had no place else to go.

The army became domesticated. Women washed laundry late at night, and for the first time in many weeks the senior officers, including the commander in chief, wore clean small-clothes and shirts and stockings. Babies wailed, and men who were awakened in the small hours of the morning cursed, felt lonely and thought of their own families. Tribesmen brought their livestock and camels with them, their donkey carts and their household belongings. Married men made camp with their families, and it became increasingly difficult to maintain an orderly, compact military organization. The rogue adventurers, who had been concerned with the problems of battalions and regiments, were forced to become judges in marital disputes. The relatively disciplined corps degenerated into an Arab mob.

But William never lost his serenity, much less his ability to control the hordes. He made valiant but vain efforts to keep up a rapid rate of march and astonished Davies and Eli by remaining cheerful when the advance was reduced to a painfully slow crawl. Only once, when the entire corps was forced to tarry for a half day at an oasis when a small boy wandered into the desert and became lost, did he admit impatience. No one but his closest associates knew it, however, and instead of ordering more than fifteen hundred men to move on, he sent his best cavalry units into the desert to search for the child.

Finally, when the boy had been recovered, he gave the order to march. What he lost in time he more than made up in the new spirit that suffused the camp of the late arrivals. Eaton Pasha, the fathers and husbands declared, was a great leader, and they professed their willingness to lay down their lives for him.

Leitensdorfer and the other adventurers fumed, but William frequently reminded them that the corps had become strong enough to defeat a garrison reinforced by Yusef's finest veterans. In spite of the slow advance, the need to purchase additional food supplies at the larger oases and the feuds caused by the attempts of the hot-blooded to seduce other men's wives, the corps had become invincible.

At an ancient castle, where numerous ruins were seen and Eli found some ancient Greek coins, there were two wells filled almost to the brim with water too bitter to drink. William, until now the complete Arab, became enough of a Westerner long enough to enjoy his first bath since the beginning of the march. Several of his immediate subordinates and the marines followed his example, while a crowd of gaping Arabs thought them mad.

Early in April a major crisis erupted when the Bey Hamet Karamanli Pasha was discovered missing one morning. William's first fear was that he had been murdered or kidnapped, but a quick investigation soon disclosed that he had become discouraged, for reasons unknown, and had started back on the long journey to Egypt accompanied by a few old, close associates who had long been his companions in adversity.

Great care was taken to conceal the news from the army, and the normal day's march was resumed, as though all were well. Encumbered by its women and children, baggage train and artillery, the corps crept westward. Meanwhile William sent two of the most reliable sheikhs and a small cavalry escort in the opposite direction to find Hamet and return with him. The commander in chief took what comfort he could in the knowledge that it would be easy enough to find Hamet, who had nowhere to go other than the oases lying toward the east, and that a few armed men could travel much more rapidly than could the heavily burdened corps.

Soon after sundown that evening the sheikhs returned with

the fugitive, and William held a grim confrontation with Hamet, in the privacy of the commander in chief's tent. The embarrassed, abashed Hamet had an excuse as feeble as it was genuine. The ultimate hour of decision was drawing nearer, and made him uncomfortable. He had run away because he found the prospect of returning to the throne of his fathers disconcerting. Never energetic or ambitious, he had grown lazier through the years, and did not look forward to assuming the responsibilities of a monarch.

William recognized the futility of lecturing him, and merely told him it was too late to turn back, adding that unless Hamet behaved, he would be taken to Derna in irons. The miserable descendant of the ferocious founder of the house of Karamanli sat cross-legged on the ground and wept.

"The General feels no sympathy for him, nor do I," Eli wrote to Miss Smith. "If he wanted to remain a beggar in exile, he should have made his position plain to us long ago."

Hamet, of course, had no real choice in the matter. His fate had been decided the moment William H. Eaton had conceived his grand design, and Hamet had been rescued, against his will, from the anonymity, genteel poverty and carefree existence which he found less of a burden than the unhappy future he did not want, had not sought and was trying in vain to elude.

It was inevitable that Hamet should cause still more troubles. A few days after his attempted desertion, he took it on himself to order the column to halt at a water hole on the plateau of the Cyrenaican desert while William had moved ahead with the advance guard to search for an oasis. Turning back when the main body did not appear, William found the Arabs at their ease, in midafternoon.

Hamet, who admitted having given the order, said he was exhausted and could not continue. The weary Arabs supported him, and real mutiny was in the air. Some of the sheikhs complained that food supplies were running low, which was true, and that as a consequence everyone was hungry.

William replied, reasonably enough, that a lack of food was

the best of all incentives to march as rapidly as possible toward Derna.

The Arabs became ugly. Farquhar and Selim the Janissary were accompanying William, and at his signal they called the Greek cavalry into battle formation. The two forces faced each other, the Christians badly outnumbered, and in the silence that followed, the sound of rifles and muskets being cocked added to the tension.

William knew a resolution of the crisis was up to him, but was himself too tired to make a speech. He dismounted and, stepping between the two groups, made the simple announcement that he was resigning as commander in chief. He would pay the wages of the Greeks, the officers, and of those Arabs who demonstrated loyalty to him. Then, accompanied only by his stepson, he would ride to the rendezvous with the American subsquadron at a small bay near Derna. From there he would return to the United States. Hamet, the sheikhs and their followers, the nomads and all the other Arabs could do whatever they pleased. If they starved in the desert, that was their concern. If Yusef's forces caught them and executed them for treason, it was no concern of a foreigner who was washing his hands of them.

The gamble succeeded. There was an immediate groundswell in the ranks of the Arabs who had been hostile only a moment earlier. Common soldiers and sheikhs alike begged William not to desert them. Hamet was shamed into adding his own requests to theirs.

Feigning reluctance, William promised to give the matter more thought, provided the march was resumed instantly. It was.

"General Eaton," William says in his *Life*, "realized that he had taken another grave risk when he invited the Arabs to fire upon him, and he knew that he could not repeat such tactics too often. Rather than give Hamet another opportunity to create havoc, he placed the craven Karamanli under the personal escort of Selim the Janissary, who, with a selected group

201

of five men ready to brave all odds, remained close to Hamet for the remainder of the march. Only by the exercise of these rigorous precautions was it possible to avoid certain strife and bloodshed."

There was no way to avoid the problem of dwindling supplies. News of the column's advance sent the supporters of Yusef into hiding, oases were deserted and it was impossible to purchase any food. Men were sent out across the desert daily in search of meat and grain, but returned empty-handed. Hamet, beset by anxieties and himself hungry, became ill and had to be strapped to his saddle.

On April 15 the corps appeared on the verge of falling apart. On that day the march began long before dawn, and the column headed toward the Mediterranean. Long after sundown the exhausted men finally reached the sea, not far from the spot where William had arranged to meet Lieutenant Hull. That he was able to come even close to the rendezvous point when he had no accurate maps or charts, and no guides who knew where to lead him, was something of a miracle. Trying to explain this phenomenon in his *Life*, he can only say, "General Eaton relied in part on his instincts, but called upon Divine Providence, knowing he needed the help of the Lord. He did not fail his humble servant, and the corps arrived less than five miles from the appointed place."

The women and children, as hungry as the men and even more tired, straggled far behind the column, and most did not arrive at the Mediterranean until late in the evening. Food supplies were gone, and there were only two small wells that stood inland, neither of them adequate for more than a small fraction of the needs of the people.

Worst of all, there was no sign of any American warships. Campfires were lighted on the beaches, driftwood being plentiful, and the members of the expedition settled down to spend a long night contemplating the certainty of starvation in the days that followed.

The events of the next morning were regarded by the Arabs

as a certain sign that William Eaton enjoyed the special protection of Allah, and thereafter their loyalty to him became fanatical. The U.S.S. *Argus* appeared from nowhere on a calm sea, sailed close to the shore and dropped anchor. Provisions were landed and the members of the expedition ate heartily for the first time in days.

Isaac Hull, who came ashore in his gig, did not at first recognize the bronzed William in his billowing Arab robes. When they finally sat down together for a talk, the commander of the subsquadron offered a logical explanation for the "miracle" of his dramatic appearance. His lookout had seen the campfires the previous night, and the squadron had moved closer to shore, but had waited until morning to identify the people on land before deciding whether to take hostile action.

While the two Americans talked, the *Hornet* sailed into the cove, also laden with supplies, and was followed by several gunboats and a ketch. Ample water was available only twenty miles away, at a point that once had been an ancient Greek port, Hull said, and arrangements were made to move the army there.

Resting and traveling slowly, the corps made its way to the water source by easy stages, with the entire force reaching its destination late on April 19.

Isaac Hull now knew beyond all doubt that William was the supreme commander of the strange army, and was horrified to find him called General by all of his subordinates. He remonstrated with the Naval Agent, and tried to tell him that he had no authority to accept a commission in an alien force while in the employ of the United States.

The corps, William blithely replied, was not alien, but was an army of his own creation.

Hull was forced to admit that its size staggered him. In fact, he sent the ketch off to the main fleet to obtain still more supplies to feed so many mouths. At last he understood the whole of William's grand design, but was in no position to forbid his fellow American to lead the motley crew of mercenaries, Tripolitanians and nomads. A brief entry in his log is revealing: "Whilst speaking with Eaton I frequently felt I was not speaking to a State Department representative, but to one who was born in the desert of Barbary and had spent his whole life there. He was not Eaton, but an Arab."

For three days the corps rested, the men regaining their strength after the hard march. Even the Arab tribesmen who had spent their entire lives in the desert were weary. Only William, making his final plans for the assault on Derna, seemed inexhaustible.

He suffered several disappointments, but took them in his stride. Commodore Barron, who was still at Syracuse, refused his request for the one hundred additional marines William wanted, saying they could not be spared. The Commodore sent only seven thousand dollars in cash, instead of the ten thousand William had requested, but softened the blow somewhat with additional ammunition and powder for the expedition's artillery.

The real blow, however, was Barron's reaction to the treaty William had signed with Hamet. It well may be that the Commodore was influenced by Colonel Lear, who felt that, as the principal American diplomatic emissary to the Barbary states, he should have a hand in the preparation of the document. Whatever his motives, which were never fully explained, Barron tried to disassociate himself and the United States from the agreement. Two pertinent statements in a letter he sent to William are significant.

In one, he said, "You must be sensible, sir, that in giving their sanction to a cooperation with the exiled Bashaw, the American Government did not contemplate the measure as leading *necessarily* and *absolutely* to a reinstatement of that Prince in his rights on the Regency of Tripoli; they appear to have viewed the cooperation in question as a *means*."

His other comment seemed to undercut the treaty, and, in fact, denied its existence. He said, "I fear the convention you were about to enter into with Hamet, and by the complexion of other measures, that a wider range may have been taken than is consistent with the powers vested in me for that particular object."

At the same time, however, the Commodore promised that the Mediterranean squadron would give its "active and vigorous support" to the land operation.

Not until much later did William learn that Barron wanted to assume no responsibility for the unique campaign, and had sent a letter of instruction to Lieutenant Hull, informing him that all final decisions with regard to the military campaign would be made by William, who would be accountable to the President and the Congress for his actions. The uneasy Barron was trying to protect himself in a situation that had no precedent.

William's first reaction to the communication he received from the Commodore was one of bitter anger. Since Barron explained that he was too ill to use a pen himself and instead had dictated the letter to Colonel Lear, it was natural for William to believe that it was the State Department representative rather than the commander in chief of the Mediterranean squadron who was trying to clip his wings and upset his master plan. For the first time since landing in Egypt, he seemed seriously disturbed.

A few hours of reflection, however, caused a change in his attitude. Regardless of what the Navy believed or wanted, he felt he had gone too far to permit an alteration of his grand scheme. If Barron wanted no part of the restoration of Hamet to the throne of Tripoli, Barron would be excluded. William assumed the entire burden of responsibility himself. If he succeeded, his glory would be all the greater; if he failed, his disgrace would be all the more ignominious.

Certainly he had little time to spend in weighing the consequences of his decision. On April 22 he received information, which seemed authentic this time, that Yusef was reinforcing the garrison at Derna. At the moment the city was being defended by approximately one thousand men, perhaps seven hundred of them foot soldiers and the rest cavalry, and at least three hundred more horsemen were traveling there from Tripoli.

Concealing the news about reinforcements from his jittery Arabs, William ordered the march resumed at dawn on April 23, arranging with Lieutenant Hull that the Navy's subsquadron would begin its blockade of Derna two days later, and would start shelling the place when the invading army appeared outside the gates.

The battle for the future of Tripoli and its relations with the United States was about to begin.

CHAPTER FOURTEEN

DERNA

After a march of three days the corps of adventurers, mercenaries and Arab volunteers finally reached their destination and camped in the hills behind the seaport city of Derna. There a number of local farmers came to the army with the news that reinforcements had indeed arrived a few days earlier, and the port was now, presumably, fairly heavily defended.

The first to become panicky, of course, was Hamet, who told William he thought he would offer his support to his brother provided Yusef granted him and his family permission to remain in the country. A number of sheikhs made elaborate plans to leave at once for their own oases in the interior. The nomads, infected by the virus of disaffection, did not pitch their own tents for the night.

It appeared that the expedition might crumble at the last moment, but William had anticipated precisely this reaction, and was able to handle it. Selim the Janissary and Lieutenant Rocco went through the bivouac, informing the men of each unit that anyone who left now would be considered a deserter, and that Eaton Pasha would hunt down and execute those who departed.

The fever subsided, a close watch was kept on Hamet to

prevent him from bolting, and the senior officers were able to concentrate on the task of capturing the city.

Derna was one of the real garden spots of the Barbary Coast, the site of an ancient Greek and Roman town, subsequently occupied by the Moors, and its people enjoyed physical comforts known to few other North Africans. The city was located in the heart of a small but exceptionally fertile plain where the soil was rich and the water, supplied by many springs, was ample for agricultural needs. The production of fruits and vegetables by farmers living outside the city limits provided the Dernans with all the food they needed, at low prices. Grass was excellent for grazing, and there were more cattle, sheep and goats than the members of the expedition had seen in months.

Because of the rocks close at hand in the hills behind the city, most houses were made of stone, and were substantial. Some of the streets were paved with cobblestones, a rarity in Barbary, and there were enough trees in the valley to provide timber for the houses of the poor. The harbor was good but was only partly sheltered, and adverse seas sometimes made it inaccessible during the late autumn, winter and early spring. That caprice had prevented the growth of Derna into one of the first ports of Barbary.

A high wall of stone was built in a semicircle around the town, protecting it from invasion by land, and two small forts that faced the sea had been sufficient to keep away marauders, but were not powerful enough to deal with nineteenth century warships equipped with long-range guns.

William found nothing unexpected in the armaments of Derna. He was so anxious to learn of conditions in the city that he accompanied the cavalry patrols he sent out on reconnaissance, much to the alarm of subordinates who wanted him to protect himself. They could not argue with his logic, however; he said that no one would recognize him in his robes, and that he would look like any one of scores of Arab horsemen.

The cavalry patrol was fortunate. The commander of the

208

garrison, although undoubtedly apprised of the enemy's approach, had been negligent in putting his troops in a state of alert. As a consequence one of the gates on the eastern side of the wall was still ajar, which William himself noticed. Accompanied by Leitensdorfer and two Greek mercenaries, he galloped through the gate, actually spending a few moments inside the defense perimeter. Then he and his companions reappeared with two prisoners, astonished members of the garrison whom they kidnapped and took back to their own camp.

The raid itself was audacious enough, but the fact that it had been made in person by the corps' commander in chief was an act so rash that, had William been a member of a real military force, he deserved a reprimand from a superior officer. His only reaction, when Lieutenant O'Bannon and Eli lectured him for having taken such a great risk, was that he had been successful.

The prisoners, interrogated separately, provided William with information that was vital. Only a small number of the reinforcements from Tripoli, perhaps one hundred and fifty in all, had already arrived at Derna. The main body of Yusef's relief corps was still one to two days' march away from the city. However, the Bey Mustafa, Governor of Derna, had long anticipated an attack, and his garrison of about eleven hundred men was ready to repel the invaders. The main defense lines were breastworks, erected inside the walls on the southeastern side of the city, opposite the hills which were the natural take-off point for an offensive operation. The seafront forts were equipped with eight 9-pounder cannon commanded by the Sheikh Muhammed el Layyas whom William knew by reputation as a courageous warrior.

An attack from the southwest would be difficult to mount, as narrow gorges cut the approaches to the city and made it almost impossible to send more than a handful of men at a time toward the walls. William, after making a study of the terrain with his lieutenants, concluded that he would have to attack from the southeast, even though the city's strongest defenses were concentrated in that sector.

He also faced another problem that increased the corps' danger. He had no idea how strong the reinforcements that had not yet reached the garrison might be, and, as they too would have to approach from the southeast, he might be trapped between two enemy armies.

His own corps outnumbered the enemy, but he knew, realistically, that his two thousand Arabs were not capable of sustaining a long siege. They were excellent horsemen, brave men who would not falter in the face of fire during a swift raid, but they would lose heart if forced to spend long, wearying weeks conducting a formal siege. Therefore, he decided, he would have to act swiftly and force the surrender of the garrison before Yusef's reinforcements arrived.

His only hope of achieving victory was to launch an overpowering attack by both land and sea, immediately. The *Nautilus* was already standing off Derna, just out of range of the defenders' guns, and William sent smoke signals inquiring about the disposition of the rest of the subsquadron. Flags fluttered from the ship's mainmast, and he learned that the *Argus* and *Hornet* would arrive later in the evening. Again he sent up smoke signals, requesting that Lieutenant Hull be notified that he intended to launch his attack at dawn the next day.

In the meantime, however, there were amenities of warfare to be observed. William sent a formal letter, under a flag of truce, to the Bey Mustafa. The communication was unusual for its bluntness. It read:

> To His Excellency, the Governor of Derna
> Sir,
>
> I want no territory. With me is advancing the legitimate Sovereign of your country. Give us passage through your city, and offer us your hand in friendship. For the supplies of which we shall need, you shall receive fair compensation.
>
> No differences of policy or religion induce us to shed

the blood of harmless men who think little and do nothing. If you are a man of liberal mind you will not balance on the propositions I offer. Hamet Bashaw pledges himself to me that you shall remain established in your government.

I shall see you tomorrow, in a way of your choice.

> William Eaton,
> Commanding,
> the Armies of the
> Bey Hamet Karamanli Pasha

Before Derna,
April 25th, 1805.

The letter was written in Arabic, but William made one slip. The date was that of the Christian calendar, not of the Muslims.

Mustafa wasted no time in sending his response, under the same flag of truce. Had he been inclined to strike a bargain or make a deal, he had waited too long, and would lose face if he opened negotiations at this final hour before the attack. So he replied courageously, in a manner appropriate to a Mohammedan warrior: *My head or yours.*

The inevitable die was cast. But William remained serene through the final preparations for combat. He summoned all of his officers to a council of war, carefully gave the verbose and the bellicose an opportunity to speak their minds, and then outlined his own battle plans. He ate a hearty meal of goat stew, and, after retiring to the privacy of his own tent, drank a mug of ale, from a small supply Isaac Hull had given him. It was typical of his sensitivity that he did not consume it in the presence of Arabs, whose religion prohibited the consumption of alcoholic beverages.

That night, although many others were restless, William slept soundly, awakening himself at four o'clock in the morning. After a breakfast of still more goat stew, he made the rounds of his troop formations, offering encouragement to his men.

The wind was favorable for sea operations, and before 5:30

A.M. the *Hornet* and *Nautilus* anchored close to the larger of the shore batteries, while Hull brought the *Argus* into the inner harbor, from which he could bombard the palace of the Governor and other buildings. The shore batteries opened fire at 5:20 A.M. on the American warships as they maneuvered into position, but they did not reply until they rode at anchor. Hull reserved for his flagship, the *Argus*, the honor of being the first to respond, and opened fire with two huge 24-pounder cannon that had been installed in the ship for the purpose.

William's operational plan was simple, and he divided his corps into four groups. Lieutenant O'Bannon commanded a striking force consisting of his handful of marines, about half of the Greeks and some of the Bedouin nomads. They would lead the direct assault from the southeast. To support them, they also had control of the corps' few cannon, which were destined to play an insignificant part in the encounter, the gunners quickly discovering they might bombard their own men during the rapid advance.

A second unit, made up in the main of Tripolitanians, was under the nominal command of Hamet, but was actually directed by Selim the Janissary, with Farquhar as his deputy. It was given the mission of approaching the city from the heights to the south, advancing carefully over rough terrain.

The bulk of the Arab cavalry—that is, men accustomed to fighting and maneuvering on horseback—was sent off to the southwest and given three duties. It was to prevent the Derna garrison from evacuating the city and trying to flee westward; it was to prevent Yusef's reinforcements from reaching the city; and it was to act as a mobile reserve, ready to move in elsewhere if needed.

The single largest body of the corps remained under William's personal command, and he decided to leave it uncommitted until he saw how action developed in the various sectors. But, as he promised Eli, "I shall taste my fill of combat before the day ends."

When the gunfire of the shore batteries and warships in the

harbor signalled the beginning of the battle, William directed O'Bannon to advance, and the marine moved his force vigorously but cautiously toward the heavily fortified southeast wall. He advanced well within rifle range, but a brisk counterfire forced him to halt and pinned him down.

In the meantime the unit supposedly commanded by Hamet managed to seize some ruins on the heights directly south of the city. There Selim the Janissary entrenched himself.

William was afraid the reinforcements from Tripoli would arrive, but the cavalry continued to see no action and his own force remained idle through the better part of the morning. A message from O'Bannon caused him considerable distress: one of the cannon blew up, and although the members of the gun crew miraculously escaped injury, the other artillery piece was damaged by the explosion, so neither could be used against the foe. William went forward himself to see if the field pieces could be salvaged, but could see that both were beyond repair.

The *Hornet* scored a great success against the more powerful of the defender's shore batteries, its guns silencing the fort. Since it was exceptionally difficult to land sailors or marines there and take possession of the place, however, it remained in the hands of troops loyal to Yusef.

For the moment it seemed as though the two sides were stalemated, but William refused to change his tactics. By continuing to apply pressure everywhere, he believed, he would compel the enemy to make a break. He was proved right in the early afternoon, when the Bey Mustafa transferred the better part of his defending force to the sector opposite O'Bannon, believing his fortified wall would keep the attackers at bay elsewhere.

William had several choices. He could reinforce Selim, send the cavalry into action against the western portion of the wall or develop the fighting in the zone where O'Bannon was hard pressed. He chose the last alternative, and personally led his own units to the marine's rescue. Deliberately, in the full knowledge of what he was doing, William forced the enlargement of the battle between the largest defending and attacking units.

As he knew, he was gambling. If the enemy repulsed him, it would be almost impossible to persuade the Arabs to make another attack the next day. Therefore the assault could not be allowed to fail. He rode up and down the lines, in view of the defenders and within their musket range, encouraging the troops. Then, in spite of the attempts of O'Bannon, Davies and Eli to dissuade him, he led the charge, riding at a wild gallop toward the wall, twirling his scimitar over his head.

This may have been the single greatest moment in William Eaton's life. Certainly it was a scene he had pictured in his mind, and he relished the role he was playing. He also displayed remarkable personal courage and enjoyed great good luck. Dozens of weapons were fired at him, and later he found five bullet holes in his robes, but was unharmed.

There was far more to his wild ride than a desire for personal glory and the pleasure of creating drama, however. William's undisciplined Arabs reacted as he had hoped they would, and, ignoring the steady fire of the defenders, advanced behind their General. The wall was taken, the gates were opened and the attackers overran the breastworks located a few yards inside the main defense line. Some defenders gave themselves up, pleading for quarter, while others fled.

William immediately took possession of the important defense works, sending O'Bannon ahead to push as far as he could. The marine took his orders literally, and was so successful that he swept aside all opposition. Lieutenant Hull, on the quarterdeck of the *Argus*, observed the scene through his glasses, and describes it succinctly in his log:

"At 3:05 P.M. Marine Lieutenant O'Bannon, with one midshipman, one sergeant and six marines, led a huge mob of Arabs down to the harbor, sweeping aside, like chaff, the defending force, which evacuated the entire eastern portion of Derna and took refuge in the western part of the city, which was ringed by its own inner wall. O'Bannon, although powder-

214

streaked, appeared to be in a festive mood, and when he saw me watching him, raised his sword to me. I immediately returned the gallant officer's salute."

William rode forward to make certain the momentum of the attack was maintained, and augmented the already successful O'Bannon with several other units. The marine promptly took possession of the principal harbor fort, known as Ras el Matariz, made captives the entire defending force holding it and raised the American flag over its ramparts.

One of the marines reported to William, who was busily consolidating his hold on the eastern part of the city, that a number of 6-inch cannon in good working order had been found inside the fort. The commander in chief immediately ordered his artillerymen to join O'Bannon, and directed the marine to begin the shelling of the western portion of Derna. William's own units launched an assault on the inner walls, and a messenger was sent to Selim, telling him to redouble his efforts.

The cavalry, which had as yet seen no action, also received orders from William to attack from the west. These blows from every quarter were more than the defenders could tolerate, and many joined the civilians who were trying to flee to the open countryside. Several squadrons of the defending cavalry managed to get away, and in time joined Yusef's relief column, commanded by General Hassan Aga. But the overwhelming majority of the garrison surrendered.

The Bey Mustafa was nowhere to be found, and not until later in the day was he discovered hiding in a mosque. According to William's *Life*, corroborated by Hull's log, the fighting ended at 4:15 P.M. when troops commanded in person by General Eaton joined a column led by Selim and occupied the palace. The official announcement, which William wrote, informed the people of Derna that their legitimate ruler, Hamet, had personally led the occupying force, but everyone knew this was a polite exaggeration. Hamet, as it happened, suffered from a rather mysterious indisposition which made it necessary for him to remain in the rear, well-protected by a personal body-guard, and not until an hour or two later did he actually arrive at the palace, suddenly but completely recovered from his malady.

After the victory had been won, William revealed that in the closing moments of the battle a bone in his left wrist had been shattered by an enemy pistol bullet. Dr. Mendrici was occupied elsewhere, so Selim applied a crude splice to the commander in chief's wrist. For the rest of his life William carried with him the results of the battle; his injury healed, but his wrist was stiff until the day he died.

Casualties among the attackers were surprisingly light, although the American marines, who had been in the vanguard all day, suffered far more, proportionately, than did other units. A marine named Thomas had been killed, and two others were wounded, one of them later succumbing to his injuries. The Greek cavalry also suffered.

There are no records to indicate how many men the defenders lost in killed, wounded or captured.

The Bey Mustafa was an immediate headache and created a continuing problem for William. The deposed Governor took refuge in the home of a wealthy Sheikh named Mansur, after whose family a portion of the city had been named, and the old Sheikh, citing the ancient traditions of the granting of sanctuary, refused to release his guest to the insistent American commander in chief. William sent Hamet to remonstrate with the Sheikh, but Mansur reminded the unhappy Hamet that he himself had at one time sought and been granted refuge under the same roof.

William was tempted to surround the house, send in some of his mercenaries and take the Governor prisoner by force. But he hesitated, afraid that the citizens of Derna might turn against Hamet. Members of the victorious Tripolitanian corps were riding out through the surrounding countryside, urging people to return to their homes and enjoy the benefits of a

216

new, just rule under a humane monarch, and a violation of the tradition of granting sanctuary would strike a sour note.

So, somewhat against his own better judgment, William allowed the Bey Mustafa to remain in the Sheikh el Mansur's home. There the former Governor conspired day and night with elements in the city loyal to Yusef, and a strong guard was posted outside the building to keep watch on everyone who entered or left, and to give a full report on their names and addresses to the commander in chief.

Many of the victorious Arabs believed the war was ended, and were prepared to spend a week celebrating, but William had other ideas. Derna, he decreed, had to be put into a state of defense at once to ward off a counterattack by Hassan Aga. Since so many Arabs balked, William made an appeal to Lieutenant Hull, who sent sailors ashore from his warships.

Forts were repaired, walls were strengthened and artillery that had been silenced was put in working order again, where possible. New breastworks were erected, and Arab "volunteers" were coaxed and threatened into building a new fort of stone on the heights from which Selim had launched his attack. The site was perfect for the defense of Derna, which no one since the ancient Romans had recognized, and the new structure stood for more than one hundred years, being known for part of that time as "Eaton's Fort" and subsequently as "the American's fort."

Although William was frantically busy and his injured wrist caused him great discomfort, he found time on April 27 to write a very long, detailed report to Commodore Barron. The communication was a masterpiece of modest understatement, and nowhere in it did William directly mention his own role as commander of the corps that had captured Derna. He inadvertantly sounded like a military man, however, particularly when he commended O'Bannon, Farquhar and a number of the Greeks for their "courage and gallantry."

Much of the report was devoted to a strong, spirited defense of William's grand scheme. Hamet, he said, was not incidental to total victory, but was essential to the establishment of a lasting peace. Using all of the arguments he had presented in his talks with President Jefferson and Secretary of State Madison, William explained in detail that Hamet would be a ruler in his own right, not a mere American puppet.

To an extent, of course, he was whistling in the dark and knew it. Hamet had already demonstrated that he was craven, lazy and had no aptitude for real leadership. Arabs responded only to men of genuine stature, so it was unlikely there would be a spontaneous uprising throughout all of Tripoli that would send Yusef into exile and place his brother on the throne as the unanimous choice of all the people of Tripoli. But, having committed himself to such a course, William would not abandon it.

He was writing from a position of strength, to be sure, and well realized it. His capture of Derna was a triumph that spoke for itself, and he was in a far better position to stand up to Commodore Barron than he would have been a few days earlier.

His letter also devoted considerable space to financial matters. He had managed, in spite of being so busy, to keep careful records of his expenditures, and his ledgers were a model of precision that would have done credit to the most meticulous Treasury Department employees. In all, he had spent $34,219.47, and he emphasized that the capture of Derna had cost the United States a remarkably small sum.

One of the strangest aspects of William's victory is that it scarcely ruffled the surface of the Navy's calm in the Mediterranean. Commodores Barron and Rodgers were, at the most, mildly impressed, and only Lieutenant Hull, who was an active participant in the battle, recognized its significance. Not until William returned to the United States would he receive the full credit due him.

If the commanders of the American forces engaged in the war with Tripoli failed to appreciate William's accomplishments, Yusef did not share their phlegm. When news of Derna's fall reached his capital, the Bashaw became so agitated that he burst into tears, and had to retire into seclusion for twenty-four hours. Suddenly he became more amenable to the idea of negotiations, and summoned Danish Consul Nissen and Captain Bainbridge of the *Philadelphia* to a conference.

William Bainbridge recorded the sense of that talk in a letter he sent, through Nissen, to Commodore Barron. He said, "The Bashaw was so much agitated at the news of the approach of his brother, that he this day declared that if it were in his power to give up the American prisoners, he would gladly do so without the consideration of money. His bravado will return, I have little doubt, and he will continue the fight until he has no real alternative but that of making peace on our terms. But his resolve has been shaken, and were the United States in a position to draw up a new treaty at this moment, the Bashaw, I am convinced, would sign it. My men cheer the names of General Eaton and Hamet, and their guards do not try to silence them. The Tripolitanian does not know, for certain, who will rule him tomorrow, and is reluctant to demonstrate his loyalty to one who may be sent into exile or even beheaded."

Had the American Mediterranean squadron been prepared to follow William's victory with a crushing naval attack on Tripoli, the war might have ended within twenty-four to forty-eight hours. But, it appears, neither Barron nor Rodgers really anticipated William's triumph, and preparations for the blockade of 1805 were proceeding at a snail's pace.

The results of this procrastination soon made themselves evident at Derna. William had hoped that a spontaneous uprising of the Tripolitanian people would begin in Cyrenaica and spread to Tripoli itself, thus forcing Yusef to abdicate. Instead, with only Derna in the hands of Hamet's supporters, men elsewhere who had shown their loyalty to Yusef were able to hedge. Once they declared themselves in Hamet's favor, Yusef would have no more to do with them, so they waited until they were sure of the wind's direction.

This created problems for William, who was engaged in an occupation he had not wanted and, in all probability, had never imagined for himself. Having estimated Hamet's abilities too highly, he was paying the penalty for his poor judgment. In brief, Hamet was incapable of ruling Derna and the surrounding countryside. Faced with the need to issue a decree or make a decision, he became so frightened that he could do nothing.

Therefore William found himself acting as the ruler of the territory he had conquered. The people of the city and its environs, who were not fooled by his attempts to pretend that Hamet was governing them, called him Bey Eaton Pasha, and treated him accordingly. Much to his embarrassment men prostrated themselves before him and begged for the privilege of kissing his shoe.

"Eaton," Isaac Hull wrote in his log, "appeared to be an Arab in all matters but that of accepting the fawning adulation of his 'subjects.' No American could stomach such abject self-humiliation, and Eaton tried to prevent the men of Derna from throwing themselves to the ground in his presence. In this endeavor he was not successful, but in all other matters he proved himself an able Governor and administrator. Had he wished, I believe he could have remained in Derna as its Governor."

Military affairs were William's primary concern, and he sent out scouts to keep a close watch on Hassan Aga, who took up a position in the hills behind Derna but, for reasons it was difficult to fathom, made no attempt to attack. Perhaps he, like other Tripolitanians, was waiting to see whether Yusef would be deposed and succeeded by his brother.

The one man who remained steadfastly loyal to the Bashaw was the Bey Mustafa, who connived against Hamet so furiously that William was tempted to seize him by force and hang him. The officers of the Navy subsquadron and his own mercenaries repeatedly urged him to make an example of Mustafa, but his own knowledge of Arab customs caused him to hold back; not even Yusef had dared to violate the principle of granting sanctuary, and the American was afraid that the whole nation would turn against Hamet if Mustafa were seized and punished.

On May 11 the problem was solved, in a manner of speaking. Mustafa was smuggled out of the city by other supporters of Yusef, and joined Hassan Aga in the hills. On May 13 the forces loyal to the Bashaw attacked Derna in force, sending their cavalry down the hills toward the city gates at about nine o'clock in the morning. The land-based artillery, supported by the warships in the harbor, began to bombard the enemy, and William's troops, stationed on the ramparts of the forts and towers, directed a steady rifle fire at the foe.

Early in the battle an Italian who had been enslaved by Yusef's supporters escaped, and was admitted through the city gates. He told William the purpose of the attack was to capture Hamet and carry him off to Tripoli in chains. As a precaution Hamet was sent out to the *Argus*, where he remained for the rest of the day, but at no time was Derna in real danger.

The attack ended soon after noon, with Hassan Aga's men fleeing to the hills. The casualty figures tell the story of the fight. Twelve of William's men were wounded and none were killed. The bodies of thirty-nine of Hassan Aga's dead were counted, and fifty-seven gravely wounded attackers were captured. According to some of them, many others were also injured.

William had proved himself as competent in defense as he had been in attack. Hassan Aga did not risk another confrontation with him, although patrols of troops loyal to Yusef continued to appear from time to time.

On May 15 William sent an urgent message to Commodore Barron, requesting reinforcements and, above all, asking that Tripoli be attacked before the benefits of his own success were dissipated. Then he settled down to grapple with such problems as the prices of vegetables, melons and meat. The farmers of the neighborhood believed they could increase prices because so many foreigners were in their midst, but William put price ceilings on all foodstuffs. The farmers grumbled, but the townspeople were grateful.

Mustafa, still persistent, tried to accomplish by stealth and chicanery what he had not been able to achieve by force. He and Hassan Aga both realized that Hamet, left to his own devices, was harmless, and that without William's support he would collapse, give up all hope of recovering his throne and probably flee into exile again. Therefore Yusef's supporters concentrated on their real foe.

A price of twenty-five thousand dollars was placed on William's head if he was killed and brought to Hassan Aga's headquarters in the hills. If captured alive, however, thirty-five thousand would be paid for him. These figures were staggering, particularly when it is remembered that most of the Tripolitanians in William's command had never earned as much as twenty-five dollars in an entire year. Eli Danielson was concerned, as were the mercenaries, and Lieutenant Hull urged William to protect himself with a bodyguard, refuse to grant daily audiences to anyone who wanted to see him and isolate himself, either in the palace or on board the *Argus*.

William refused to consider these or any other suggestions. Arabs, he wrote in his *Life*, respected an individual's courage above all else. If a man demonstrated that he was fearless, he would be treated accordingly, but if he proved himself craven, "wild dogs disguised as men would tear his flesh from his bones."

He continued to walk the streets of Derna without fear, each afternoon he received anyone who wanted to see him and, in the manner of Ottoman sultans, tried to right the wrongs and ameliorate the grievances presented to him. Perhaps, as Eli suggested in a letter to Miss Smith, the fatalism of the Moslems had pervaded his own thinking, and he believed that if his time to die had come, he would die.

Whatever his private reaction to the enemy's reward offer may have been, his own conduct was magnificent, and he won not only the respect of the people of Derna, but of the enemy. According to Captain Bainbridge, Murad Reis was lavish in his praise of "the General" after word of William's attitude reached Tripoli. "If all Americans were like Eaton," Bainbridge quoted the renegade Scotsman as saying, "we would have lost the war long ago."

What William himself wanted was victory, a total capitulation by Yusef, and as the days dragged without any sign that hostilities soon would cease, the conqueror of Derna, its *de facto* governor, began to wonder whether all his efforts had been in vain.

CHAPTER FIFTEEN

THE END OF A DREAM

Through the long winter and spring of 1805 various units of Commodore Rodgers' squadron had been maintaining at least a partial blockade of Tripoli. Rodgers himself supervised these activities, frequently sailing to Tripolitanian waters from Syracuse or from Malta, which he was using as a provisioning station. His efforts in maintaining pressure on Yusef were negated, however, by Colonel Lear, who was engaging in a spirited correspondence with the Bashaw.

During this critical period, while William was marching across the desert and capturing Derna, Lear proved himself abysmally shortsighted. Convinced that a peace could be negotiated on mutually advantageous terms, he dickered with Yusef, who still refused to abandon the principle of obtaining ransom for the officers and sailors of the *Philadelphia* crew who remained his prisoners.

The capture of Derna drastically altered the situation. Yusef realized he would be fortunate to keep his throne, and suddenly became more amenable, according to advices reaching Commodore Barron from Consul Nissen and Captain Bainbridge. So Commodore Rodgers returned to Tripoli in the

Essex, putting in at Malta to take Colonel Lear with him. The frigate reached Yusef's capital on the morning of May 26.

Simultaneously with directing the opening of what he hoped would become the final negotiation of peace terms, Commodore Barron inserted a sharp needle into the balloon that had been William Eaton's dream. So ill that he was being forced to leave Syracuse and return to the United States, Barron was still able to see clearly what William so stubbornly refused to recognize, that Hamet Karamanli was incapable of uniting the Tripolitanian people behind him, and that the United States was forced to deal with Yusef.

In a letter dated May 27, Barron expressed himself to William in specific terms, saying, "If the Bey Hamet, after having been put in possession of Derna, his former government and the district in which his interest is said to be most powerful, has not in himself energy and talent, and is so destitute of means and resources, as not to be able to move on with successful progress, seconded by our naval forces acting on the coast, he must be held unworthy of further support, and the cooperation as a measure too expensive and too little pregnant with hope and advantage to justify its further prosection."

Adding insult to mortal injury, Barron forwarded the sum of two thousand dollars in cash, all the money he could spare.

Rodgers succeeded his predecessor as commander of the Mediterranean squadron and assumed direct personal responsibility for the negotiations.

The entire diplomatic community at Tripoli urged Yusef to settle for terms his foes would find satisfactory, and even the representatives of his fellow Barbary Coast monarchs, increasingly nervous because of William's capture of Derna, wanted the Bashaw to make peace at almost any price. But Yusef demurred: thickheadedness was a family trait and Hamet was not the only member of the clan lacking in mental agility.

In brief, Yusef still clung to the principle of collecting ransom for each of the Americans he held captive. The forthright John Rodgers broke off the negotiations and ordered all ships of the squadron standing off Tripoli to strip for action.

William was not surprised when he learned the talks had broken down. He entertained no more respect for Yusef than he held for Hamet, and was astonished that the Navy's senior officers thought one brother was superior to the other. Although still busy governing Derna, with patrols of his troops quietly enlarging the area under his control, William began the preparation of a long letter to Commodore Rodgers justifying his own stand and pleading for help. Freely admitting that Hamet was a frail reed, he said Yusef was no stronger, and he insisted that only by following his own plan could the United States achieve a lasting, beneficial peace in Barbary. The letter took many days to write, and meanwhile events began to move at a rapid pace.

Isaac Hull received orders on June 4 to withdraw his subsquadron from Derna and return to Syracuse, bringing William and other Christian members of the expedition with him. The indignant William refused to leave, and the embarrassed Hull agreed to postpone his own departure until he received a reply to the indignant protest that William now wrote to Rodgers. The *Nautilus* sailed off for Tripoli with the letter, and William continued to act as the ruler of Derna and its environs.

While these exchanges were taking place, the bombardment of Tripoli was resumed, and the fire of the American gunners on board the frigates was so devastating that Yusef finally realized he was beaten. On June 3 he raised the white flag and agreed to relinquish his American prisoners in return for a token, the payment of a small sum as ransom that would enable him to save face. He and Colonel Lear signed the preliminary treaty that same day.

While the *Philadelphia's* officers and men were in the process of being set free late in the afternoon of June 3, Commodore Rodgers wrote another hasty note to Naval Agent Eaton. The new American commander in the Mediterranean had a great deal on his mind, and June 3 was a particularly busy day. Under the best of circumstances, however, Rodgers was a blunt sailor unaccustomed to tact and finesse.

In the event that William had not already left Derna, he wrote, all Americans in that city, together with other Christians desiring evacuation, were to leave on board the frigate *Constellation*, which he was sending from Tripoli at once. The communication was abrupt, its language was cold and the tone was that of a high official addressing a menial subordinate. Although Rodgers knew that William had captured Derna and was administrating it, he elected not to lard his letter with the sweet balm of praise that had made Commodore Barron's communications to William relatively inoffensive.

Rodgers did not know it, but he was creating a storm.

By sheer coincidence, June 11 was a doubly significant day. Hassan Aga and the Bey Mustafa made one final attempt to dislodge William from Derna, but failed miserably. Nearly one hundred of their followers were killed or wounded and, showing the common sense Arabs always displayed under such circumstances, they made their peace with the American. Not only was Derna secure, but William could march unopposed to Benghazi whenever he chose.

At sundown on June 11, less than two hours after the conclusion of an informal agreement between William and his foes, the *Constellation* sailed into the harbor of Derna. Captain William Campbell, the frigate's commander, sent an officer ashore with two letters for William, one from Lear containing a copy of the peace treaty with Yusef, the other Commodore Rodgers' brief, abrupt note.

William, his own victory complete, felt he had been betrayed by bunglers who knew nothing of the Barbary Coast. He was infuriated by the payment of a token ransom to Yusef, which he neither forgot nor forgave, and his bitterness on the subject, which he made no attempt to conceal from President Jefferson, Secretary Madison or the members of both Houses of Congress after his return to the United States, was responsible for the sudden retirement of Tobias Lear from a career with the Government.

The tone of Commodore Rodgers' letter was personally annoying to a man who had marched hundreds of miles across the desert, won a great victory and then, with an enemy price on his head, had administered a Tripolitanian province with great efficiency. Until now William had been serene in the face of countless disappointments, but his patience was exhausted and he lost his temper.

He blasted so hard at the junior lieutenant who had come ashore that the officer returned to the *Constellation* and summoned Captain Campbell. The surprised Campbell had himself rowed ashore, and found William ensconced in the palace, attired in Arab dress, the monarch of all he surveyed.

Commodore Rodgers, William announced, could go to the devil. He and his men were not evacuating Derna.

Campbell, unable to deal with the situation, sent a message to the Commodore. The *Hornet* sailed for Tripoli that same night with his letter, and William continued to govern Derna —and with it most of Cyrenaica—in Hamet's name.

Ten days later the *Hornet* returned with instructions for Campbell. He was ordered to use persuasion if possible, force if necessary, to embark all Americans and other Christians. The embarrassed Campbell showed the letter to William as they dined together—on stewed goat meat—at the palace. According to William's *Life*, both were at their ease. Under the circumstances, this must have been something of an exaggeration.

Campbell asked William's intentions.

"I cannot dishonor the men who have achieved America's greatest victory since our nation won her independence," William allegedly replied. "It would be a disgrace beyond my ability to endure if our friends in the Navy were to bombard American heroes. Therefore, Captain Campbell, we will accompany you."

William knew, however, that he could not leave Derna with-

228

out making some provisions for the future government of the city and province. He was the only authority there, Hassan Aga and the Bey Mustafa having retired deep into the desert interior, and he was afraid there would be riots, looting and a general lack of order after his departure. He also had to deal with Hamet.

His interview with the unfortunate brother of the Bashaw was one of the most painful experiences William had ever been forced to endure. Until now Hamet had known nothing of what had transpired at Tripoli, and William laid all the facts before him. Once again Hamet's hope of regaining his throne vanished and, as far as William knew, no provisions had been made for his future in the treaty that Colonel Lear had made with Yusef.

All William could do was invite Hamet to accompany him on the *Constellation*, and extend an uncompromising personal promise that under no conditions would he be handed over to a vindictive Yusef.

Hamet seemed relieved that he would not become his nation's monarch, but he did express nervousness over the reception his brother would give him. By this time his faith in William was so great that he accepted the American's promise, however, and he was the first to go aboard the *Constellation*, accompanied by his few retainers.

William had many arrangements to make before he himself could leave. He worked for thirty hours without rest or sleep. He appointed the most efficient and honest of the local officials to act as "temporary" custodians of the Derna government. He paid off the Tripolitanians and other mercenaries, using all of his own funds in the process. It might be added that when he finally went on board the *Constellation* he had "only a few small coins" in his purse.

Without exception the Greeks decided to seek their fortune elsewhere, as did the European adventurers, none of whom were averse to a making a voyage to Tripoli at the expense of the United States Navy. They were rowed out to the *Constella-*

tion, and Tripolitanian troops took up sentry duty at the empty palace.

The last to leave were the marines and William. "There were tears in General Eaton's eyes," Lieutenant O'Bannon later told a Joint Committee of the Senate and House of Representatives, "when he stepped into the gig. But he did not look back at Derna."

Conditions in Derna became chaotic, precisely as William had feared. Real peace was not restored until Yusef sent a pledge granting amnesty to all who had been associated with his brother. Eventually the Bey Mustafa returned from the hills, and the people of Derna resumed their quiet lives. But there had been a permanent change that plagued the Bey Mustafa and his successors, who were constantly reminded by irate citizens that the government had been far more efficient during the reign of the American. Derna did not forget William Eaton.

By the time the *Constellation* reached Tripoli, Colonel Lear had completed the preparation of the final treaty with Yusef, and both had signed it. William, no longer caring that he was supposedly under the direction of Commodore Rodgers and that Lear was his State Department superior, created a furor when he read the document.

There were no provisions in it for the protection of Hamet and his family, and when Lear told him it was too late to amend the treaty, William again lost his temper. Unless the treaty was amended, he said, he would conduct a personal war against Yusef and drive him from his throne.

Lear knew he meant every word, as did Rodgers, who was beginning to revise his opinion of the redoubtable Eaton. The treaty was amended. Yusef promised full protection to Hamet, his wives and his children, who could live where they pleased in the realm provided that Hamet made no future attempt to regain the throne. Hamet was relieved to make such a pledge and the brothers were reconciled.

The officers and sailors of the *Philadelphia's* crew, now resting on board other American warships anchored in Tripoli harbor, crowded onto the decks and cheered William. The people of Tripoli turned out by the thousands to see him when he went ashore to thank Consul Nissen for his help. Lieutenant O'Bannon praised him lavishly, and so did Lieutenant Hull, for whom John Rodgers felt great respect.

The Commodore began to see William in a new light, although William, deeply hurt, maintained a stiff, formal reserve in the presence of the Commodore. Rodgers invited him to dine, privately, on board the *Constitution*, and the two men made their peace with each other. Before the evening ended Rodgers heard the full story of William's incredible saga, and thereafter he became a staunch, vocal admirer of the man he always called "General."

He also admired the crisp financial report that William submitted, through him, to Secretary of the Navy Smith. The entire Derna expedition, including the cost of administering the city and province, had cost $59,108.58. Of this sum, $20,000 had come out of William's own pocket.

Rodgers regretted privately—and, later, publicly—the payment of a "token" sixty thousand dollars to Yusef for the release of the *Philadelphia's* crew. As the Commodore wrote to Secretary Smith, "If General Eaton accomplished what he did with a trifle less than sixty thousand, I cannot but wonder what he would have done had he been given the additional sixty thousand that has now been paid into the coffers of the Bashaw."

In July the American squadron finally left Tripoli, most of William's adventurer-rogues preferring to remain behind and seek their future fortunes in Barbary and other parts of Islam. Precisely what became of most is not known, and they disappeared into the sleazy limbo from which they had emerged.

All of Barbary was now at peace with the United States, and the size of the squadron that reached Syracuse on July 16, 1805, was a notification to the heads of every pirate state that the new nation across the Atlantic had become a power to be

231

respected. Under Rodgers' command were six frigates, four brigs, two schooners, three ketches and one sloop. There were also fifteen gunboats, and even the British were impressed by the Americans' seamanship and gunnery.

William's feat in capturing Derna had a far more sobering and lasting effect on the rulers of Barbary than did the size and power of the squadron, however, and did much to counteract the effect of the payment of the "token" tribute to Yusef. "In Tunis, Algiers and Morocco," Commodore Rodgers wrote to Secretary Smith, "the rulers of Barbary tremble at the name of Eaton. They will not attack our shipping again as long as General Eaton lives and is capable of mounting attacks against them."

William did his best for the rogues who had served with him. Farquhar traveled to the United States, where he became a citizen. He applied for a commission as an officer in the Marine Corps, and was made a Lieutenant after William, O'Bannon and Rodgers warmly endorsed him.

Leitensdorfer vanished, turned up a few months later in Sicily and then worked his way across the Atlantic as a crew member of an American merchantman. He was penniless, and his request to the United States Government that he be re-imbursed and recognized for his services as adjutant of General Eaton's corps was ignored until William intervened. Then Leitensdorfer was given employment in the War Department as a cartographer, work for which he was ill suited.

William continued to battle for him, and eventually Leitensdorfer was granted one year's wages equivalent to those of a captain in the United States Army. He migrated to the Ohio Valley, where he established a homestead under the name of Leitensdorfer, and just before the outbreak of the War of 1812 he married a girl of German extraction. No more is known of him.

On August 6, 1805, William Eaton and Eli Danielson ended their own adventure in the Mediterranean and sailed for home on board the *Constellation*. William was in a thoroughly unhappy frame of mind. Ironically, he had won the glory he had so avidly sought, but no longer found it satisfying.

Far more important to him now was the principle of forcing the rulers of Barbary to respect the United States, and he was convinced that Tobias Lear had betrayed his country by paying $60,000 in tribute to Yusef Karamanli Pasha. "The United States," he said in his formal report to Secretary Smith, "must be respected by the pirate nations, and we will never achieve such respect by paying blackmail." He thoughtfully made copies of the report for the President, Secretary of State and the chairmen of appropriate Congressional committees.

He held Lear solely to blame for what he considered an inadequate treaty that would perpetuate the intolerable situation of the past, that had negated his own efforts and had compromised the integrity of the United States not only in Barbary, but in the eyes of the civilized world. He exaggerated the situation, of course, and was not altogether fair in holding Lear alone responsible for the treaty. Commodore Barron, although ill at Syracuse, had been aware of Lear's negotiations, and if he did not specifically approve of the step-by-step progress, he did not actively disapprove, either.

Since Barron continued to hold his formal supreme command of American forces in the Mediterranean during the period the negotiations were in progress, the ultimate responsibility was his, but he was a sailor, not a diplomat, and William pointed no accusing finger at him. Technically, Commodore Rodgers should have shared the blame, too, since he succeeded Barron immediately prior to the signing of the treaty by Lear and Yusef. However, he had been functioning for months as the operational commander of sea operations, he knew almost literally nothing of the complicated diplomatic maneuvers that had been taking place, and it would have been grossly unjust to condemn him, too.

So William reserved all his fire for Lear. The long, meticulously documented report was cogent, lucid and devastating. The frustrations of years went into its preparation, and Lear was damned as a shortsighted ignoramus who had betrayed American principles at a time when a genuine, permanent victory could have been achieved.

In years to come, William predicted gloomily, the United States would face a similar situation in Barbary, and would be compelled to send another expedition to the Mediterranean. Lear, he declared, would have to answer for the American lives that would be lost and the money of American taxpayers that would be squandered.

A full inquiry into the whole matter should be made, at once, by both the Executive and Legislative branches of the Government, William urged. He granted that it was too late to recover the $60,000 that had been paid to Yusef. "When a Barbary corsair closes his hairy fist over a bag of American silver," he said dramatically, "it is never seen again."

But the bulk of the American squadron had remained in the Mediterranean, Commodore Rodgers was an exceptionally able officer, and the men under his command had proved their worth in naval operations. Yusef and the other monarchs of Barbary were afraid of American sea power. They wanted no early resumption of hostilities. Therefore it was obvious, William said, that now was the time to insist on a renegotiation of the treaty. Now, while the capture of Derna and the bombardment of Tripoli, relatively light though it had been, were still fresh in the minds of every North African pirate, was the appropriate moment for the United States to take an uncompromising stand on behalf of the principles that Tobias Lear had subverted.

William closed the report in a blaze of righteous indignation, writing, "It was my invariable opinion, and I invariably endeavored to impress it both by argument and effort, that the conclusion of a peace treaty with Tripoli ought to be delayed until all our means of chastisement were brought to bear on the enemy. But the instrument the most imposing, that which the enemy undoubtedly greatly dreaded, and on which our country had fixed its chief hope and reposed its honor, was at no time utilized to its full extent—*our Squadron*! Our gallant Commodore was given no opportunity to use, to the full, the awesome fire power that could have levelled the barbarian's city of Tripoli to the ground.

"And our Commissioner, empowered to negotiate for the United States by our Government, negotiated out of our hands an important post in the enemy's dominions, next in population and consequence to his capital—*without any equivalent whatever.* The effort and sacrifices entailed in the capture of Derna, the suffering of brave men and the death of many, including intrepid Americans, was in vain. Derna was returned to the tyrant of Tripoli as a free gift.

"Was it not worth, to the Bashaw Yusef, the freedom of the three hundred Americans from the frigate *Philadelphia* who had been his helpless slaves and whom he had humiliated through so many harrowing months of confinement? Could our Commissioner not have traded Derna for the prisoners, at the very least, without discarding the principles, honor and integrity of the United States by paying a coward's ransom to the tyrant?

"Thus, tho' it was our business, and tho' we had most amply the means to dismantle the enemy, instead of this, we have established him in a more safe situation to do us and mankind mischief, than he possessed before the war; or than he could have possessed without the war.

"By expelling and rendering forever impotent his rival, we have relieved him of his most dangerous adversary.

"The Bashaw Yusef has gained and made secure a kingdom for himself, and, after him, his sons.

"What have we gained by the war? What benefit has accrued to the United States by the suffering of the *Philadelphia's* officers and men, six of whom died in captivity? What benefit has accrued to the United States by the death of two members of the Marine Corps who accompanied the Bey Hamet on his march to Derna? These dead, and the noble Europeans and Africans who joined hands with us in a noble enterprise—and

235

who lost their lives in that effort—cry out from their shallow graves for justice.

"However the peace with Tripoli may be received by the United States, these are circumstances in which both our interest and our honor are so deeply involved that they cannot but induce an inquiry. I earnestly pray that this inquiry will be conducted with all due dispatch, so that wrongs may be righted, insofar as it is not already too late to right them."

William had ample opportunity to revise and polish his report on the long, often-delayed, stormy voyage. The *Constellation* put into Gibraltar, and was detained there for several weeks while Captain Campbell tried to buy supplies for his passengers and crew. The naval war between England and France was increasing in its intensity, Spain had become deeply involved, and it was difficult to buy food.

Some of the officers and men from the *Philadelphia* were traveling on board the *Constellation* and were anxious to return home. Campbell sympathized with them, and did what he could, but it nevertheless took him a long time to purchase what he needed.

William, his report written, no longer seemed to care whether or when he reached the United States. He became a victim of severe depression and spent endless hours alone, either in his cabin or on deck, staring out at the water. He lost his appetite and ate so sparingly that his clothes no longer fitted him. His hair began to turn white, a process that continued through the rest of the voyage, and although he had always cared about his appearance, it did not matter to him when Eli told him that he now looked distinguished.

He was indifferent to the welcome he might receive at home, and scarcely gave the subject any thought. Convinced that the major work of his life had been done in vain, he grieved for what he believed to be the lost honor and integrity of the United States. He no longer enjoyed being called General, even though Campbell, his officers and the men from the *Philadelphia* addressed him by no other title.

Autumn gales in the Atlantic seemed to revive his interest in life, he seemed immune from seasickness for the first time, and his appetite increased.

"All that has gone before," he grimly told Eli, who duly reported the statement in a letter to Miss Smith, "is but a prelude. My first concern, when we reach home, must be the recovery by the United States of the honorable position she deserves in the Barbary states. I am prepared to fight for this cause until the end of my days."

The glory seeker and adventurer had matured, and truly deserved the garlands of a hero.

CHAPTER SIXTEEN

THE HERO

William Eaton landed at Baltimore on November 5, 1805, and, accompanied by his stepson, went on to Washington in a hired coach. The following morning, while Eli procured funds for them from William's accounts, bought them shirts and boots and other necessities, and made arrangements with a tailor to visit their lodgings later in the day, the Hero of Derna plunged into the first of a long series of conferences with Secretaries Smith and Madison, as well as meetings with members of the Senate and House of Representatives.

The angry, indignant William had an ax to grind, and intended to hone its edges to a razorlike sharpness. Nothing else mattered to him, and he was so preoccupied that, although his appearance always had been important to him, several days passed before he found the time to keep an appointment with the tailor. His new suits could wait. So, it appeared, could Eliza. More than a week passed before he wrote her a brief letter to the effect that he had returned to the United States. By then he knew he would be remaining in Washington for at least a month or two, but he did not invite her to join him; he was content to let her stay in Brimfield, and was in no hurry to be reunited with her.

Since little was known of William's exploits when he reached the United States, the country awakened slowly to its recognition of him as a national hero, and more than a fortnight elapsed before an explosion of enthusiastic admiration took place. But when people realized what he had done they more than made up for their previous neglect.

The first to become aware of William's accomplishments was Secretary Smith, who praised him lavishly in private and in public. James Madison's attitude was more restrained. Tobias Lear, his subordinate, was directly responsible for the treaty that William considered shameful and was attacking with ferocious energy, so the Secretary of State awarded the Hero of Derna a laurel wreath bearing few leaves.

Commodore Preble, more than any other individual, called William to the attention of the American public. The former commander of the Mediterranean squadron wrote a letter of congratulations, made copies of it and thoughtfully sent them to the press. He said, in part, "The arduous and dangerous services you have performed have justly immortalized your name, and astonished not only your own country but the world. If pecuniary resources and naval strength had been at your command, what would you not have done?

"As one familiar with every aspect of the multitudinous problems you faced in Barbary, I salute you, sir! You have acquired immortal honors and established the fame of your country in the East! It gives me pride to be your compatriot!"

The alerted newspapers printed long articles on William's march to Derna and, in an age when few editors felt compelled to be restricted by the demands of accurate reporting, they vied with each other in attempts to tell exciting, lurid stories. Overnight an unknown Naval Agent became a popular figure everywhere. Parents of newborn babies named their sons for William, and in at least forty towns from New Hampshire to Georgia, thoroughfares were called General Eaton Street.

The Administration was embarrassed by the outburst of adulation. While it was true that peace had been established in Barbary and the crew of the *Philadelphia* released, tribute had been paid to the Bashaw and a principle had been violated. Jefferson and Madison were vulnerable, as they well knew. The President's enemies scoffed at him, saying he had sacrificed honor for expediency, and William unexpectedly found himself in the storm center of a hot political tempest which he had neither the experience nor the temperament to weather.

The astute Jefferson, sending the Lear treaty to the Senate for confirmation, spent the better part of his covering message praising William and hinting that the Administration should share in his glory. Secretary Madison adroitly followed the same line.

Public dinners attended by many public officials of consequence were tendered William in Washington, Richmond and Baltimore. He was the lion of the hour, fife and drum corps serenaded him in the street beneath his bedroom window, and counties in Kentucky, Pennsylvania and Ohio were renamed in his honor. But the plaudits gave him no satisfaction.

At the Washington banquet, attended by four members of the Cabinet, eleven senators and a number of congressmen, he startled his audience with a fighting speech. He could not enjoy rich food, he declared, when Hamet Karamanli, to whom the United States owed an obligation, was a beggar. He could not accept the congratulations of fellow citizens, no matter how sincere their good wishes, when Tobias Lear had caused the United States everlasting shame by paying blackmail to the savage ruler of Tripoli.

"I don't want your kind words of welcome, your rich food and your fine wines!" he cried. "I demand justice! Let there be an inquiry into the sorry state of this nation!"

As it happened, resolutions were pending in both Houses of Congress, which had intended to give William a special commendation and a gold medal. But his belligerence forced the Administration to close ranks, and instead of passing the resolutions by an almost automatic voice vote, Administration sup-

240

porters summoned William to meetings of a Joint Committee appointed to make the investigation he had demanded.

The hearings began in January, 1806, and dragged on for months. The former Secretary of War, Timothy Pickering, for whom William had named a mud fort in Georgia, was now a senator from Massachusetts, and was his champion. At odds with the President on a number of issues, Pickering lost no opportunity to badger, annoy and harass the Administration.

The erratic Congressman John Randolph of Virginia, formerly the leader of the House, but now a man without political party ties, also came to William's aid. Considered by many to be the most persuasive and colorful orator of the day, Randolph made speech after speech in the Committee hearings, picturing Hamet Karamanli as a destitute, broken man forcibly separated from his family by a conniving President Jefferson and Secretary Madison. The portrait he painted was so touching, so convincing, that he began repeating his addresses on the floor of the House itself.

Had William allowed the legislators to fight his battles for him, he might have escaped unscathed from the political maelstrom. But he insisted on giving testimony himself, day after day, and the adherents of the President and Secretary of State, who were no novices in political warfare, were forced to retaliate. William was subjected to long, arduous cross-questioning. Attempts were made to trip him, confuse him, make him look foolish.

His greatest error was inadvertent. A new senator had been appointed from Kentucky to fill an unexpired term, and, at twenty-nine, was actually under the age required by the Constitution for a seat in the upper chamber. Henry Clay, neither a supporter nor an opponent of the Administration, was looking out for his own interests and was a young man very much in a hurry to blaze a trail for himself. His questioning of William was deliberate, methodical and profound.

The personalities of the two men clashed. William was increasingly impatient, Clay increasingly sardonic. Instead of

241

speaking softly and winning another friend, William treated the new Senator caustically, and made himself an implacable foe. Clay, with his own reputation to maintain, felt the need to destroy the credibility of the witness, and the two clashed repeatedly.

Clay's real opposition to William became manifest on the floor of the Senate, where he argued long and brilliantly against the award of a medal to a man who had dared to give himself the title of General and had led an expedition of rogues and mercenaries against his nation's foes. Pickering leaped to William's defense, but was no match for Clay, and the vote on the granting of a medal and commendation was delayed.

When hearings were postponed, William took his case to the country. He went to Philadelphia, where a public parade was held in his honor and a mammoth banquet was given for him. He traveled to New York, where he made four addresses in two days and was tendered another banquet. Early in 1806 he decided, perhaps for the sake of appearances, that it was time to see his wife, and went to Brimfield.

In a changing, busy world, the relationship of the Hero of Derna and his wife remained unaltered. William spent about ten days with Eliza, quarreled with her incessantly, and finally fled to Boston. The Massachusetts militia offered him balm for his wounds by holding a cavalry and infantry review for him on Boston Common. With Senator Pickering pulling strings behind the scenes, the Legislature invited General Eaton to deliver an address, which he did, lashing out at his critics, attacking Lear's treaty and once again demanding "peace with honor for our beloved nation."

The Massachusetts Legislature gave him a wild, standing ovation, and then, expressing its admiration in more concrete form, voted him a grant of ten thousand timber-rich acres in its Maine district. William accepted the gift with gratitude, and thought that perhaps the tide was turning in his favor.

During the summer adjournment of Congress he again went to Washintgon, this time on personal business, and presented his bill for twenty thousand dollars to the Navy, State and

Treasury Departments. If he expected to be paid immediately, as several passages in his *Life*, indicate, he was doomed to be disillusioned. All three copies of the bill were forwarded to the President, and Jefferson, who was in an uncomfortable spot, did nothing. If he approved, he would seem to be supporting a man who was acting in opposition to his Administration, but if he disapproved, he would arouse the wrath of a national hero's followers. Consequently he thought it best to delay until William became calmer—and Lear's treaty was ratified by the Senate.

William, however, became increasingly exercised after receiving a letter from the pitiful Hamet. Now in Sicily, Hamet wrote that he was penniless, that his brother had threatened him, forcing him to flee from Tripoli again, and that he had no funds to take him to Egypt, where his family was starving. Several covering letters from officers of the Mediterranean squadron substantiated the truth of Hamet's assertions.

Armed with fresh ammunition, William raised his voice more loudly in protest. He had received invitations from scores of cities and towns throughout the United States, inviting him to make addresses, and he went on an extensive tour, traveling as far west as Pittsburgh, and as far south as Nashville. Everywhere he received a hero's welcome, and everywhere he told the same story, always reading the letter from Hamet at a climactic moment in his talk.

He was traveling alone these days. Eli, who had married Miss Smith, had been given a commission as a lieutenant in the Navy, and was in active training for sea duty. For the first time in years William was unattended.

He made an impressive appearance. Meticulously dressed, he carried a gold-headed cane, but apparently went to great lengths to conceal the stiffness of his wrist that had been caused by the wound he had suffered at Derna. He wanted no pity, and had no desire to win support for his cause by arousing sympathy. His hair was completely white now, and he looked like an elderly, distinguished—and healthy—lion.

In the autumn, after a visit to more than a score of cities, the lion returned to Washington. His tour had created pressures on the members of Congress, who were reluctant to deny honors to a man so obviously the favorite of the electorate. The bill to grant a medal to General Eaton was again submitted to both Houses, and this time it passed with only token opposition. For whatever it was worth, William was now entitled to wear the medal on his coat, but his attempts to block Lear's treaty were less successful.

The President and Secretary of State had been doing their own homework, and the treaty with Tripoli was ratified, on the grounds that it was easier to accept what Lear had done than it would be to reopen negotiations with Tripoli and, in all probability, be forced to fight another war in order to obtain better and higher-principled terms.

The ratification of the treaty renewed William's fury, and the entire question of Hamet's relationship with the United States was referred to the special Joint Committee of the Senate and House that, once the treaty had been ratified, no longer had any other reason for being. William was the first witness called to testify, and repeated much that he had said earlier.

Meanwhile his friends were making no secret of the fact that his own request for reimbursement by the Government was "lost" on the President's desk. They portrayed him as a hero in financial need, which was inaccurate, of course; the better part of his own fortune was intact, he had been given the deed to the huge grant of land made to him by Massachusetts, and his wife's property was untouched, too.

But Jefferson was embarrassed and irritated and sent the request for funds to the Joint Committee. The change in atmosphere was indicated very rapidly when the Committee approved the demand and recommended that William be paid in full. The House Appropriations Committee gave its approval, as did the Senate Foreign Affairs Committee, and a bill authorizing the Treasury Department to repay William in full was passed by both Houses and signed by the President in February, 1806. The Treasury, acting with almost unprecedented speed, paid William within forty-eight hours.

The long hearings of the Joint Committee came to an end in March, 1806, and its report was made public one month later. A few members, notably Senator Clay, abstained from signing the report; no one dissented.

The report, 473 pages long, completely vindicated William and supported every position for which he had been fighting. What particularly impressed impartial observers was the fact that a majority of Committee members were active supporters of President Jefferson. William had won a political victory as resounding as his triumph in Tripoli. Among the many points made by the Committee were:

1. General Eaton received official congratulations for his resourcefulness and intrepidity in organizing a campaign and carrying it to a successful conclusion almost single-handed.

2. Contrary to allegations made by his foes, General Eaton had acted under authority granted to him by the President, and by members of the Cabinet acting in the name of the President.

3. Assurances of support given to Hamet Karamanli by representatives of the United States had been valid and had been made in good faith.

4. "However unpleasant the task, the Committee are compelled by the obligation of truth and duty to state that Colonel Lear . . . appears to have gained a complete ascendency over Commodore Barron . . . to have assumed command of peace negotiations in the name of the Commodore, to have dictated every measure, to have paralyzed every military operation by sea and land; and finally, without properly utilizing the fleet before Tripoli, without consulting the safety of the ex-Bey or his army, and against the opinion of Commodore Rodgers and all senior officers of the fleet, to have entered into convention with the reigning Bashaw, by which, contrary to his instructions, he stipulated to pay him sixty thousand dollars."

5. "The Committee are of the opinion that the order issued to General Eaton to evacuate Derna was improper, it being

245

understood that the Committee attach no blame whatever to Commodore Rodgers, he having been placed by Colonel Lear in a position which gave him no alternative, and which forced him to issue such instructions."

6. "The Committee . . . will not condescend to enter into consideration of pretended reasons assigned by Colonel Lear to palliate the management of the affairs of the negotiation. . . . They appear to the Committee to have no foundation in fact, and are used rather as a veil to cover an inglorious deed, than solid reason to justify the negotiators' conduct."

7. *"The Committee roundly condemns, now and for all time, the payment of tribute by the United States of America, for any reason whatsoever, to any foreign potentate."*

8. The Committee expressed its belief that, had William's plan been carried out in full, the *Philadelphia* prisoners would have been rescued without the payment of ransom, and without endangering their lives. Further, "although not themselves members of the military . . . the Committee offer to General Eaton their felicitations on the sagacity of his plan."

9. Hamet had been betrayed, the Committee concluded, and recommended that he be compensated "so that none of the Muhammedan faith may claim that he suffered from a breach of faith perpetrated by Christians."

Congress acted swiftly, and both Houses adopted the report without change. Bills were rushed through Congress and signed by the President appropriating the sum of two thousand, four hundred dollars to be paid at once to Hamet Karamanli, and, in addition, granting him an additional two hundred dollars per month from the Treasury of the United States for the rest of his life.

Pensions were voted to fifteen other persons who had been members of the Derna expedition, among them Leitensdorfer, now in the United States, and all of the marines who had participated.

Although the Committee recommended no financial compensation for William himself, Congress voted him, for life, the pension of a brigadier general in the Regular Army.

In both principle and practice William had won everything he had sought, even though, as he told Senator Pickering, "Yusef doesn't understand words. Only deeds have meaning to him, and the day will come when he will once again demand ransom from us."

That prediction was fulfilled in 1809, when the Bashaw ran short of funds. The American squadron stationed in the Mediterranean reverted to the "Eaton plan," brought Hamet out of retirement and once more made him Governor of Derna. But the same old mistakes were repeated, Hamet was given insufficient support and Yusef sent him into permanent exile and retirement in Egypt.

William, thanks to his pension, was now legally entitled, through the back door, to call himself General. He used the title for the rest of his days, as did everyone who had intercourse with him. He had won recognition as one of his country's leading citizens, and it was universally agreed that he had won the honor.

His own financial situation was comfortable, however, and he had no need for the pension. So, after mulling the matter for some days, he wrote a long-winded letter to President Jefferson, accepting the honor and "a payment of one dollar per year, as a token of the services I have been privileged to render my country in an hour of her need." He graciously declined the pension itself, a gesture that won him many more admirers.

William's popularity was now at its peak, and he confided to Secretary Smith, his good friend, that he hoped the President would find a place for him in the Army as a Brigadier General. Pickering, although not on too cordial terms with the Executive branch of the Government, passed along the "hint."

Neither President Jefferson nor Secretary Madison held any grudge against William for the fight he had waged, although the Administration had suffered a blow in the eyes of the public because it was responsible, in the final analysis, for what Tobias Lear had done. Jefferson and Madison were themselves men of high honor and principle, and realized that there had been no personal bias or malice in the attack that William had launched.

According to the correspondence of Pickering, which is substantiated by that of John Randolph and, oddly, that of Henry Clay, Jefferson would have found employment for William had there been an opening for him. But there were only a handful of places for brigadier generals in the Administration of a President determined to maintain peaceful relations with all countries.

The few posts that required a brigadier general, most of them the command of frontier districts where Indian raids were frequent, were already filled. In fact, several brigadier generals with lifelong military records of distinction had been retired from active duty because there were no positions available for men of their high rank.

When Pickering conveyed the bad news to his friend, William replied that he would enjoy serving as a military attaché, which would give him the chance to use his talents as a diplomat as well as those of a soldier. But his rank stood in his way. The United States maintained major legations in three European capitals, London, Paris and Madrid. In each of these cities the post of military attaché was held by a lieutenant colonel, and it would have been presumptuous of the young United States to replace an incumbent with an officer of much higher rank.

This time Secretary Madison conveyed the unhappy news to the Hero of Derna. Although he admired and respected William, places on the legation staffs were already filled by officers who could be replaced only by their peers.

William found himself with nothing to do, no causes for which to crusade, and no post in the Government. Having already made several triumphal tours—at his own expense—he was tired of banquets, cheering crowds and serenading fife and

248

drum corps. For the moment he had no plans, no future and no idea of what might lie ahead for him. He was sure of only one thing: under no circumstances did he intend to retire to Brimfield and spend the rest of his days under the same roof with Eliza.

CHAPTER SEVENTEEN

THE DECLINE AND DEATH OF A HERO

For a time in the spring of 1807 William toyed with the idea of entering politics. Senator Pickering encouraged him, as did other friends, and he had seen enough of both senators and congressmen during his long sojourns in Washington to believe he could serve people as efficiently as they could. His first opportunity came when a delegation of citizens wrote to him from his congressional district, urging him to stand for a seat in the House of Representatives. The timing of their letter suggests that Pickering may have been responsible for the offer.

A strong conviction had grown in William since his return to the United States from Barbary. The countless hours of cross-interrogation he had endured on the Joint Congressional Committee's witness stand had given him an intense dislike of political parties and party politics. So he replied to the suggestion that he run for Congress with a countersuggestion: he would accept, he said, only if he could run without being branded with a party affiliation. The United States, he declared, would be ruined by party politics, which were divisive. He believed democracy would survive only if parties were abolished.

The gentlemen who had extended him the offer did not

renew it or press him to change his mind. They simply retired, silently, and did not get in touch with him again.

The stand William had taken paid dividends that summer, in a minor way. Without his knowledge, much less agreement, the electorate of Brimfield and environs voted him a seat in the Massachusetts Legislature. He was startled when the news reached him. He had been thinking of himself as a national leader—he always thought exclusively in sweeping terms—and the idea of representing a rural constituency in a state legislature was something of a letdown. Nevertheless he replied gracefully to the letter informing him of his election. He was honored, he said, and would take his seat in Boston as soon as more pressing business in Washington permitted him to come home.

It was true that urgent business prevented him from traveling to Massachusetts, but that business was in Richmond, Virginia, and he was under subpoena to appear there. In brief, he was scheduled to be a key witness in the trial of Aaron Burr for treason, and the man destined to become the greatest Chief Justice of the Supreme Court in the history of the United States, John Marshall, was presiding.

Although it is impossible to summarize the career of Burr in a few words, enough can be related to make clear the impact of his trial on the country. A Revolutionary War hero who had risen through the ranks to the command of a brigade, Burr had gone into the law, married brilliantly and had risen to national power as a member of the United States Senate from New York. In 1800 he had opposed Jefferson for the Presidency, had received as many electoral votes and, with the election thrown into the House of Representatives, had lost there on the thirty-sixth ballot.

Under the system used at that period, he was elected Vice President, and served ably in the post for four years. After leaving office, hoping to renew his attempt to become President by being elected Governor of New York, he revived an old and bitter quarrel with New York's other leader, Alexander Hamilton. They duelled, Hamilton was killed, and Burr's hopes of winning high office were forever ruined.

Burr purchased a huge tract of land in the Louisiana Territory, admittedly intending to settle there himself and to attract Army veterans. There were so many rumors regarding his intentions that Jefferson, always uneasy about him, had him brought to trial on grounds of treason.

According to some stories, Burr merely intended to carve a new state out of the wilderness, and, as its leader, return to the national political scene.

Some people, however, said that if the United States became embroiled in a war with Spain, which many deemed likely, Burr intended to invade Spain's huge North American possession, Mexico, either on behalf of the United States or for his own profit.

General James Wilkinson, commander of the Army of the West, who was actually himself a traitor in the pay of Spain, fanned the flames of the President's suspicions by telling Jefferson that Burr intended to create an army of his own, separate the states of the West from the United States and set up his own government.

No one knew precisely what to believe, newspapers printed fresh rumors that grew wilder every day, and the atmosphere was so tense that Federal troops were called out to protect Burr and the principal witnesses in the trial.

William, prior to his departure for Islam on the expedition that had won him renown, had become acquainted with Burr in Washington. They had dined together on a number of occasions and sometimes had strolled together through the streets of the town. Much of Burr's activity has remained unexplained for more than a century and a half, so it is impossible to determine to what extent William may have become involved with him. Perhaps, had he not gone to the Mediterranean, William might have been tempted to join Burr's Louisiana Territory colony.

But it seems unlikely that the Hero of Derna was a party to

any anti-American plot, assuming that Burr was engaged in such a plot. On the contrary, William proved himself something of a superpatriot in a time of crisis.

Late in 1806, Colonel George Danielson, a veteran of the American Revolution who had been the brother of Eliza's first husband, received a letter from Burr that disturbed him. Believing it indicated that Burr intended to establish his own nation in the West at the expense of the United States, he sent the communication to William, who was in Washington and therefore in a position to take whatever action he deemed appropriate.

William read the letter, agreed with Colonel Danielson and immediately went to the Executive Mansion; although his relations with Jefferson were somewhat strained in December, 1806, he felt that only the President was capable of dealing with so serious a matter.

Jefferson did not take as grave a view of the communication as did William and Colonel Danielson. Perhaps it hinted of treasonable activity, he said, but perhaps it did not. In any event, he added it to his growing file of evidence against Aaron Burr.

For the moment there was nothing more that William could do in the matter, but everywhere feeling against Burr continued to mount, rumors flew more thickly, and at last, in the spring of 1807, the President felt compelled to act. Burr was brought to trial late in May, 1807, in Richmond, and William was summoned there as a Government witness.

The atmosphere in Richmond was one of hysteria. Men who were usually calm and sensible spoke darkly of lynching Burr and his associates. The United States was said to be in peril, foreign powers were expected to launch surprise attacks at any moment, and there were pessimists who voiced the conviction that the nation would have to fight another major war in order to maintain its independence. Justice Marshall found it difficult to maintain an air of impartiality in his courtroom, and only a great jurist could have succeeded, as he did.

But only in the court itself was there ordered tranquility. Richmond was enjoying its unprecedented notoriety, citizens gathered by the hundreds to watch the country's great and near-great enter and leave the courtroom, relax at taverns and disappear with young "ladies" who had come to the town in unprecedented numbers.

General William Eaton arrived in Richmond early in June, and at once found himself the center of attention. Everyone had heard of the handsome and distinguished Hero of Derna, it was said he had evidence that would send Burr to the gibbet and he was followed by admiring throngs wherever he went.

William had the best time of his life. Himself vindicated by Congress, its gold medal prominent on his nattily tailored coat, he relished the adulation. His own future plans were uncertain. He was waging no battle for honor or principle, and after so many months of anxiety, he was able to shed his cares. He did, with rather pathetic results.

In brief, his sojourn in Richmond was one of the least attractive periods of his life. Flattered by those who liked to be seen in the company of important men, he allowed them to buy him meals and liquor. According to a number of contemporary accounts, he frequently drank to excess during the four and one half months he spent in Richmond. Long denied congenial feminine companionship, he consorted with the young women of dubious virtue, and more often than not had an overnight guest at his inn lodgings. The trial seemed interminable, and he joined in card games, sometimes gambling recklessly. For the first time he behaved with the abandon of a rake and reprobate, but did not care.

"Wherever the rum flows, trollops abound and the gaming tables are crowded," wrote a contemporary diarist, "there General Eaton may be found."

William loved his unprecedented fling, but found it expensive. By the time he left Richmond, late in the autumn of 1807, his reputation had been permanently tarnished. National heroes, he discovered, were expected by the public to comport

themselves with circumspection. No one objected too strongly
if a great man occasionally drank one glass of rum too many,
vanished with a pretty harlot or played an infrequent game of
twenty-one for high stakes. But no one of stature could drink
heavily every day, always be seen in the company of prostitutes
and reserve a regular place at the gaming tables. Ordinary
mortals could err, but heroes were required to set an example
for lesser men.

The trial itself did William no good either. Burr and the
lawyers helping him defend himself attacked William fero-
ciously, trying to destroy his standing as a witness. His entire
past was reviewed, and the defense bore down on his own
court-martial. In vain he protested that he had been cleared
by the War Department, and the whole country learned that
the Hero of Derna had suffered the embarrassment, if not the
disgrace, of a court-martial in 1796.

The defense also tried to prove William licentious, cited his
unhappy relationship with his wife and produced evidence to
the effect that he had taken many mistresses through the years.
His manservant, Aletti, was called to the stand, and was forced
to admit that his master had slept with many women. The
newspapers printed every word they could glean, often exaggerating the truth and twisting facts.

The climax of his unfortunate experience took place one
night in September, when his tavern companions persuaded
him to dress up in his Arab robes. A trollop appeared in a
hastily contrived version of harem attire and William, befuddled by drink, made love to her in public, finally falling unconscious across a tavern table. A number of newspaper editors
and reporters covering the trial were present and gave the
American people a discreet but damaging account of the hero's
conduct.

William found, as had many before and after him, that a
man's stature was destroyed when people snickered at him.

The court rendered a verdict of "not guilty," and Aaron
Burr was set free, although many people continued to cling to

the belief that he was a traitor. The great and near-great left Richmond. William had nowhere to go except Brimfield. He had no other business in Washington, his depravity had ruined whatever chances he might have had to win a new Government appointment, and respectable men were somewhat uneasy in his presence. Whether he liked it or not, he had to make a peace of sorts with his wife.

Why did this sober, energetic and industrious man suddenly fall apart in Richmond during the Burr trial? Why did he behave as he had never done in all his life?

It is difficult to answer such questions with any degree of certainty, but a study of the years immediately preceding William's strange breakdown provide the clues that unravel the mystery. For a very long time he had taken no holidays, and his march on Derna had been exhausting. The many months he had spent in Washington and traveling around the country had tired him still more, and he had known no relief from his cares. He was lonely, in spite of the crowd's applause that no longer had meaning for him. He felt that Lear's treaty of peace with the Bashaw had ruined his life's work. Perhaps he was showing his contempt for the human race.

By the time he came to Richmond, certainly, he had become a cynic. Lear's treaty and his enforced evacuation of Derna had been severe blows from which he had never recovered. His countless hours of fencing on the witness stand of the Joint Congressional Committee had reinforced his low opinion of politics and partisan politicians. And the verdict rendered in the Burr case disgusted him.

William was convinced of Burr's guilt, and had wagered five thousand dollars that he would be convicted. Although his own knowledge of the law was limited, he believed justice had been subverted. He left Richmond with the feeling that the last of the principles to which he had clung was a sham, like all the others.

There is also the possibility that he lacked the inner fiber to utilize his hero's standing and climb still higher. But, it must be remembered, he had already been told that there was no place for him in the Government. So he had two alternatives: he could retire from public life, spending his time with Eliza in Brimfield or cultivating his wilderness estate in Maine, or he could run for high public office. He found both choices distasteful.

So it was a disillusioned man who traveled north from Richmond. Washington was busy with its own concerns, Philadelphia was disinterested in a hero whose triumphs had already been celebrated, New York was indifferent, and the citizens of New Haven and Providence yawned. William's already battered vanity had suffered a series of crushing blows by the time he reached Brimfield.

The acidity of Eliza's tongue made him feel no better, and after spending his customary few, uncomfortable days in her presence, he fled to Boston. There the Legislature was meeting, and a seat was waiting for him. The refuge was a relatively humble one, but he sought any port in a storm.

A fresh, humiliating experience awaited him. When he arrived at the chamber of the Legislature and stood at the rear with the sergeant at arms, waiting to be escorted to the speaker's rostrum to take the oath of office, he heard himself being discussed on the floor. Other members, unaware that he had arrived, were criticizing his conduct in Richmond, quoting from the accounts of his revels in the Boston press, and questioning the right of one so depraved to sit in the august assembly where John and Sam Adams, John Hancock and other patriots had made history.

William might have been wise to retire and return at a later, more propitious hour. But he had never run away from an enemy in his life and his pride rooted him to the spot. Finally, when there was a brief pause in the speechmaking, he started down the aisle, accompanied by the red-faced sergeant at arms. Members who recognized William gasped, and a murmur ran through the chamber.

Had the new representative from Brimfield taken his seat

with quiet dignity after being sworn in, something might have been salvaged. But William insisted on defending himself, and no sooner was he escorted to his seat than he demanded the floor and delivered a savage, impassioned attack on his critics.

Freshman members of the Legislature were expected to remain silent until they learned the customs of the House, and even men who were inclined to sympathize with William found it difficult to forgive his vicious assault on their colleagues. The ranks of his enemies, according to one newspaper account, doubled within the hour.

Thereafter William tried to create a niche for himself in the Legislature and in Boston society, but failed in both efforts. He had recognized his own inability to get along in politics, and remained a military man of action congenitally disinclined to cope with the subtleties of political warfare. He was the outsider, and with the sheen of his exploits somewhat tarnished by his recent conduct, was treated, rather condescendingly, as an amateur by the professional politicians.

His conviction that political parties were a curse that would destroy American politics won him no friends in the Legislature, either. He was the only member who did not belong to a political party and his incessant attacks on all parties made his colleagues nervous. Some, feeling sorry for him, urged him to refrain from his criticism, but he mistakenly thought they were asking him to be silent because they were afraid of him and he redoubled the fury of his assaults on the political party system.

It is not surprising that he soon became the most shunned man in the Legislature. He was totally without influence, was assigned to no committees of importance and was given no real responsibilities. Sensitive to the insults, he would have left the Legislature had there been some other place for him to go.

His attempts to create a circle of friends for himself in Boston ended in disaster, too. Although he was a New Englander by birth, he had become a Westerner by temperament. Most men of substance in Boston lived quietly, dressed conservatively and, if inclined toward the pleasures of the flesh, enjoyed them discreetly.

William refused to be a hypocrite. The whole world knew his wife was a virago, he said, and it was common knowledge that he could not abide her company for more than a few days at a time. Therefore he made no attempt to hide his affairs, but openly took young ladies of the evening to his quarters. He enjoyed wearing gaudy, Arab-like cloaks in cold weather, he rode a spirited stallion that sometimes disrupted traffic in Boston's narrow, cobbled streets, and his booming laugh soared above the conversation of others in the genteel taverns.

As a consequence, the gentlemen of Boston were inclined to shy away from him. He found companionship chiefly with those who were still impressed by his exploits in Barbary and enjoyed being seen with a man they still regarded as a hero. William knew they were using him and sometimes complained because he invariably paid the bar bills, but he had little choice. If he shunned these men, he would be alone.

Only one family chose to disregard the ban that society placed on William. It happened to be the most prominent in Massachusetts. Former President John Adams, now living in retirement, occasionally invited General Eaton to dine at his Quincy home, and Senator John Quincy Adams, who was retired from public life by his political enemies in 1808 and taught rhetoric at Harvard College before returning to the political career that would lead him, too, to the Presidency, saw fit to dine with General Eaton at the Bunch o' Grapes and other taverns when he wished.

"The old fox and the young," an anonymous newspaper commentator declared in print, "are the only men in Massachusetts who dare to set their own rules, seek company that amuses them and close their ears to gossip. One would need great courage to tell a President of the United States that he forgets himself when he breaks bread with a General who is no General, but a lout."

William sent a clipping of the newspaper attack to Lieutenant

259

Eli Danielson with the notation, "I consort with Presidents and their kin, but am not good enough for the great gentry of Boston."

When William rode out to Quincy or accompanied Senator Adams to a tavern he was the sober, carefully dressed man who had made such a good impression on high-ranking Government officials before he learned new, bad habits in Richmond. He drank sparingly, spoke in a well-modulated voice, and dispassionately discussed the great issues of the day. But on other occasions he seemed a totally different person. He consumed huge quantities of flip, a deadly concoction of rum and sherry. He consorted with disreputable persons and was so raucous that innkeepers and tavern owners dreaded his unannounced arrival at their establishments.

It is difficult to determine whether William really drank to excess frequently during this period, or whether he was putting on an act out of a sense of defiant bravado. Some Bostonians and members of the Legislature were certain that he was rarely sober. But Aletti, who lived with him and looked after him, later declared that he drank spirits only occasionally and in moderation. Eli, who was not present, but who regularly corresponded with him, made the same claim.

One fact is certain: it was during this trying time that William began to write his autobiography, which would be published anonymously, and his clear, incisive writing was not the work of an alcoholic. Perhaps he chose an unfortunate way of thumbing his nose at those who were avoiding him; whether he knew it or not, he alone suffered.

The Hero of Derna was destined to drink more bitter tea. In the autumn of 1808 he declared himself a candidate for re-election to the Legislature, but his constituents failed to support him and retired him to private life. His mortification was complete. He returned to Brimfield broken in spirit.

He and Eliza managed to establish a truce long enough for her to become pregnant; the result of this union was William, Jr., who grew up to enjoy a long career in the Army. On subsequent visits to his wife he sired several other children who led undistinguished lives and about whom little is known.

To put it charitably, William was no more a model father than he was an ideal husband. Too far advanced in middle age to settle down into domesticity, he wandered restlessly through New England, sometimes absenting himself from home for months, sometimes for weeks. At no time, however, did he attempt to visit the sweetheart of his youth. Derna apparently cured him of that daydream.

Someone told him of the grand estate that Major General Henry Knox, Washington's first Secretary of War, had built for himself in Maine, neglecting to add that the cost of maintaining the place had virtually bankrupted the corpulent Knox. In any event, William decided that what one hero could do, another could emulate.

He began making regular journeys to the grant of timberland the Massachusetts Legislature had given him. After surveying the property, he hired men to clear land for his manor house and its subsidiary buildings. Eliza, unexpectedly rearing a family in middle age, had no interest in the project, and William himself sometimes wondered whether the tract was too isolated for a man who enjoyed convivial company.

Nevertheless he continued to make plans with dogged enthusiasm that sometimes seemed strained, and frequently sent sketches to Eli for his approval. William took it for granted that Eli, after his retirement from the Navy, would move to the grant and live there with his family in a house of his own. No one enjoyed a closer relationship with William than his stepson.

Occasional attempts were made by some of William's former friends in Washington to find him a place of honor in the Government, but the Hero of Derna had become his own worst enemy. He was sometimes asked, as he meandered through New England, to address citizens' groups. He always complied, and in his speeches lashed out with impartial fury at every figure in public life except former President Adams. America's relations with England were deteriorating and James Madison, who succeeded Thomas Jefferson as President in March, 1809, was making strenuous efforts to prevent a major war. New England was strongly opposed to war, too, and William offended both the Administration and his listeners by accusing them of cowardice.

He simultaneously attacked the congressional group known as the War Hawks, led by Henry Clay, whom he charged with a reckless disregard of the national welfare and future. Some of his more virulent addresses found their way into print and the newspapers eventually were read in Washington. Systematically, it appeared, William was cutting himself off from everyone who might be helpful to him.

In spite of these growing eccentricities, he kept up a steady correspondence with men he had known in Barbary, among them Danish Consul Nissen, who was now his nation's principal representative in all of the Barbary States, and the unfortunate Hamet Karamanli, who enjoyed his last, pathetic fling in 1809 and then retired to a drab life of rural obscurity in the Egyptian interior. Aware of every nuance in the region, William sent long letters of advice to President Madison and Secretary of State James Monroe.

Most of his suggestions were sound and it might have been possible to establish a lasting peace more quickly in North Africa if the Government had followed them. But by now William was regarded in responsible quarters as an unstable man, and the receipt of his communications was politely acknowledged by Presidential and State Department underlings. It is doubtful that Madison or Monroe actually read any of his numerous letters.

In the summer of 1810, while residing "temporarily" in a log cabin on the Maine property that he and several local hired men had built, William became severely ill with gout. Unable to leave the cabin and too proud to write for assistance, he languished helplessly. The summer was unusually cold and damp, he found it difficult to maintain a fire in the hearth, and by early autumn he was also crippled by rheumatism. Unknown benefactors finally carried him on a long journey to Boston, where he received medical attention.

In the autumn of 1810 he returned to Brimfield, looking like a very old man, but retaining enough vigor to sire yet another child. At Brimfield he also found financial troubles awaiting him. He had grown increasingly careless in recent years and so many creditors were clamoring for payment that he was obliged to sell five thousand acres of the Maine tract in order to pay his debts.

That sale destroyed the last of his dreams, and he was no longer able to picture himself as a country squire. His reasons for wanting to live were becoming fewer, and he could no longer numb himself with liquor. In fact, ever since the physician in Boston had rationed his consumption of spirits, rum had made him deathly ill.

Still unable to remain long in one place, he went off to New Haven to visit relatives. It was on this journey that he began to read and write avidly, perhaps in the hope of blinding himself to the realities of life. Relatives, including his wife, were bombarded with sonnets and other poems that he wrote with feverish haste. All were inferior and some were pathetically infantile.

By now he had virtually completed the writing of his *Life,* which Eli, stationed in New York, was editing for him. Its publication, William believed, would rehabilitate his reputation. Eli, who may or may not have agreed with his conclusion, took care not to disillusion him.

Returning to Brimfield for Christmas, 1810, William expected to find Eli and his wife there. Instead the greatest and most cruel blow he had yet suffered awaited him. Eliza had just received word that Lieutenant Eli Danielson had been killed by a fellow officer in a duel.

William's grief was so intense that he broke down. A physician had to give him laudanum to calm him. He had truly loved Eli, and found it almost impossible to accept the young man's tragic death. For some days he was confined to his bed, and aroused himself only when a passing remark by Eliza made him fearful that Eli's good reputation had been lost.

What had caused the duel? The letters from brother officers were vague. William stirred sufficiently to send a barrage of letters to everyone he knew. Reassuring replies soon soothed him. Eli had been blameless, and his opponent, who had been at fault throughout, was being court-martialed.

Writing in the trembling hand of an old, ill man, William sent a letter to Commodore Rodgers. It was a rambling, semi-coherent communication which said repeatedly that the duel would not have taken place had Rodgers been present to prevent it.

John Rodgers replied with a warm letter of condolence.

President Madison and many others from whom William had not heard in years sent their sympathies. Each, in return, received a brief acknowledgment written in the trembling hand.

But Eli was gone, nothing would bring him back, and William completely lost his own desire to live. By January, 1811, he no longer had the use of his legs and was forced to remain in bed. He made no objection and, in fact, didn't seem to care.

His one immediate concern was the financial future of Eli's widow, and he sent off anxious letters to her father, to the Navy Department and to John Quincy Adams, asking for information. All sent him similar replies, which the young widow herself confirmed. She was not in want, her own family was taking care of all her present and future financial needs, and she never would starve.

She sent William her love, telling him at some length how great Eli's regard for him had been. Having heard that William himself was ailing, she promised to visit him as soon as her own grief became less intense. The communication was addressed only to William; Eliza, the dead officer's mother, was not included.

William knew he was dying, and put his own affairs in order. Mysterious correspondence with publishers in Brookfield,

Massachusetts, where the *Life* was printed, lead to the conclusion that he arranged for the posthumous publication of his autobiography. He took care, however, to destroy the correspondence with E. Merriam and Company by burning it in his bedroom hearth. Whether he paid for the publication is unknown. The publishers remained discreetly silent on the subject and presumably themselves pocketed the profits, the book selling at a brisk pace for a number of years after its initial publication.

As nearly as can be ascertained, William was not interested in earning money from the *Life*. Nor did he make arrangements for his family to receive royalties. His one concern was his reputation. He was anxious that his story be told.

Eli's widow and his own good name having been assured a future worthy of them, William transferred his attention to his own forthcoming demise. He wrote a new will which indicated that he possessed an irreverent sense of humor that, until then, had rarely found expression.

First, with all due solemnity, he left all his worldly goods to "my beloved wife Eliza, whom I have always cherished, and whose love has comforted me through the long years of our marriage." He said it with a straight face.

He requested Eliza to share her inheritance with their children, and to his oldest son, William, Jr., he left his sword, his Barbary scimitar and the boots he had worn on the march to Derna.

He took care in his will to discuss his own coffin: "Let me beg of you not to make it of pine, for I cannot bear the smell of it; and take care not to place me on my back, for in that position I am very subject to nightmares."

Still writing solemnly, William also requested that his superb stallion be shot and buried with him. Whether this request was serious or was a last, eccentric joke is a secret he took with him to his grave.

By May 1 the time for humor was at an end. William suffered intense, unending pain, and even laudanum administered in heavy doses gave him only temporary relief. He was expected to die at any moment, but lingered, sometimes delirious, and surprised his doctors with his obstinacy. On one occasion, when lucid, he turned quietly to Eliza, who sat beside him, and remarked, "Never, in all the time we have been married, have you and I spent so much time together. I regret I didn't arrange to die much sooner, and even more, I regret any pain I have caused you."

Eliza burst into tears, and they were reconciled.

Late on the evening of June 1, 1811, General William H. Eaton expired in his sleep.

The seal on his will was broken the next morning by members of the Danielson family, and everyone was stunned by William's demand that his stallion be shot and buried with him. Soon all of Brimfield was agog. The entire neighborhood took part in the debate. Some argued that a will was a sacred document, and that it was mandatory to observe its injunctions, while others claimed that it would be an act of wanton cruelty to shoot the horse. Finally common sense prevailed, and two of Eliza's cousins, who were in charge of the arrangements, decided it would be stupid to kill a valuable animal. Soon thereafter the horse was sold and Eliza was grateful for the cash she received.

Care was taken to bury William in a coffin of oak rather than of pine. He was given a military funeral, with the honors of a brigadier general, and the local militia paraded to and from the cemetery. It was the second time that Eliza had buried a brigadier general.

For reasons unknown, no headstone was erected to mark William's grave. Years later, when Eliza died, she was placed beside him in another unmarked grave.

But, thanks to William's own foresight, his *Life* provided him with a monument more lasting than a headstone. Having discovered that the fame he once had sought was fleeting, he had taken no chances.

A POSTSCRIPT

William Eaton's overnight rise to renown was equalled only by his swift decline into anonymity. Rarely has a man been accorded a place in history with such fanfare, only to lose it again with such breathtaking speed. Like sports stars of a later era, he was a hero one day and a bum the next.

In part, of course, his own personality failings were responsible for the swift decline of his reputation. Until he went to Richmond to testify in Aaron Burr's treason trial, Eaton behaved with the grave decorum befitting a man who had won a campaign against his nation's enemies almost single-handed. He was modest at times when modesty was a virtue, he made no undue claims for recognition and he fought valiantly for principle.

Perhaps, as I have suggested in the main text of this biography, the strains of the march to Derna and the long, often futile struggle with hostile congressmen wore Eaton down. He won his victory in Washington, and perhaps suffered a psychological reaction that unsettled him. Whatever the reasons, his drinking, gaming and wenching in Richmond turned nearly everyone of stature against him, as did the sorry spectacle he made of himself in the Massachusetts Legislature.

Even more important than his own actions in causing the decline of his reputation, however, was the War of 1812, which broke out so soon after his death. New national heroes performed deeds of valor and were duly recognized. Men who had been associated with Eaton in the Mediterranean led the young United States Navy to great glory. General Andrew Jackson defeated British veterans at New Orleans, and the people of the United States were as awed as were Europeans that semi-trained American frontiersmen were able to win such a decisive victory in combat with the elite redcoats who had beaten Napoleon Bonaparte's "invincible" legions.

Eaton's war was a "little" war. At no time were more than six or seven thousand American fighting men involved in it. Inevitably, then, it was virtually ignored, coming as it did between two far more significant struggles, the Revolution, in which America won her independence, and the War of 1812, in which she maintained it. All too often the general historian has been forced by limitations of space to reduce the Barbary campaign to a footnote.

Only in the present day, when it is possible to take the long view, can we begin to appreciate Eaton's accomplishments. He, more than anyone else, served notice on the civilized and semicivilized worlds that the United States was a growing power that could be neither slighted nor insulted. Great Britain failed to heed the warning of his example and suffered a defeat in the War of 1812.

Above all, however, Eaton must be remembered for his own personal achievements, which have been likened to those of T. E. Lawrence a little more than a century later. It is no exaggeration to say that Eaton was America's "Lawrence of Arabia."

The reader interested in delving into Eaton's story in more detail will find it fascinating to read *Life of the Late General William Eaton, Principally Collected from His Correspondence and Other Manuscripts*, published in Brookfield, Mass., by E. Merriam and Company. The 1813 edition, in my opinion, is the best.

Among the studies I found helpful in the preparation of this work were *General William Eaton, the Failure of an Idea*, by Francis Rennell Rodd, George Routledge & Sons, Ltd., London,

1933; and *A Memorial Sketch of William Eaton,* by the Reverend A. W. H. Eaton, a direct descendant, which was privately published in Boston in 1893. A later edition, published in 1896, contained long excerpts from Eaton's private correspondence and journals which, to my knowledge, have been printed nowhere else.

Samuel Edwards

INDEX